Emily Holt

It Might Have Been

Emily Holt

It Might Have Been

ISBN/EAN: 9783337143176

Printed in Europe, USA, Canada, Australia, Japan

Cover: Foto ©Andreas Hilbeck / pixelio.de

More available books at **www.hansebooks.com**

It Might Have Been

The Story of
The Gunpowder Plot

BY

EMILY SARAH HOLT

AUTHOR OF "MISTRESS MARGERY," "THE KING'S DAUGHTERS,"
"LETTICE EDEN," "JOYCE MORRELL'S HARVEST," ETC.

" Remember, remember the Fifth of November,
Gunpowder Treason and Plot ·
I see no reason why Gunpowder Treason
Should ever be forgot."

" What we will, yet lack the power to do,
Be it for good or ill, God counts it done."
SAMUEL CARTER HALL.

NEW EDITION

LONDON
JOHN F. SHAW AND CO.
48 PATERNOSTER ROW

PREFACE.

"THERE is a way that seemeth right unto a man, but the end thereof are the ways of death." That is one of the main lessons to be learned from the strange story of the Gunpowder Plot.

The narrative here given, so far as its historical portion is concerned, is taken chiefly from original and contemporaneous documents. It has been carefully kept to facts—in themselves more interesting than any fiction —and scarcely a speech or an incident has been admitted, however small, for which authority could not be adduced.

Those of my Readers who have made the acquaintance of *Lettice Eden*, and *Joyce Morrell's Harvest*, will meet some old friends in this tale.

THE principal Authorities consulted in preparing this Volume are the following:—

The Gunpowder Plot Book, and other Domestic State Papers of the reigns of James I. and Charles I.

Harleian MS., No. 360, "Religious Tracts" (a decided misnomer).

Additional MSS., Nos. 6177, 6178, "Excerpta from Burghley Papers."

Foley's Records of the English Province of the Society of Jesus.

Gerard's Condition of Catholics under James I.

Greenway's Narrative of the Gunpowder Plot.

Jardine's Criminal Trials, and his Narrative of the Gunpowder Plot.

CONTENTS.

"Lost, lost!" cried Langham as Percy. ......

IT MIGHT HAVE BEEN.

CHAPTER I.

THE LAST NIGHT IN THE OLD HOME.

"Which speaks the truth—fair Hope or ghastly Fear?
God knoweth, and not I.
Only, o'er both, Love holds her torch aloft,
And will, until I die."

FIDDLE-DE-DEE! Do give over snuffing and snivelling and sobbing, and tell me if you want your warm petticoat in the saddle-bag. You'd make a saint for to swear!"

More sobs, and one or two disjointed words, were all that came in answer. The sobbing sister, who was the younger of the pair, wore widow's mourning, and was seated in a rocking-chair near the window of a small, but very comfortable parlour. Her complexion was pale and sallow, her person rather slightly formed, and her whole appearance that of a frail, weak little woman, who required perpetual care and shielding. The word require has two senses, and it is here used in both. She needed it, and she exacted it.

The elder sister, who stood at the parlour door, was

about as unlike the younger as could well be. She was quite a head taller, rosy-cheeked, sturdily-built, and very brisk in her motions. Disjointed though her sister's words were, she took them up at once.

"You'll have your thrum [1] hat, did you say? Where's the good of crying over it? You've got ne'er a thing to cry for."

Another little rush of sobs replied, amid which a quick ear could detect the words "unfeeling" and "me a poor widow."

"Unfeeling, marry!" said the elder sister. "I'm feeling a whole warm petticoat for you. And tears won't ward off either cramp or rheumatism, my dear—don't think it; but a warm petticoat may. Will you have it, or no?"

"Oh, as you please!" was the answer, in a tone which might have suited arrangements for the speaker's funeral.

"Then I please to put it in the saddle-bag," cheerily responded the elder. "Lettice, come with me, maid. I can find thee work above in the chamber."

A slight sound behind the screen at the farther end of the parlour, which sheltered the widow from any draught proceeding from the window, was followed by the appearance of a young girl not hitherto visible. She was just eighteen years of age, and resembled neither of the elder ladies, being handsomer than either of them had ever been, yet not sufficiently so to be termed beautiful. A clear complexion, rosy but not florid, golden-brown hair and plenty of it, dark grey eyes shaded by dark lashes, and a pleasing, good-humoured, not self-conscious expression—this was Lettice, who said in a clear musical voice, "Yes, Aunt," and stood ready for further orders.

---

[1] The thrum is the fringed end of a weaver's web; a thrum hat was made of very coarse tufted woollen cloth.

As the door shut upon the aunt and niece, the former said, as if to the sister left behind in the parlour—

"A poor widow! Ay, forsooth, poor soul, that you are! for you have made of your widowhood so black a pall that you cannot see God's blue sky through it. Dear heart, but why ever they called her Faith, and me Temperance! I've well-nigh as little temperance as she has faith, and neither of them would break a cat's back."

By this time they were up in the bedchamber; and Lettice was kept busy folding, pinning, tying up, and smoothing out one garment after another, until at last her aunt said—

"Now, Lettice, bring thine own gear, such as thou wilt need till we light at Minster Lovel, for there can we shift our baggage. Thy black beaver hat thou wert best to journey in, for though it be good, 'tis well worn; and thy grey kirtle and red gown. Bring the blue gown, and the tawny kirtle with the silver aglets[1] pendant, and thy lawn rebatoes,[2] and a couple of kerchiefs, and thy satin hat. Thou wert best leave out a warm kerchief for the journey."

"And my velvet hood, Aunt, and the green kirtle?"

"Nay, I have packed them, not to be fetched out till we reach London. Thou mayest have thy crimson sleeves withal, an' it list thee."

Lettice fetched the things, and her aunt packed them in one of the great leather trunks, with beautiful neatness. As she smoothed out the blue kirtle, she asked—

"Lettice, art thou sorry to be gone?"

"Truly, Aunt, I scarce know," was the answer. "I am sorry to leave Aunt Milisent and my cousins, and Aunt Frances"—but Aunt Frances was an evident after-thought—"and I dare say I shall be sorry to leave all the places I know, when the time comes. But then so many of us

---

[1] Tags, spangles.   [2] Turn-over collars.

are going,—you, and Grandmother, and Aunt Edith, and Cousin Aubrey, and Aunt Faith—and there are so many new places to see, that on the whole I don't think I am very sorry."

"No, very like not, child."

"Not now," said a third voice, softly, and Lettice looked up at another aunt whose presence she had not previously noticed. This was certainly no sister of the two plain women whose acquaintance we have just made. Temperance Murthwaite had out-lived her small share of good looks, and Faith's had long since been washed away in tears; but Edith Louvaine had been extremely beautiful, and yet was so notwithstanding her forty years. Her hair was dark brown, with a golden gleam when the sun caught it, and her eyes a deep blue, almost violet. Her voice was sweet and quiet—of that type of quietness which hides behind it a reserve of power and feeling. "At eighteen, Lettice, we are not commonly sorry to leave home. Much sorrier at thirty-eight: and at eighty, I think, there is little to leave but graves."

"Ay, but they're not all dug by the sexton," remarked Temperance, patting the blue kirtle to make it lie in the hole she had left for it. "At any rate, the sorest epitaphs are oft invisible save to them that have eyes to see them."

Edith did not answer, and the work went on. At length, suddenly, the question was asked—

"Whence came you, Edith?"

"From Mere Lea, whither I have been with Mother and Aubrey, to say farewell."

"And for why came you hither? Not to say farewell, I reckon."

"Nay," replied Edith, smiling. "I thought I might somewhat help you, Temperance. We must all try to spare poor Faith"

" Spare poor Faith ! " repeated Temperance, in a sarcastic tone. "Tell you what, Edith Louvaine,—if you'd think a bit less of sparing her, and she'd think a bit more of sparing you, it would be a sight better for poor Faith and poor Edith too."

" I ? I don't want to be spared," answered Edith.

"No, you don't, and that's just it. And Faith does. And she oughtn't. And you oughtn't."

" Nay, Temperance. Remember, she is a widow."

"Small chance of my forgetting it. Doesn't she tell me so six dozen times a day ? Ask Faith to do any thing she loveth not, and she's always a widow. I've had my thoughts whether I could not be an orphan when I'm wanted to do something disagreeable. What think you ?"

" I think your bark is worse than your bite, Temperance," said Edith, smiling.

"I'm about weary of barking," answered Temperance, laying smooth a piece of cobweb lawn. "I think I'll bite, one of these days. Deary me, but there are widows of divers sorts ! If ever there were what Paul calls 'a widow indeed,' it is my Lady Lettice; and she doesn't make a screen of it, as Faith does, against all the east winds that blow. Well, well ! Give me that pin-case, Lettice, and the black girdle yonder; I lack somewhat to fill up this corner. What hour must we be at Selwick, Edith ?"

" At five o' the clock the horses are bidden."

"Very good. You'll bide to supper ? "

"Nay, not without I can help you."

" You'll not help me without you'll tell Faith she's a snivelling lazy-bones, and that you'll not, I know. Go and get your beauty-sleep—and comfort Lady Lettice all you can."

When Edith had departed, and the packing was finished, the aunt and niece went down to supper. It consisted of

Polony sausages, sweetmeats, and an egg-pie—a Lanca-
shire dainty, which Rachel the cook occasionally sent up,
for she was a native of that county.   During the entire
meal, Faith kept up a slow rain of lamentations, for her
widowhood, the sad necessity of leaving her home, and
the entire absence of sympathy which she experienced in
all around her : till at last her sister inquired—

"Faith, will you have any more pie ? "

"N—o," said Faith with a sob, having eaten nearly
half of it.

"Nor any more sausage ? "

"Oh no ! " she answered, heaving a weary sigh.

"Nor sucketts [1] neither ? "

Faith shook her head dolefully.

"Then I'll help you to a little of one other thing, which
you need sorely ; and that's a bit of advice."

Faith moaned behind her handkerchief.

"As to quitting home, that's your own choice ; so don't
go and pretend to fret over it.   And as to sparing you,
you've been spared a deal too much, and I've been a fool
to do it.   And just bethink you, Faith, that if we are
now to make one family with my Lady Lettice and
Edith, you'd best be thinking how you can spare them.
My Lady Lettice is a deal newer widow than you, and
she's over seventy years on her back, and you've but
forty——"

"Thirty-nine," corrected Faith in a choked voice.

"And she's leaving her home not from choice, but
because she has no choice ; and she has spent over fifty
years in it, and is like an old oak which can ill bear up-
rooting.   I only trust those Newcastle Louvaines will get
what they deserve.   I say it's a burning shame, never to
come forward nor claim aught for fifty years, until Sir
Aubrey and both his sons were gone, and then down they

[1] Sweetmeats ; subsequently spelt *succades.*

pounce like vultures on the widow and her orphan grandson, and set up a claim, forsooth, to the estate—after all
these years! I don't believe they have any right—or at
any rate, they've no business to have it: and if my Lady
Lettice had been of my mind, she'd have had a fight for
it, instead of giving in to them; and if Aubrey Banaster
had had a scrap of gumption, he'd have seen to it. He
is the eldest man of the family, and they're pretty nigh
all lads but him. Howbeit, let that pass. Only I want
you, Faith, to think of it, and not go treating my Lady
Lettice to a dish of tears every meal she sits down to,
or she'll be sorry you're her daughter-in-law, if she isn't
now; and if her name were Temperance Murthwaite it's
much if she wouldn't be."

"Oh, you can say what you like—you always do——"

"Beg your pardon, Faith; I very generally don't."

"You haven't a bit of feeling for a poor widow. I
hope you may never be a widow——"

"Thank you; I'll have a care of that. Now, Lettice!
jump up, maid, and don your hat and mantle, and I will
run down with you to Selwick while there's a bit of light.
My Lady Lettice thought you'd best be there to-night,
so you could be up early and of some use to your Aunt
Edith."

It was not Temperance Murthwaite's custom to let the
grass grow under her feet, and the three miles which lay
between the little house at Keswick and Selwick Hall
were put behind her and Lettice when another hour was
over.

Selwick Hall stood on the bank of Derwentwater, and
was the residence of Lettice's grandmother, the widowed
Lady Louvaine, her daughter Edith, her grandson Aubrey,
and Hans Floriszoon, the orphan nephew of an old friend,
Mynheer Stuyvesant, who had been adopted into the
family when a little child. It was also theoretically the

abode of Lettice's Aunt Faith, who was Aubrey's mother, and who practically flitted from the one house to the other at her rather capricious will. It had become her habit to depart to Keswick whenever her feelings were outraged at Selwick; and as Faith's feelings were of that order which any thing might outrage, and nobody knew of it till they were outraged, her abode during the last six years had been mainly with the sister who never petted her, but from whom she would stand ten times more than from the tenderer hearts at Selwick.

Lettice's hand was on the door when it opened, and there stood her Cousin Aubrey.

"Good even, Aunt Temperance," said he. "You are right in time for supper."

"Thank you, Master Aubrey Late-hours," replied she; "'tis a bit too late for my supper, and Lettice's likewise, without she can eat two of a night. How is it with my Lady Lettice? I hope, lad, you help and comfort her all you can."

Aubrey looked rather astonished.

"Comfort her?" he said. "She's all right."

"How old are you, Aubrey?"

"Why, Aunt Temperance, you know I was twenty last month."

"One makes blunders betimes, lad. That speech of thine sounded about ten."

"What mean you, Aunt Temperance?"

"Nay, lad, if God have not given thee eyes and brains, I shall be ill-set to do it.—Run in, Lettice. No, I'm not coming—not while to-morrow morning. Remember to be up early, and help all you can—both of you. Good even."

Temperance shut the door, and they heard her quick foot tread sharply down the gravel walk.

"I say, 'tis jolly moving house, isn't it?" said Aubrey.

" I can't think why Aunt Temperance supposes that Grandmother or any body should want comforting."

" Well, we are young, and she is old," replied Lettice ; " I suppose old folks care more about those things, perhaps."

" Oh, 'tis but because they are lazy and have the rheumatism," said Aubrey, laughing. " Beside, Grandmother cares not about things like Mother. Mother's for ever fretting, but Grandmother's always cheery."

The cousins left the deep whitewashed porch and the oak-panelled hall, and went forward into the chief sitting-room of the house, known as the great parlour. The word " withdrawing-room " was still restricted to palaces and palatial mansions, and had not descended so low as to a country gentleman's house like Selwick Hall. The great parlour was a large room with a floor of polished oak, hung with tapestry in which the prevailing colour was red, and the chairs held cushions of red velvet. On the tiled hearth a comfortable fire burned softly away, and in a large chair of dark carved wood beside it, propped up with cushions of red velvet, sat an old lady of seventy-six, looking the very picture of comfort and sweetness. And though " her golden hairs time had to silver turned," and she was now a widow indeed, and desolate, some of my readers may recognise their old friend Lettice Eden. Her eyes, though a little sunken, kept their clear blue, and her complexion was still fair and peach-like, with a soft, faint rose-colour, like a painting on china. She had a loving smile for every one, and a gentle, soothing voice, which the children said half cured the little troubles wherein they always ran to Grandmother. Aunt Faith was usually too deep in her own troubles, and Aunt Edith, though always kind, was also invariably busy ; while there was considerable hesitation in making an appeal to Aunt Temperance, who might answer it with a box on the ear instead of a comforting

B

kiss, or at best had an awkward way of turning the tables
on the plaintiff by making him out to be the offender
instead of the defendant. But nobody ever hesitated to
appeal to Grandmother, whose very rebukes fell as softly
as rose-leaves, and were always so justly deserved that
they had twice the effect of those which came from
perpetual fault-finders. Aubrey had grown up in this
atmosphere, but it was much newer to his cousin Lettice,
the daughter of Dudley Murthwaite and Helen Louvaine.
Until she was twelve years old, Lettice had dwelt with
her father at Skiddaw Force, her Aunt Temperance having
supplied the place of the dead mother who had faded
from her child's memory, for Helen passed away when
her daughter was only two years old. It had not been
exactly Dudley's choice which had placed Temperance in
that position. He would have preferred his wife's youngest
sister, Edith, to fill the vacant place of mother to his
little girl; but Edith firmly though kindly declined to
make her home away from Selwick Hall. The natural
explanation of course was that she, being the only unmarried daughter of the house, preferred to remain with
her parents. Edith said so, and all her friends repeated
it, and thought it very natural and proper. And no one
knew, except God and Edith, that the reason given was
only half the truth, and that the last place in this world
which Edith Louvaine could take was the place of that
dead sister Helen who had so unconsciously taken the one
thing which Edith coveted for herself. Thus thrown back
on one of his own sisters, Dudley tried next to persuade
Faith to make her home with him. It might have been
better for Faith if she had done so. But she liked the
more luxurious life of Selwick Hall, where she had only
to represent herself as tired or poorly to have any exertion
taken for her by some one else; and she was one of those
unconscious impostors who begin by imposing on them-

selves. Whatever she wished to do, she was always capable of persuading herself that she ought to do. Faith
therefore declined to remove to her brother's house. The
last resource was Temperance, who, when appealed to,
averred herself perfectly ready to go wherever she was
most wanted. One baggage-horse would be enough for
her luggage, she thanked goodness; she had two gowns
for winter and two for summer, and no reasonable woman
ought to have any more. As to ruffs and puffs, cuffs and
muffs, she troubled herself with none of those ridiculous
vanities. A plain laced bodice and skirt were good
enough to work in, and a pair of stout shoes to keep her
out of the mire, with a hat and kerchief for outdoor wear,
and a warm cloak for cold weather. Her miscellaneous
possessions were limited to a big work-basket, two silver
spoons and a goblet, and three books—namely, a copy of
the four Gospels, a Prayer-book, and Luther on the Lord's
Prayer. Packing and unpacking were small matters in
these circumstances, and Temperance's change of residence was the affair of an afternoon. Six years afterwards her brother Dudley died; and Temperance, taking
into consideration the facts that Skiddaw Force was a very
lonely place, having no house within some miles save a
few isolated cottages of charcoal-burners and shepherds;
that a small house at Keswick belonged to Lettice; and
that the child's grand-parents on the mother's side were
desirous to have her near them, let the house at Skiddaw
Force, and came to live at Keswick.

The family at Selwick Hall had once been much larger
than now. All were gone but these few—Milisent to
another home; Anstace, Walter, and Helen lay in the
churchyard, and Ned, the father of young Aubrey, under
the waves of the North Atlantic; and then Mynheer
Stuyvesant, the old Dutch gentleman who had been
driven from his own land for the faith's sake, and having

been the boys' tutor, had stayed for love after necessity
was over, took his last journey to the better country ; and
dear, honest, simple Cousin Bess Wolvercot, friend and
helper of all, went to receive her reward, with—

> " Nothing to leave but a worn-out frame,
>   And a name without a stain ;
> Nothing to leave but an empty place,
>   That nothing could fill again "——

and after that, Lady Lettice felt herself growing old. The
evening shadows crept further, and her right hand in
household affairs was gone; but with the constant love
and aid of Edith, she held on her way, until the sorest
blow of all fell on her, and the husband who had been
ever counsellor and comforter and stay, left her side for
the continuing City. Since then, Lettice Louvaine had
been simply waiting for the day when she should join him
again, and in the interim trying through growing infirmities to " do the next thing,"—remembering the words
uttered so long ago by his beloved cousin Anstace, that
some day the next step would be the last step.

When Sir Aubrey Louvaine died, at the age of seventy-
nine, two years before the story opens, Aubrey, his grandson and namesake, became the owner of Selwick Hall:
but being under age, every thing was left in the hands of
his grandmother.

The pang of Lady Louvaine's bereavement was still
fresh when another blow fell on her. Her husband had
inherited Selwick from a distant cousin, known in the
neighbourhood as the Old Squire. The Old Squire's
two sons, Nicholas and Hugh, had predeceased him, Sir
Aubrey had taken peaceable possession of the estate, and
no one ever doubted his title for fifty years, himself least
of all. Three months after his death, Lady Louvaine was
astounded to receive a lawyer's letter, claiming the Sel-

wick lands on behalf of one Oswald Louvaine of Newcastle, a young man who asserted himself to be the grandson of the long-deceased Hugh. His documentary proofs
were all in order, his witnesses were numerous and positive, and Lady Louvaine possessed no counter-proof of
any kind to rebut this unheard-of claim. After a vain
search among her husband's papers, and a consultation
with such of her friends and relatives as she judged suitable, she decided not to carry the matter into a court of
law, but to yield peaceable possession to young Oswald,
on consideration of his giving her a writ of immunity from
paying back dues of any kind, which indeed it would have
been quite out of her power to discharge. Sir Aubrey's
income was comfortably sufficient for the family wants,
but there was little to spare when both ends had met.
Mr. Oswald accepted the terms as an immense favour on
his part; and at the age of seventy-six Lady Louvaine
was deprived of the home wherein she had dwelt for
fifty-six years, and summoned like Abraham to go forth
into the land which God would show her.

Where to go was the next question. Her daughter
Milisent, with her husband Robert Lewthwaite, would
gladly have received her, and implored her to come to
them; but nine children, a full house, and a small income, barred the way in that direction. No offer of a
home came from Red Banks, where the children of her
eldest daughter Anstace lived, and where the income
was twice as large as at Mere Lea, while the family
did not amount to half the number. Temperance Murthwaite trudged up to Selwick to offer the tiny house which
was part of Lettice's little patrimony, actually proposing
herself to go to service, and leave Lettice in her grandmother's care. This Faith regarded as a cruel injury, and
Lady Louvaine would not hear of it. From her daughter-
in-law, Mrs. Walter Louvaine, at Kendal, came a sweetly-

perfumed and sweetly-worded letter, wherein the writer offered—a thousand apologies, and a dozen excuses for not receiving her dear and revered mother. Her grief in having so to write, she assured them, was incalculable and inconsolable. She begged that it might be taken into consideration that Diana was shortly to be married, and would require a trousseau—which, she did not add, comprised a pound of gold lace, and six pairs of silk stockings at two guineas the pair: that Montague, being in a nobleman's household, was an appalling expense to her; that the younger boys were growing up and would require situations found for them, while Jane and Frances would some day need portioning: all which facts were so many heavy burdens,—and had not the Apostle said that he who neglected to provide for his own was worse than an infidel? Lady Louvaine received this letter with a slight sigh, a gentle smile, and "Poor Frances!" But the usually calm, sunny temper of Edith was not proof against it. She tore the letter in two and flung the fragments into the fire.

"Edith, my dear daughter!" ejaculated her astonished mother.

"Mother, I can't stand it!" was the response. "I must either do this or something worse. And to drag in the Apostle Paul as a prop for such hypoc——I'll just go and churn, and perhaps I can talk like a Christian when I come back!"

Such things as these did not move Lady Louvaine. But there were two things which did move her, even to tears. The first was when Hans brought her a little box in which lay five silver pieces, entreating her to accept them, such as they were—and she found after close cross-examination that part of the money was the boy's savings to buy cherished books, and part the result of the sale of his solitary valuable possession, a pair of silver buckles.

The other took place when notice was given to all the servants. Each received his or her wages, and a little token of remembrance, with bow or courtesy, and an expression of regret on leaving so kind a mistress, mingled with good wishes for her future welfare: all but one. That one was Charity, the under-housemaid from Pendle. Charity rolled up her arms in her apron, and said curtly —"Nay !"

" But, Charity, I owe you this," responded her mistress in some surprise.

"If you're bound to reckon up, my Lady, betwixt you and me, there mun be somewhat set down o' tother side o' th' book," announced Charity sturdily. "Yo' mun mind you 'at yo' took me ba'at [1] a commendation, because nob'ry [2] 'd have me at after Mistress Watson charged me wi' stealing her lace fall, 'at she found at after amongst her kerchiefs; that's a hundred pound to th' good. And yo' nursed me through th' fever—that's another. And yo' held me back fro' wedding wi' yon wastrel [3] Nym Thistlethwaite, till I'd seen a bit better what manner of lad he were, and so saved me fro' being a poor, bruised, heart-broke thing like their Margery is now, 'at he did wed wi'—and that counts for five hundred at least. That's seven hundred pound, Madam, and I've nobut twelve i' th' world—I'm bankrupt. So, if you please, we'll have no reckonings, or I shall come off warst. And would you please to tell me when you look to be i' London town, and where you'll 'light first ? "

"My good Charity ! they named thee not ill," answered Lady Louvaine. "I trust to be in London the end of March—nigh on Lady Day; and I light at the White Bear, in the King's Street, Westminster."

"Pray you, Madam, how many miles is it hence ? "

"'Tis about two hundred miles, Charity."

---

[1] Without.   [2] Nobody.   [3] Scoundrel.

For a moment Charity was silent. Then she said, "An't like you, Madam, I'd fain go the first o' March."

Lady Louvaine was a little surprised, for she had given her servants a month's notice, which would expire on the fifteenth of March. However, if Charity preferred to be paid in time instead of money, that was her own affair. She assented, and Charity, dropping another courtesy, left the room.

Lady Louvaine's house in London had been obtained through the Earl of Oxford, a distant cousin of her husband, in whose household her son Walter had long before taken unwholesome lessons in fashion and extravagance. The Earl, now in his grand climacteric, had outlived his youthful frivolity, and though he had become a hard and austere man, was yet willing to do a kindness to his kinsman's widow by engaging a house for her, and offering for her grandson a squire's place which happened to be vacant in his household. She would have preferred some less showy and more solid means of livelihood for Aubrey, whose character was yet unfixed, and whose disposition was lighter than she liked to see it: but no other offered, and she accepted this.

A few days before the time for departure, up trudged Temperance Murthwaite again.

"Madam," said she, "I'm something 'feared I'm as welcome as water into a ship, for I dare guess you've enough to do with the hours, but truth to tell, I'm driven to it. Here's Faith set to go after you to London."

"Poor child! let her come."

"I can get as far as 'poor,' Madam, but I can go no further with you," answered Temperance grimly. "Somebody's poor enough, I cast no doubt, but I don't think it's Faith. But you have not yet beheld all your calamities. If Faith goes, I must go too—and if I go, and she, then must Lettice."

"Dear Temperance, I shall be verily glad."

"Lady Lettice, you're too good for this world!—and there aren't ten folks in it to whom I ever said that. Howbeit, you shall not lose by me, for I purpose to take Rachel withal, and she and I can do the housework betwixt us, and so set Edith free to wait on you. Were you thinking to carry servants, or find them there ? "

" I thought to find one there. More than one, methinks, we can scarce afford."

" Well, then for that shall Rachel serve : and I'll work the cost of my keep and more, you shall see. I can spin with the best, and weave too ; you'll never come short of linen nor linsey while I'm with you—and Lettice can run about and save steps to us all. What think you ?—said I well ? "

" Very well indeed, my dear : I were fain to have you."

" Then you'll look for us. Good-morrow ! "

The last evening was a busy one for all parties, and there was little time to spare for indulgence in remembrance or regret. It was two hours later than usual, when Lettice at last lay down to sleep and even then, sleep seemed long in coming. She heard her Aunt Edith's soft movements in the neighbouring gallery, where she was putting final touches to the packing, and presently they slid unconsciously into the sound of the waterfall at Skiddaw Force, by the side of which Lettice was climbing up to the Tower of London. She knew nothing of the tender, cheerful " Good-night, Mother dear ! " given to Lady Louvaine—of the long, pathetic gaze at the moonlit landscape—of the silently-sobbed prayer, and the passionate rain of tears—such different tears from those of Faith !—which left a wet stain upon Edith's coverlet. It was hard to leave the old home—hard to leave the new graves. But the next thing the young niece heard was only—" Time to rise, Lettice ! " spoken in the usual brighi manner—and, looking up, she saw Aunt Edith fully dressed.

Lettice sprang up in a fright, and scrambled into her clothes with all the haste possible. She, who was to have helped Aunt Edith, to be fast asleep in bed when she was ready! It was not many minutes before Lettice was dressed, but her morning prayer had in it sundry things which were not prayers.

Breakfast was nearly over when a curious rolling sound was heard, followed by the tramp of horses: and Aubrey jumped up to look, for it was half-an-hour too soon for the baggage-horses to be brought. He had to run into the porch-chamber to see what it was, and before he returned came old Roger the serving-man, with a letter in his hand, which he gave to his mistress. She opened the letter, but finding it somewhat difficult for dim eyes to make out, she gave it back to Roger, desiring him to read it.[1] So Roger read:—

"MADAM,—Since I need be in London this next week-end, where I look to tarry some time, and am offered a seat in my good Lord of Northumberland's caroche, it were pity that my caroche should go thither empty, in especial when so good and old a friend is likewise on her journey. May I therefore beg that your Ladyship will so far favour me as to use the caroche as your own, from this day until Friday week, when, if it serve your convenience, it may return to me at Radcliffe House? My servants have orders to obey your Ladyship's directions, and to serve you in all regards as myself.

"I kiss the hands of fair Mistress Edith, and beg my best compliments to your young gentlemen, and am, Madam, yours to my little power,   DILSTON."

[1] This was quite a common occurrence at that time, when men-servants were usually better educated, and ladies and gentlemen much less so, than now.

Aubrey had come back whilst Roger was reading, and scarcely gave him leave to make an end of the letter.

"Madam, 'tis my Lord Dilston's caroche, with six great Flanders horses, and three serving-men, all as fine as fiddlers, and never a soul in the caroche——"

"Truly, this is of the Lord's goodness," said Lady Louvaine. "I did indeed fear the journey on horseback, but there seemed none other means."

"The like did I for you, dear Mother," added Edith. "I am most thankful for my Lord Dilston's kindly proffer. It shall ease the journey to you more than all we could do."

Lady Louvaine bade Edith write an answer, and ordered Roger to take back to Mere Lea the three saddle-horses lent her by Mr. Lewthwaite, explaining why they were no longer needed. It was then settled that the four ladies and Lettice should travel in the coach, Aubrey, Hans, and Rachel going on horseback.

Hans had gone out, and they saw him talking in the front with Lord Dilston's postillion. Now he came back.

"Well, Hans, what wormed you out of the postillion?" inquired Aubrey.

"His master's goodness," said Hans.

"Have you a bit left for me? or do you want it all for yourself?"

"It is all for my Lady. My Lord Dilston was meaning to have gone to Town himself in his own caroche, till he heard of your Ladyship's trouble, and then he cast about to know of some friend that was going, so he might leave it for you. Then he heard of my Lord of Northumberland, and he begged a seat in his caroche; and Madam Penelope stuffed the caroche with all the cushions that were in the house, and a hamper of baked meats, and wine, and a great fur mantle to lap your Ladyship in; and my Lord bade the postillion to drive very soft, that you should not be shaken, without you told him to go fast, and the footmen were to have a care of you and save you all that they could. Said I not well, his goodness?"

"Truly, Hans, you did so," answered Edith; "and right thankful should we all be, first to the Lord, and then to my Lord Dilston, that my dear mother can now journey in safety and comfort."

Lady Louvaine said, softly, "Bless the Lord! and may He bless this kind friend! Truly, I marvel wherefore it is that every one is so good to me. It must be, surely, for my dead Aubrey's sake."

"Oh, of course," said young Aubrey, laughing; "they all hate *you*, Madam, you may be sure."

His grandmother smiled on him, for she understood him.

Now came the Murthwaite sisters trudging up the path, Temperance carrying a heavy basket, and Faith bearing no greater weight than her handkerchief, behind which, as usual, she was weeping.

"Good morrow, Madam," said Aunt Temperance as she came in. "A fine day for our journey."

"You're to ride in a caroche, Aunt Temperance!" cried Aubrey.

"Who—me? No, I thank you, my young Master. I never set foot in such a thing in my life, nor never will by my good will. I like the feel of a horse under me well enough; but that finicky gingerbread thing, all o'er gilding—I'd as soon go on a broomstick. Whose is it?"

"'Tis my Lord Dilston's, that hath most kindly proffered it to Mother for the journey," replied Edith. "We had settled that we four, with Lettice, should journey therein; but if you would rather be on horseback, Temperance——"

"That would I, by ten mile," said she. "I hate being cooped up in a four-post bed, with all the curtains drawn;

and that lumbering thing's no better. Faith'll go, I don't doubt; any thing that's a bit smart and showy'll take her : and Lettice may please herself. I dare say the child will have a fantasy to ride in a caroche for once in her life."

"Indeed, Aunt, I would like it," answered Lettice, "for very like I may never have such another chance while I live."

"Truly, that's little like," retorted Temperance with a laugh. "So have thy ride, child, if thou wilt. — Dear heart ! Lady Lettice, I ask your pardon."

"For what, Temperance, my dear ? "

"Taking your place, Madam, instead of my own. Here am I, deciding what Lettice shall do or not do, when you being in presence, it belongs to you to judge."

Lady Louvaine gave her gentle smile.

"Nay, if we must stand upon our rights, you, Temperance, as her father's sister, have the right to choose."

"Then I choose to obey you, Lady Lettice," said Temperance with a courtesy.

"Madam," now announced Hans from the door, "the baggage is packed, and the caroche awaiteth your Ladyship."

Edith helped her mother to rise from her chair. She stood one moment, her hand on Edith's arm; and a look came into her eyes such as a drowning man might give to the white cliffs whereon his home stood, where his wife and his little children were waiting for him. So she stood and looked slowly round the chamber, her eyes travelling from one thing to another, till she had gone all over it. And then she said, in a low, pathetic voice—

"'Get thee out of thy country, and from thy father's house, unto the land that I will show thee.' Once before I had that call, and it led me to him who was the stay and blessing of my life. Yet again I go forth: O my

Father, let it lead to Thee, unto Thy holy hill, and to Thy tabernacle! Remember Thy word unto Thy servant, wherein Thou hast caused me to hope—'Certainly I will be with thee,'—'I will not fail thee, nor forsake thee,'— 'Fear not, for I have redeemed thee: I have called thee by thy name; thou art Mine.' Lord, keep Thine own!— Now, my children, let us go hence with God."

In something like a procession they went forth from Selwick Hall. Lady Louvaine first, leaning on Edith and Hans, to whom Aubrey was always ready to resign troublesome duties; then Faith, Temperance, Aubrey, and Lettice.

At the door stood the great coach, painted in dark mulberry-colour and picked out with gilding, the lining and cushions of blue: and harnessed to it were the six great horses, dark roan, with cream-coloured manes, knotted likewise in blue. The servants wore mulberry-coloured livery, corded with blue.

Lady Louvaine took her place on the right hand of the coach, facing the horses, Faith being at her side. Opposite sat Edith, and Lettice by the door.

"Aunt Temperance!" called out Aubrey from the door-step, "you shall have my horse, if you will; I am going in the caroche."

"You are *what*, Sirrah?" demanded Aunt Temperance, with the severity of at least one Lord Chief Justice.

"I shall ride in the caroche," repeated Aubrey calmly.

"Northumberland, Cumberland, Westmoreland, and Durham!" was the awful answer.

The young people knew what that meant. When Temperance said "Dear heart!" she was just a little surprised or put out; when it was "Lancaster and Derby!" she was very much astonished or provoked; but when she supplicated the help of "Northumberland, Cumberland, Westmoreland, and Durham!" it meant from

Aunt Temperance what swearing would from any one else.

"I should like to know, if you please, Mr. Aubrey Louvaine, whether you are a king, a sick woman, or a baby?"

"Well, Aunt, I don't think I am any of them at present."

"Then you have no business to ride in a caroche till you are. I never heard of such a thing in my life. A man to ride in a caroche! We shall have them hemming handkerchiefs to-morrow."

"You won't have me," said Aubrey.

"I won't have you in there," retorted Temperance bluntly, "without my Lady Lettice call you in, and that she won't. Will you, Madam?"

"Certainly not, my dear, after your decision," she replied. "Indeed, I do think it too effeminate for men, persons of high honour except, or them that are sick and infirm."

"That rascal's not sick, any more than he's a person of honour.—Thee bestride thy horse, lad—without thou canst find an ass, which would suit with thee better.—Now, Hans, come and help me to mount."

When all were mounted, the six great horses tugged and strained at the big coach, and with a good push from the four farm-servants, it moved forwards, at first slowly, then faster. The farm-servants stood bareheaded, to see the family depart, crying, "God bless you, my Lady, and bring you home in peace!"

Faith sank back sobbing into the corner, and there were tears in Edith's eyes which she would not let fall.

"Farewell!" said Lady Louvaine, leaning forward. "Farewell, my good, kind old friends—Thomas, William, Isaac, and Gideon—I wish you God's blessing, and a better head than I."

"Nay, nay, that'll ne'er be, nor couldn't, no wise!" cried old Gideon, and the rest all echoed his "Nay, nay!"

"Farewell!" said his mistress again, somewhat faintly, as she sank back into the corner. "Friends, God will bless me, and He shall bring me home in peace."

CHAPTER II.

THE JOURNEY TO LONDON.

" And yet, I do remember, some dim sense
  Of vague presentiment
Swept o'er me, as beyond the gates we turned
  To make the long descent."

AT the bridge-end, as they came up, were Milisent and her husband, with seven of their nine children,—even little Fortune, but five years old, whom Milisent lifted into the coach and set on her Aunt Edith's knee, saying " she should say all her life that she had sat in my Lord Dilston's caroche." Then Milisent came in herself and sat down for a moment between her mother and Faith, whilst her husband talked with Aubrey, and all the children crowded about Hans, always a favourite with children. After a few minutes' conversation, Robert came up to the coach-door with—"Time to go, Milly. We must not tarry Mother on her journey, for she is like to be weary enough ere she come to its end."

Then Milisent broke down, and threw her arms around her mother, and cried,—"O Mother, Mother, how shall I do without you? Must I never see you again?"

"My Milisent," said Lady Louvaine, " I shall not carry God from thee. And thou wilt surely see me again, sweet heart, where we shall part no more for ever."

c

For a few minutes Milisent wept as if her heart would break; then she wiped her eyes, and kissed them all round, only breaking down a little again when she came to her sister Edith.

"O Edith, darling sister, I never loved thee half well enough!"

Edith was calm now. "Send me the other half in thy letters, Milly," she replied, "and I will return it to thee."

"Ay, we can write betimes," said Milisent, looking a little comforted. Then to her niece,—"Now, Lettice, I look to thee for all the news. The first day of every month shall we begin to look out for a letter at Mere Lea; and if my sister cannot write, then must thou. Have a care!"

"So I will, Aunt," said Lettice.

Milisent alighted with a rather brighter look—she was not wont to look any thing but bright—Robert took his leave and then came all the cousins pouring in to say good-bye. So the farewells were spoken, and they went on their journey; but as far as they could see until hidden by the hill round which they drove, Milisent's handkerchief was waving after them.

Lady Louvaine bore the journey better than her daughters had feared; and our friends deemed themselves very happy that during the whole of it, they were not once overturned, and only four times stuck in the mud. At the end of the fourth day, which was Friday, they came up to the door of the Hill House at Minster Lovel. And as they lumbered round the sweep with their six horses, Edith cried joyously, —"Oh, there's old Rebecca!"

To Edith Louvaine, a visit to the Hill House was in a sense coming home, for its owner, her father's cousin, Joyce Morrell, had been to her almost a second mother. When people paid distant visits in the sixteenth century, it was not for a week's stay, but for half a year, or at least a quarter. During many years it had been the custom that visits of this length should be exchanged between Selwick Hall and the Hill House at Minster Lovel alternately, at the close of every two years. But Edith, who was Aunt Joyce's special favourite, had paid now and then a visit between-times; and when, as years and infirmities increased, the meetings were obliged to cease for the elders, Edith's yearly stay of three or four months with the old and lonely cousin had become an institution instead of them. Her feeling, therefore, was much like that of a daughter of the house introducing her relatives to her own home; for Lady Louvaine was the only other of the party to whom the Hill House had been familiar in old times.

Its owner, the once active and energetic old lady, now confined to her couch by partial paralysis, had been called Aunt Joyce by the Louvaines of the second generation ever since their remembrance lasted. To the younger ones, however, she was a stranger; and they watched with curious eyes their Aunt Edith's affectionate greeting of the old servant Rebecca, who had guarded and amused her as a baby, and loved her as a girl. Rebecca, on her part, was equally glad to see her.

"Run you in, Mrs. Edith, my dear," said she; "you'll find the mistress in the Credence Chamber. Eh, she has wearied for you!—Good evening, Madam, and I'm fain to see your Ladyship again. Would you please to allow of my help in 'lighting?'"

While Rebecca and Hans assisted her mother to descend, Edith ran into the house with as light and fleet a step as if she were fourteen instead of forty, and entered a large, low chamber, hung with dark leather hangings, stamped in gold, where a bright lamp burned on a little table, and on a low couch beside it lay an old lady, covered over with a fur coverlet. She had a pleasant, kindly old face, with fresh rose-colour in her cheeks, and snow-white hair; and her face lighted up when she saw Edith, like a candle set in a dark window. Edith ran to her, and cast her arms about her, and she said, "My Edith, mine own dear child!" as tenderly as if she had been her own mother.

Lady Louvaine followed her daughter, leaning on Hans and Rebecca, who took her up to the couch, and set her down in a large chair furnished with soft cushions, which stood close beside, as if it were there on purpose. She laid her hand upon Joyce's, who fondled it in both hers. Then Joyce gave a little laugh.

"Lettice, dost thou wonder to hear me laugh?" asked she. "I seemed like as if I saw, all at once, that sunshine afternoon when thou camest first over from the Manor House, sent of my Lady Norris to make friends with us. Dost remember?"

"And thou camest tripping lightly down the stairs, clad of a russet gown, and leddest me up to see Anstace. 'Do I remember it!' Ah, Joyce, my sister, there be sore changes since that day!"

"Be there so?" said Joyce, and smiled brightly enough. "A good number of miles nearer Home, Lettice, and a good number of treasures laid up for both of us, where neither moth nor rust shall hurt them. My treasures are all there which are not likewise thine. And now let me see the new gems in thy jewel-box. Who art thou, my maid?"

"I am Lettice Murthwaite, Madam, if you please."

"My dear heart, I do not please to be called Madam. I am thine Aunt Joyce. Come here and kiss me, if thou wilt."

Lettice knelt down by the couch, and kissed the old lady.

"There is not much of Nell here, Lettice," said Joyce to Lady Louvaine. "'Tis her father the child is like.

Now then, which of these two lads is Aubrey—he with
the thinking brow, or he with the restless eyes?"

Lady Louvaine called Aubrey, and he came up.

"Why, thou art like nobody," said Aunt Joyce.
"Neither Ned nor Faith, nor any of Ned's elders. Lettice,
where is Faith? hast not brought her withal?"

Faith was in the hall, listening to a lecture from
Temperance, embellished by such elegancies as "Stuff and
nonsense!" and "Listen to reason!" which ended up at
last with "Lancaster and Derby!" and Faith came slowly
in, with her everlasting handkerchief at her eyes.

"Nay, Faith, sweet heart, no tears!" cried the old lady.
"Sure there's nought to weep for this even, without thou
art so dog-weary that thou canst not keep them back."

"Mistress Morrell, I wish you good even," said Temperance, coming in after her sister. "If you'll but learn
Faith to keep that handkerchief of hers in her pocket,
you'll have done the best work ever you did since we saw
you last in Derwent-dale. She's for ever and the day
after a-fretting and a-petting, for why she'd better tell
you, for I'm a Dutchman if I can make out."

Aunt Joyce looked from one to the other.

"So unfeeling!" came Faith's set form, from behind the
handkerchief. "And me a poor widow!"

The old lady's face went very grave, and all the cheeri-
ness passed out of it.

"Faith, you are not the only widow in the chamber,"
she said gently. "Temperance, my dear, she is weary,
maybe."

"She hasn't got a bit of call," rejoined Temperance.
"Sat all day long in my Lord Dilston's smart caroche,
lolling back in the corner, just like a feather-bed. Mistress
Joyce, 'tis half ill-temper and half folly—that's what
it is."

"Well, well, my dear, we need not judge our neigh-

bours.—Edith, my child, thou knowest the house as wel
as I; wilt thou carry thy friends above? Rebecca hath
made ready My Lady's Chamber for my Lady "—with a
smile at her old friend—" and the Fetterlock Chamber for
Faith and Temperance. The Old Wardrobe is for thee
and Lettice, and the lads shall lie in the Nursery."

Names to every room, after this fashion, were customary
in old houses. The party were to stay at Minster Lovel
for four days, from Friday to Tuesday, and then to pursue
their journey to London.

In the Old Wardrobe, a pleasant bedchamber on the
upper floor, Lettice washed off the dust of the journey,
and changed her clothes when the little trunk came up
which held the necessaries for the night. Then she tried
to find her way to the Credence Chamber, and—as was
not very surprising—lost it, coming out into a long pic-
ture-gallery where she was at once struck and entranced
by a picture that hung there. It represented a young
girl about her own age, laid on a white couch, and dressed
in white, but with such a face as she had never seen on
any woman in this life. It was as white as the garments,
with large dark eyes, wherein it seemed to Lettice as if
her very soul had been melted; a soul that had gone down
into some dreadful deep, and having come up safe, was
ever afterwards anxiously ready to help other souls out
of trouble. She would have thought the painter meant
it for an angel, but that angels are not wont to be in-
valids and lie on couches. Beside this picture hung
another, which reminded her of her Grandfather Louvaine;
but this was of a young man, not much older than Aubrey,
yet it had her grandfather's eyes, which she had seen in
none else save her Aunt Edith. Now Lettice began to
wonder where she was, and how she should find her way;
and hearing footsteps, she waited till they came up, when
she saw old Rebecca.

"Why, my dear heart, what do you here?" said she kindly.

"Truly, I know not," the youthful visitor answered. "I set forth to go down the stairs, and missed the right turning, as I guess. But pray you, Rebecca, ere you set me in the way, tell me of whom are these two pictures?"

"Why," said she, "can you not guess? The one is of your own grandfather, Sir Aubrey Louvaine."

"Oh, then it is Grandfather when he was young. But who is this, Rebecca? It looks like an angel, but angels are never sick, and she seems to be lying sick."

"There be angels not yet in Heaven, Mistress Lettice," softly answered the old servant. "And if you were to live to the age of Methuselah, you'd never see a portrait of one nearer the angels than this. 'Tis a picture that old Squire —Mistress Joyce's father—would have taken, nigh sixty years since, of our angel, our Mistress Anstace, when she was none so many weeks off the golden gate. They set forth with her in a litter for London town, and what came back was her coffin, and that picture."

"Was she like that?" asked Lettice, scarcely above her breath, for she felt as if she could not speak aloud, any more than in church.

"She was, and she was not," said old Rebecca. "Them that knew her might be minded of her. She was like nothing in this world. But, my dear heart, I hear Mrs. Edith calling for you. Here be the stairs, and the Credence Chamber, where supper is laid, is the first door on your left after you reach the foot."

On the Saturday evening, as they sat round the fire in the Credence Chamber, Edith asked Aunt Joyce if old Dr. Cox were still parson of Minster Lovel.

"Nay," said she; "I would he were. We have a new lord and new laws, the which do commonly go together."

" What manner of lord ? " inquired Edith.

" And what make of laws ? " said Temperance.

" Bad, the pair of them," said the old lady.

" Why, is he a gamester or drunkard ? " asked Lady Louvaine.

" Or a dumb dog that cannot bark ? " suggested Temperance.

" Well, I'd fain have him a bit dumber," was Aunt Joyce's answer. " At least, I wish he'd dance a bit less."

" Dance ! " cried Edith.

" Well ! " said Aunt Joyce, " what else can you call it, when a man measures his steps, goes two steps up and bows, then two steps down and bows, then up again one step, with a great courtesy, and holds up his hands as if he were astonished—when there's nothing in the world to astonish him except his own foolish antics ? "

" But where doth he this ? " said Lady Louvaine: " here in the chamber, or out of door ? "

" Dear heart ! in the church."

" But for why ? "

" Prithee ask at him, for I can ne'er tell thee."

" Did you ne'er ask him, Aunt ? " said Edith.

" For sure did I, and gat no answer that I could make aught of: only some folly touching Catholic practice, and the like. And, 'Master Twinham,' said I, 'I know not well what you would be at, but I can tell you, I lived through the days of Queen Mary, and, if that be what you mean by Catholic practices, they are practices we don't want back again.' Well, he mumbled somewhat about being true to the Church, and such like: but if he be an honest man, my shoes be made of Shrewsbury sweet bread. We tumbled all such practices out of the Church, above forty years gone; and what's more, we'll not stand to have them brought in again, though there be some may try."

"They will not bring any such folly in while the Queen liveth, I guess," answered Edith.

"Amen! but the Queen, God bless her! is seventy this year."

"Would you have her live for ever, Aunt Joyce?" asked Aubrey.

"Would she could!" she answered. "As to this fellow, I know not what he'll be at next. He told me to my face that a Papist was better than a Puritan. 'Well, Mr. Twinham,' said I, 'you may be a Papist, but I am a Puritan, and there I tarry till I find somewhat better.'"

"Why, Joyce!" said Lady Louvaine, smiling, "thou wert not wont to call thyself a Puritan, in the old days when thou and Bess Wolvercot used to pick a crow betwixt you over Dr. Meade's surplice at Keswick."

"No, I wasn't," said she. "But I tell you, Lettice, there be things human nature cannot bear. A clean white surplice and Christ's Gospel is one thing, and a purple vestment and an other Gospel is another. And if I'm to swallow the purple vestment along with the white surplice, I'll have neither. As to old Bess, dear blessed soul! she's in her right place, where she belongs; and if I may creep in at a corner of Heaven's door and clean her golden sandals, I shall be thankful enough, the Lord knows."

"But, Mrs. Morrell! sure you never mean to say that surplices be giving place to purple vestments down this road!" cried Temperance in much horror.

"Children," said the old lady very solemnly, "we two, in God's mercy, shall not live to see what is coming, but very like you will. And I tell you, all is coming back which our fathers cast forth into the Valley of Hinnom, and afore you—Temperance, Faith, and Edith—be old women, it will be set up in the court of the Temple. Ay, much if it creep not into the Holy of Holies ere those three young folks have a silver hair. The Devil is coming, children: he's safe to be first; and in his train are the priests and the Pope. They are all coming: and you'll have to turn them out again, as your grandfathers did. And don't you fancy that shall be an easy task. It'll be the hardest whereto you ever set your shoulders. God grant you win through it! There are two dangers afore you, and when I say that, I mean not the torture-chamber and the stake. Nay, I am thinking of worser dangers than those—snares wherein feet are more easily trapped, a deal. List to me, for ere many years be over, you will find that I speak truth. The lesser danger is if the Devil come to you in his black robes, and offer to buy you with that which he guesseth to be your price—and that shall not be the same for all: a golden necklace may tempt one, and a place at Court another, and a Barbary mare a third. But worse, far worse, is the danger when the Devil comes in his robes of light; when he gilds his lie with a cover of outside truth; when he quotes Scripture for his purpose, twisting it so subtilely that if the Spirit of God give you not the answer, you know not how to answer him. Remember, all you young ones, and Aubrey in especial, that no man can touch pitch and not be defiled. 'Evil communications corrupt good manners': and they corrupt them worst and quickest when you see not that they be evil. If you think the scales be falling from your eyes, make very sure that they are not growing on them. And you can do that only by keeping very close to God's footstool and to God's Word. Be sure of this: whatsoever leads you away from that Book leads you wrong. I care not what it be—King or Pope, priest or layman, blind faith or blind reason,—he that neglects and sets aside the Word of God, for whatever cause, and whatever thing he would put in his place—children, his ways incline unto Hell, and his paths unto the dead. Go not after him, nor follow him. Mark my words, and see, twenty and yet more forty years hence, if they come not true."

Aubrey whispered to Lettice, " What made her pick out me ' in especial,' trow ? I'm not about to handle no pitch."

But Hans said, with his gravest face, "·I thank you, Madam," and seemed to be thinking hard about something all the rest of the evening.

On the Sunday morning, all went to church except the two old ladies, who could honestly plead infirmity.

When they came out, Lettice, who was burning to speak her mind, exclaimed,—" Saw you ever a parson so use himself, Aubrey ? Truly I know not how to specify it—turning, and twisting, and bowing, and casting up of his hands and eyes—it well-nigh made me for to laugh ! "

" Like a merry Andrew or a cheap Jack," laughed Aubrey.

" I thought his sermon stranger yet," said Hans, "nor could I see what it had to do with his text."

" What was his text ? " inquired heedless Aubrey.

" 'Thou shalt love the Lord thy God,' " repeated Hans.

" Ay, and all he did, the hour through," cried Lettice, "was to bid us obey the Church, and hear the Church, and not run astray after no novelties in religion. And the Church is not the Lord our God, neither is religion, so far as I see."

" I mind Sir Aubrey once saying," added Hans, " that when a bride talked ever of herself, and nothing of her bridegroom, it was a very ill augury of the state of her heart."

" But saw you those two great candlesticks on the holy table ?—what for be they ? " said Lettice.

" Oh, they be but ornaments of the church," answered Aubrey, carelessly.

"But we have none such in Keswick Church: and what is the good of candlesticks without candles?"

"The candles will come," quietly replied Hans.

"Ah! you're thinking of what the old gentlewoman said last night—confess, Master Sobersides!" said Aubrey.

"I have thought much on it," answered Hans, who walked along, carrying the ladies' prayer-books; for the road being dirty, they had enough to do in holding up their gowns. "And I think she hath the right."

"Hans, I marvel how old thou wert when thou wert born!" said Aubrey.

"I think, very like, about as old as you were," said Hans.

"Well, Mr. Louvaine, you are a complete young gentleman!" cried his Aunt Temperance, looking back at him. "To suffer three elder gentlewomen to trudge in the mire, and never so much as offer to hand one of them! Those were not good manners, my master, when I was a young maid—but seeing how things be changed now o' days, maybe that has gone along with them. Come hither at once, thou vagrant, and give thine hand to thy mother, like a dutiful son as thou shouldest be, and art not."

"Oh, never mind me!" sighed Faith. "I have given over expecting such a thing. I am only a poor widow."

"Madam," apologised Hans, very red in the face, "I do truly feel ashamed that I have no better done my duty, and I entreat you not——"

"I was not faulting thee, lad," said Temperance. "We have already laden thee with books; and it were too much to look for thee to do thine own duty and other folks' too. It's this lazy lad I want. I dare be bound he loveth better to crack jests with his cousins than to be dutiful to his old mother and aunts."

"Temperance, I am only thirty-nine," said Faith in an injured voice. "I am the youngest of us three."

"Oh deary me! I ask your pardon," cried Tempe-

rance, with a queer set of her lips. "Yes, Madam, you
are; Edith is an old woman of forty, and I a decrepit
creature of forty-five; but you are a giddy young thing
of thirty-nine. I'll try to mind it, at least till your next
birthday."

Lettice laughed, and Aunt Temperance did not look
angry, though she pulled a face at her. Edith smiled,
and said pleasantly—

"Come, Aubrey, hand thy mother on my side; I will
walk with Lettice and Hans."

"Aunt Edith," said Lettice, "pray you, why be those
candlesticks on the holy table, with never a candle in
them?"

"I cannot tell, Lettice," replied she; "I fear, if the
parson dared, there would be candles in them, and belike
will, ere long."

"Think you Aunt Joyce is right in what she said last
night?"

"I fear so, Lettice," she answered very gravely. "We
have not yet seen the last, I doubt, of Satan and his
Roman legion."

The same afternoon, Lettice had a talk with old Rebecca,
which almost frightened her. She went up to the gallery
for another look at the two pictures, and Rebecca passing by, Lettice begged that if she were not very busy,
she would tell her something about them. In reply she
heard a long story, which increased her reverential love
for the dead grandfather, and made her think that "Cousin
Anstace" must have been an angel indeed. Rebecca had
lived in the Hill House for sixty years, and she well
remembered her mistress's sister.

"Mind you Queen Mary's days, Rebecca?" asked
Lettice.

"Eh, sweet heart!" said the old servant. "They could
ne'er be forgot by any that lived in them."

"Saw you any of the dreadful burnings?"

" Ay, did I, Mrs. Lettice," said she,—"even the head and chief of them all, of my Lord's Grace of Canterbury. I saw him hold forth his right hand in the flame, that had signed his recantation : and after all was over, and the fire out, I drew nigh with the crowd, and beheld his heart entire, uncharred amongst the ashes. Ah my mistress! if once you saw such a sight as that, you could never forget it, your whole life thereafter."

"It must have been dreadful, Rebecca!" said Lettice.

" Well, it was, in one way," she answered: "and yet, in another, it was right strengthening. I never felt so strong in the faith as that hour, and for some while after. It was like as if Heaven had been opened to me, and I had a glimpse of the pearly portals, and the golden street, and the white waving wings of the angels as he went in."

" Saw you the Bishops burned, Rebecca—Dr. Ridley and Dr. Latimer?"

"I did not, Mrs. Lettice; yet have I seen them both, prisoners, led through Oxford streets. Dr. Ridley was a man with a look so grave that it was well-nigh severe : but Dr. Latimer could break a jest with any man, and did, yea, with his very judges."

" Were you ever in any danger, Rebecca?—or Mrs. Morrell?"

"I never was, Mrs. Lettice; but my good mistress was once well-nigh taken of the catchpoll.[1] You ask her to tell you the story, how she came at him with the red-hot poker. And after that full quickly she packed her male, and away to Selwick to Sir Aubrey and her Ladyship, where she tarried hid until Queen Elizabeth came in."

" Think you there shall ever be such doings in England again?"

" The Lord knoweth," and old Rebecca shook her white

[1] Constable.

head. " There's not a bit of trust to be put in them snakes of priests and Jesuits and such like : not a bit ! Let them get the upper hand again, and we shall have the like times. Good Lord, deliver us from them all!"

Lettice went down, intending to ask Aunt Joyce to tell her the story of the red-hot poker; but she never thought of it again, so absorbed was she with what the two old ladies were saying as she came in. They did not hear her enter: and the first word she heard made her so desirous of more, that she crept as softly as she could to a seat. Curiosity was her besetting sin.

" She used not to be thus," said Lady Louvaine. " Truly, I know not what hath thus sorrowfully changed the poor child; but I would some means might be found to undo the same. Even for some years after Ned's death, I mind not this change; it came on right slowly and by degrees."

Lettice felt pretty sure that " she " was Aunt Faith.

" 'Tis weakness, I suppose," said Lady Louvaine, in a questioning tone.

" Ay, we are all weak some whither," replied Aunt Joyce ; " and Faith's weakness is a sort to show. She is somewhat too ready to nurse her weaknesses, and make pets of them. 'Tis bad enough for a woman to pet her own virtues; but when she pets her vices, 'tis a hard thing to better her. But, Lettice, there is a strong soul among you—a rare soul, in good sooth ; and there is one other, of whose weakness, and what are like to be its consequences, I am far more in fear than of Faith's."

" Nay, who mean you ? " asked Lady Louvaine in a perplexed voice.

" I mean the two lads—Hans and Aubrey."

" Hans is a good lad, truly."

" Hans has more goodness in him than you have seen the end of, by many a mile. But Aubrey ! "

"You reckon not Aubrey an ill one, I hope?"

"By which you mean, one that purposes ill? Oh no, by no means. He is a far commoner character—one that hath no purpose, and so being, doth more real ill than he that sets forth to do it of malicious intent."

"Are you assured you wrong not the lad, Joyce, in so saying?"

"If I do, you shall full shortly know it. I trust it may be so. But he seems to me to have a deal more of Walter in him than Ned, and to be right the opposite of our Aubrey in all main conditions."

"Ah," sighed the widow, in a very tender tone, "there can be no two of him!" Then after a little pause, "And what sayest thou to Lettice—my little Lettice?"

The concealed listener pricked up both her ears.

Aunt Joyce gave a little laugh. "Not so very unlike an other Lettice that once I knew," said she. "Something less like to fall in the same trap, methinks, and rather more like to fall in an other."

"Now, tell me what other?"

"I mean, dear heart, less conceit of her favour,[1] and more of her wisdom. A little over-curious and ready to meddle in matters that concern her not. A good temper, methinks, and more patience than either of her aunts on the father's side: as to humility—well, we have none of us too much of that."

"Joyce, wouldst thou like to have us leave Lettice a while with thee? She could wait on thee and read to thee, and be like a daughter to thee. I will, if thou wouldst wish it."

"Nay, that would I not, Lettice, for the child's own sake. It were far better for her to go with you. There is an offer thou couldst make me, of that fashion, that my self-denial were not equal to refuse. So see thou make it not."

---

[1] Beauty.

"What, now? Not Hans, trow?"

"Edith."

"O Joyce!"

"Ay, dear heart, I know. Nay, fear not. I'll not take the last bud off the old tree. But, thyself saved, Lettice, there is none left in all the world that I love as I love her. Perchance she will find it out one day."

"Joyce, my dear sister——"

"Hold thy peace, Lettice. I'll not have her, save now and again on a visit. And not that now. Thou shouldst miss her sorely, in settling down in thy new home. Where shall it be?"

"In the King's Street of Westminster. My good Lord Oxford hath made earnest with a gentleman, a friend of his, that hath there an estate, to let us on long lease an house and garden he hath, that now be standing empty."

"Ay, that is a pleasant, airy place, nigh the fields. At what rent?"

"Twenty-four shillings the quarter. Houses be dearer there than up in Holborn, yet not so costly as in the City; and it shall not be far for Aubrey, being during the day in the Court with his Lord."

"Lettice, you shall need to pray for that boy."

"What shall I ask for him, Joyce?"

"'That he may both perceive and know what things he ought to do, and also may have grace and power faithfully to fulfil the same.' Don't let him rule you. He is very like to try it, the only man in a family of women—for he shall make little account of Hans Floriszoon, though there is more sense in Hans's little finger than in all Aubrey's brains. If I can see into the future, Aubrey is not unlike to push you o'er, and Hans to pick you up again. Have a care, Lettice. You remember when Walter was in Court, with my Lord Oxford?"

"O Joyce!"

Lettice wondered what they meant, for she had never heard of her Uncle Walter being with Lord Oxford. She had never much liked Uncle Walter. He was always rather stiff and stern, and he used to come down sharply on niece or nephew if they did any thing wrong, yet not like her Grandfather Murthwaite, who was slow and solemn, and seemed to mourn over their evil deeds; but Uncle Walter was quick and sharp, and he snapped at them. They were under the impression that he never could have done a naughty thing in the whole course of his life, because he always seemed so angry and astonished to see the children do so. Lettice, therefore, was curious to hear about Uncle Walter.

"Well," said Aunt Joyce, "not exactly the same, yet too like. He'll take the colour of his company, like Walter: and he shall be evenly free-handed with his money——"

Lettice stared, though there was nothing to stare at but Aunt Joyce's big grey cat, curled up in the window-seat. Uncle Walter a spendthrift! she could not even imagine it. Did she not remember her Cousin Jane's surprise when her father gave her a shilling for a birth-day present? When Lettice listened again, Aunt Joyce was saying—

"He's no standing-ground. Whatso be the fantasy of the moment, after it he goes; and never stays him to think what is like to come thereof, far less what might come. But that which causes me fear more for him than Walter, is the matter of friends. Walter was not one to run after folks; he was frighted of lowering himself in the eyes of them he knew, but methinks he ran not after them as Aubrey doth. Hast ever watched a dog make friends of other dogs? for Aubrey hath right the dog's way. After every dog he goes, and gives a sniff at him;

and if the savour suit, he's Hail, fellow, well met! with him the next minute. Beware that Aubrey makes no friend he bringeth not home, so far as you can: and yet, Beware whom he bringeth, for Lettice' sake. 'Tis hard matter: 'good for the head is evil for the neck and shoulders.' To govern that lad shall ask no little wisdom; and if thou have it not, thou knowest where to ask. I would his mother had more, or that his father had lived. Well! that's evil wishing; God wist better than I. But the lad 'll be a sore care to thee, and an heavy."

"I fear so much, indeed," said Lady Louvaine, and she sighed.

Then Edith came in, and exclaimed, "What, all in the dark?" and Aunt Joyce bade her call Rebecca to bring light. So the naughty Lettice slipped out, and in five minutes more came boldly in, and no one knew what she had heard.

As they sat round the fire that evening, Aunt Joyce asked suddenly, "Tell me, you three young folks, what be your ambitions? What desire you most of all things to be, do, or have?—Lettice?"

"Why, Aunt, I can scarce tell," said Lettice, "for I never thought thereupon."

"She should choose to be beautiful, of course," suggested Aubrey. "All women do."

"Marry come up, my young Master!" cried his Aunt Temperance.

"Oh, let him be, Temperance," answered Aunt Joyce. "He knows a deal more about women than thou and I; 'tis so much shorter a time since he was one."

Temperance laughed merrily, and Aubrey looked disconcerted.

"I think I care not much to be beautiful, Aunt, nor rich," said Lettice: "only sufficient to be not uncomely nor tried of poverty. But so far as I myself can tell what I do most desire is to know things—all things that ever there be to know. I would like that, I think, above all."

"To know God and all good things were a very good and wise wish, Lettice," was Aunt Joyce's answer; "but to know evil things, this was the very blunder that our mother Eve made in Eden. Prithee, repeat it not. Now, Aubrey, what is thy wish?"

"I would like to be a rich king," said he.

"Were I a fairy queen, Aubrey, I would not give thee thy wish: for thou couldst scarce make a worser. 'They that will be rich fall into temptation and a snare,' and they that seek power be little behind them. 'Godliness is great riches,' lad, 'if a man be content with that he hath.'"

"Methinks, Aunt, that is one of your favourite texts," remarked Edith.

"Ay," said she, "it is. 'Enough is as good as a feast.' Hans, 'tis thy turn."

Hans had sat gravely looking into the fire while the others talked. Now he looked up, and answered—

"Madam, I am ambitious more than a little. I desire to do God's will, and to be content therewith."

"Angels could win no further," answered Aunt Joyce, with much feeling in her voice. "Ay, lad; thou hast flown at highest game of all."

"Why, Aunt!" said Aubrey, "never heard I a meaner wish. Any man could do that."

"Prithee do it, then," replied Aunt Joyce, "and I for one shall be full fain to see thee."

"No man ever yet fulfilled that wish," added Edith, "save only Christ our Lord."

Lady Louvaine sighed somewhat heavily; and Joyce asked, "What is it, dear heart?"

"Ah!" said she, "thy question, Joyce, and the children's

answers, send me back a weary way, nigh sixty years gone, to the time when I dwelt bowerwoman with my Lady of Surrey, when one even the Lady of Richmond willed us all to tell our desires after this manner. I mind not well all the answers, but I know one would see a coronation, and an other fair sights in strange lands : and I, being then young and very foolish, wished for a set of diamond, and my Lady of Richmond herself to be a queen. But my Aubrey's wish was something like Hans's, for he said he desired to be an angel. Ah me! nigh sixty years!"

"He hath his wish," responded Aunt Joyce softly. "And methinks Hans is like to have his also, so far as mortal man may compass it. There be some wishes, children, that fulfil themselves : and aspirations after God be of that sort. 'He meeteth them that remember Him.' Lettice, I trust thou mayest have thy wish to a reasonable length, so far as is good for thee : and, Aubrey, I can but desire the disappointment of thine, for it were very evil for thee. But thou, Hans Floriszoon, 'go in peace; and the God of Israel grant thee thy petition that thou hast asked of Him.'"

It was hard work for those two old friends to part, each knowing that it was almost certain they would never again meet until they clasped hands in the Paradise of God. When it came to the farewell, Lady Louvaine knelt down, though with difficulty—for Joyce could not raise herself—and the adopted sisters exchanged one long fervent embrace.

"O Joyce, my friend, my sister! my one treasure left to me from long ago! We shall never kiss again till——"

Lettice Louvaine's voice was lost in sobs.

"Maybe, dear heart—maybe not. Neither thou nor I can know the purposes of God. If so, farewell till the Golden City!—and if thou win in afore me at the pearly

portals, give them all my true love, and say I shall soon
be at home."

"Farewell, love! There is none to call me Lettice but
thee, left now."

"Nay, sweet heart, not so. '*I* have called thee by
thy name.' There will be One left to call thee 'Lettice,'
until He summon thee by that familiar name to enter the
Holy City."

So they journeyed on towards London.

It was on the afternoon of the twenty-fourth of March
that they sighted the metropolis at last from the summit
of Notting Hill. They drove down the Oxford road,
bounded on either side by green hedges, with here and
there a house—the busy Oxford Street of our day—turned
down the Hay Market to Charing Cross, and passed by
Essex Gate and its companion portal, the Court Gate,
through "the Court," now known as Whitehall, emerging
upon "the King's Street." There was no Parliament
Street in those days.

As they turned into King Street, it struck the elders
of the party that there seemed to be an unusual stir of
some kind. The streets were more crowded than usual,
men stood in little knots to converse, and the talk
was manifestly of a serious kind. Lady Louvaine bade
Edith look out and call Aubrey, whom she desired to
inquire of some responsible person the meaning of this
apparent commotion. Aubrey reined in his horse accordingly, as he passed a gentleman in clerical attire, which
at that date implied a cassock, bands, and black stockings. Had Aubrey known it, the narrowness of the
bands, the tall hat, the pointed shoes, and the short
garters, also indicated that the clergyman in question was
a Puritan.

"Pray you, Sir, is there news of import come?" inquired
the youth: "or what means this ado?"

The clergyman stopped suddenly, and looked up at his questioner.

"What means it?" he said sadly. "Friend, the great bell of Paul's was rung this morrow."

"I cry you mercy, Sir! Being a countryman, I take not your meaning."

"The great bell of Paul's," explained the stranger, "tolls never but for one thing, and hath been silent for over forty years."

"Good lack! not the plague, I trust?" cried Aubrey.

"Would it were no worse! Nay, this means that we are sheep without a shepherd—that she who hath led us for three-and-forty years, who under God saved us from Pope and Spaniard, can lead us no more for ever. Lad, no worser news could come to Englishmen than this. Queen Elizabeth hath passed away."

So, under the shadow of that dread sorrow, and that perilous uncertain future, they entered their new home.

CHAPTER III.

HOW IT FIRST BEGAN.

"O Conspiracy!
Sham'st thou to show thy dangerous brow by night,
When evils are most free? Oh, then, by day,
Where wilt thou find a cavern dark enough
To mask thy monstrous visage?"—*Shakspere.*

THE new home was the midmost of three contiguous houses, standing on the western side of King Street, and nearly opposite to what is now the entrance to New Palace Yard. They were a little larger and more pretentious than most of the houses in this street, and a good-sized garden ran backwards from each towards St. James's Park. As every house had then its name and a signboard to exhibit it—numbers being not yet applied to houses—these were no exception to the rule. That one of the trio nearest to the Abbey displayed a golden fish upon its signboard; the middle one hung out a white bear; while from the northernmost swung a panel representing an extremely stiff and angular creature apparently intended to suggest an angel. The young people made merry over their sign, Aubrey insisting that Hans was the White Bear, and Lettice retorting that it was Aubrey himself.

Hans and Aubrey sprang from their horses at the door; and while the latter rang the bell, the former busied him-

self in helping the ladies to alight. Whether any one
would be inside the house was a problem requiring solu-
tion; and they thought it worth while to ascertain this
before going further. In a moment, quick steps were
heard approaching, and the door was opened by a woman
who hardly showed herself behind it.

Lady Louvaine came in first, leaning on Hans.

"Good evening," she said to the portress. "It was
good of my Lord Oxford to provide—nay! Charity!"

"Ay, Madam, it's me," said the familiar voice of the
old servant, whom her mistress believed she had left
behind in Cumberland.

"Why, old friend! when camest thou hither?"

"You'd best sit you down afore you hear folks their
catechisms," said Charity, coolly, leading the way to a
pleasant parlour hung and upholstered in green, where a
fire was burning on the hearth, and a large cushioned
chair stood beside it. "When did I come? Well, let's
see!—it was o' Tuesday last."

"But how?" queried her mistress, in a tone which was
a mixture of astonishment and perplexity.

"Same how as I get to most places, Madam—on my
feet."

"You walked to London, Charity?"

"Ay, I did. I'm good for fifteen miles at a stretch."

"And whence gat you the money for your lodging?"

Charity laughed. "I never paid a halfpenny for
lodging nobut[1] once, and that was th' last night afore I
got here. Some nights I lay in a barn upo' th' hay: but
most on 'em I got took in at a farm-house, and did an
hour or two's work for 'em i' th' morn to pay for my
lodging and breakfast. But some on 'em gave it me right
out for nought—just for company like. I bought my

[1] Except, only. This, now a Northern provincialism, is an archaism at
least as old as the fourteenth century.

victuals, of course: but I should ha' wanted them wherever I'd been."

"And what led you to wish for life in London, Charity?"

"Eh! bless you, I want none to live i' London. It's a great, smoky, dirty place."

"Then what did you want?"

"I wanted yo'," said Charity, with a nod at her mistress. "Lady Lettice, yo'll not turn me away? If things is so bad you cannot afford to keep me, you shalln't: I can earn enough by my spinning half th' day, and serve you i' t' other half. But yo'll want two: I'm sure Rachel can ne'er do all th' work, and you'd best have me, for nob'ry else 'll put so much heart into 't as I shall. Do let me stop, for I cannot abear to leave you."

It was a moment before Lady Louvaine could speak. Then she held out her hand to Charity.

"My faithful Charity, I will not turn thee away! So long as I have two loaves of bread, thou mayest be sure of one."

"Thank God, that's all right!" said Charity with a sigh of evident relief. "We's [1] get on famous, Rachel and me, and nother on us 'll feel as if we'd been cast away of a desert island, as I've been feeling afore yo' come. Eh, but it is a town, is this!"

"Charity, I wonder how you won in the house," said Edith. "My Lord Oxford——"

"I've got a bit more gumption, Mrs. Edith, than you credit me with. I brought a letter to my Lord, or I should ne'er ha' looked to get in else."

"A letter!—from whom?"

"Fro' Mrs. Joyce Morrell, to tell him who I were, and a bit more, I reckon."

"I asked my Lord Oxford of his goodness to speak to some upholder [2] to send in a little necessary furnishing,"

---

[1] We shall.   Upholsterer.

said Lady Louvaine, looking round, "such as were strictly needful, and should last us till we could turn us about: but methinks he hath done somewhat more than that."

"You'll turn you round middling easy, Madam," answered Charity. "Th' upholder were bidden to put th' house to rights all through, and send the bill to Mistress Joyce. She gave me lodging fro' Setterday to Monday, and bade me see to 't that yo' had all things comfortable. 'Don't split sixpences,' she saith; 'the bigger the charges the better, so long as they be for true comfort and not for gimcracks.' So, Madam, I hope we've hit your Ladyship's liking, for me and Mrs. Joyce, we tried hard—me at choosing, and she at paying. So that's how it were."

And dropping a quick courtesy, Charity departed with too much alacrity for thanks.

Lady Louvaine's eyes followed her.

"The lines are fallen unto us in pleasant places," quoted Edith, softly.

"Ay," answered her mother. "And the pillar of the cloud hath gone before."

Charity found Rachel in the kitchen, carrying a carpet-bag and a great bundle, and gazing round her with a bewildered air.

"Well, lass, what's ta'en thee?" was her greeting.

"Eh, Charity Ashworth, is that thee? Where art thou fro'?"

"Where are we both come to? That's more to th' purpose."

"I'm banished my country, that's all I know," said Rachel, blankly. "I'm glad to see thee, schuzheaw."[1]

"Dost thou mean to carry yon for th' rest o' thy life?"

---

[1] Nevertheless. This strictly Lancastrian provincialism is supposed to be a corruption of "choose how." Its exact pronunciation can hardly be put into English letters.

demanded Charity, laying hands on the carpet-bag.
"Come, wake up, lass, and look sharp, for there'll be
some supper wanted."

A very expressive shake of Rachel's head was the
response. But she set down the bundle, and began to
unfasten her sleeves for work. Sleeves were not then
stitched to the gown, but merely hooked or buttoned in,
and were therefore easily laid aside when needful.

"What's the price o' eggs this road on?" asked she.

"Nought. We 'n getten th' hens to lay 'em. Down i'
th' market they're four a penny."

"Eggs—four a penny!" ejaculated the horrified cook.

"Ay—they're a bonnie price, aren't they? Ten to a
dozen the penny at Keswick. Chickens be twopence and
threepence a piece."

Rachel turned and faced her colleague with a solemn
air. "Charity Ashworth, wilt thou tell me what we've
come here for?"

"'To do our duty in that state of life to which it shall
please God to call us,'" said Charity, sturdily. "There's
twenty hens i' yon yard at th' end o' th' garden, and two
cows i' th' shippen, and three black pigs i' th' sty,—
Mistress Joyce ordered 'em—and two pairs o' hands, and
two brains, and two hearts, and the grace o' God: and if
thou wants aught more, thou'lt have to ask Him for it.
So now let's be sharp and see to th' supper."

As they sat at breakfast the next morning, which was
Lady Day and Sunday, Lady Louvaine said—

"I would fain know what manner of neighbours we
shall have here, whether pleasant or displeasant; for some
of our comfort shall hang thereon."

"Oh, there's a capital fellow at the Golden Fish," cried
Aubrey. "His name is Tom Rookwood, and his sister
Dorothy is the prettiest girl I have seen this month. I
know nought of the Angel."

"Ah!" said Hans, and shook his head, "I have seen the Angel."

"And is he angelic?" responded Aubrey.

"There be angels good and ill," Hans made answer. "Madam, I were best forewarn you—there's a tongue dwelleth there."

"What manner of tongue, Hans?" said Lady Louvaine, smiling.

"One that goes like a beggar's clapdish," said he; "leastwise, it did all the while I was in the garden this morning. She greeted me o'er the wall, and would know who we were, and every one of our names, and what kin we were one to the other, and whence we came, and wherefore, and how long we looked to tarry—she should have asked me what we had to our breakfast, if I had not come in."

"And how much toldest her?" inquired Temperance.

"Not a word that I could help," answered Hans. "Indeed, that is the only comfort of her—that she asks questions so fast you can scarce slide in an answer. She was free enough with her information as well—told me her name, and how many children she had, and that she paid three-and-fourpence the yard for her perpetuance gown."

"And what is her name?" asked Faith.

"Silence Abbott," said he.

"She scarce answers to it, seemingly," replied Temperance.

"Where made you acquaintance with your Tom Rookwood, Aubrey?" said his grandmother.

"At the door," said he. "His father is a gentleman of Suffolk, a younger son of Rookwood of Coldham Hall. He has three sisters,—I saw not the other two; but I say, that Dorothy's a beauty!"

"Well!" replied Temperance. "Folks say, 'As mute

as a fish'; but it seems to me the Golden Fish is well-nigh as talkative as the Angel. Mind thy ways, Aubrey, and get not thyself into no tanglements with no Dorothys. It shall be time enough for thee to wed ten years hence."

"And have a care that Mr. Rookwood be himself an upright and God-fearing man," added his Aunt Edith.

"Oh, he's all right!" answered Aubrey, letting Dorothy go by. "He saith he can hit a swallow flying at eighty paces."

"More shame for him!" cried Edith. "What for should he hit a swallow?"

"He has promised to show me all sorts of things," added Aubrey.

"Have a care," said Lady Louvaine, "that he lead thee not into the briars, my boy, and there leave thee."

The Monday morning brought a visitor—Mrs. Abbott, from the Angel, after whose stay Edith declared that a day's hard work would have fatigued her less of the two inflictions. This lady's freedom in asking questions, without the remotest sense of delicacy, was only to be paralleled by her readiness to impart information. The party at the White Bear knew before she went home, that she had recently had her parlour newly hung with arras, representing the twelve labours of Hercules: that she intended to have roast veal to supper: that her worsted under-stockings had cost her four-and-sixpence the pair: that her husband was a very trying man, and her eldest son the cleverest youth in Westminster.

"Worsted stockings four-and-sixpence!" cried Temperance. "What a sinful price to pay! And I declare if they ask not three shillings and fourpence for a quarter of veal! Why, I mind the time when in Keswick it was but sixteen pence. Truly, if things wax higher in price than now they are, it shall be an hard matter to live. This very morrow was I asked a shilling for a calf's head of the butcher, and eightpence for a lemon of the costard-monger, whereat I promise you I fumed a bit; but when it came to threepence a-piece for chickens,—Lancaster and Derby! It shall cost us here ever so much more to live."

"It shall not," said Hans. "There be five acres of garden, and save for foreign fruits and spices, you shall ask little of the costardmonger shortly."

"But who is to dig and dress it?" moaned Faith. "Aubrey cannot, all the day with his Lord, even if he were not away o' nights: and Charity shall have too much to do."

"I have two hands, Madam," answered Hans, "and will very quickly have a spade in them: and ere I do aught else will I set the garden a-going, that Rachel and Charity can keep it in good order, with a little overlooking from you."

"Me!" cried Faith, with a gasp of horror.

"Right good for you!" said her sister. "I'll not help at that work; I shall leave it for you. As to foreign fruits and spices, we'll have none of them, save now and then a lemon for the Lady Lettice—she loves the flavour, and we'll not have her go short of comforts—but for all else, I make no 'count of your foreign spice. Rosemary, thyme, mint, savory, fennel, and carraway be spice enough for any man, and a deal better than all your far-fetched maces, and nutmegs, and peppers, that be fetched over here but to fetch the money out of folks' pockets: and wormwood and currant wine are every bit as good, and a deal wholesomer, than all your sherris-sack and Portingale rubbish. Hans, lad, let's have a currant-bush or two in that garden; I can make currant wine with any, though I say it, and gooseberry too. I make no count of your foreign frumps and fiddlements. What's all your Champagne but just gooseberry with a French name to it? and

how can that make it any sweeter? I'll be bounden half
of it *is* made of gooseberries, if folks might but know.
And as to your Rhenish and claret, and such stuff, I would
not give a penny for the lot—I'd as soon have a quart of
alegar. Nay, nay! we are honest English men and women,
and let us live like it."

"But, Temperance, my dear," suggested Lady Louvaine,
with a smile, "if no foreign fruits had ever been brought
to England, nor planted here, our table should be somewhat scanty. In truth, we should have but little, I believe, save acorns and beechnuts."

"Nay, come!" responded Temperance; "wouldn't you
let us have a bit of parsley, or a barberry or twain?"

"Parsley!" said Lady Louvaine, smiling again. "Why,
Temperance, that came first into England from Italy the
year Anstace was born—the second of King Edward." [1]

"Dear heart, did it so?" quoth she. "And must not we
have so much as a cabbage or a sprig of sweet marjoram?"

"Sweet marjoram came in when thou wert a babe,
Temperance; and I have heard my mother say that
cabbages were brought hither from Flanders the year my
sister Edith was born. She was five years elder than I,
and died in the cradle."

"Well!" concluded Temperance, "then I'll hold my
peace and munch my acorns. But I reckon I may have a
little salt to them."

"Ay, that mayest thou, and honey too."

The next day, the Golden Fish swam in at the door;
and it came in the form of Mistress Rookwood and her
daughter Gertrude, who seemed pleasanter people than
Mrs. Abbott. A few days afterwards came the Rector,
Mr. Marshall, with his wife and daughter; and though—
or perhaps because—Agnes Marshall was very quiet, they
liked her best of any woman they had yet seen. Before

[1] This was a revival; for "persille" is found on the Rolls of Edward II.

they had stayed long, the Rector asked if Lady Louvaine had made acquaintance with any of her neighbours. She answered, only with two houses, the one on either side.

Mr. Marshall smiled. "Well, Mistress Abbott means no ill, methinks, though her tongue goeth too fast to say she doth none. Yet is her talk the worst thing about her. Tell her no secrets, I pray you. But I would warn you somewhat to have a care of the Rookwoods."

"Pray you, Sir, after what fashion?" asked Lady Louvaine. "If I know from what quarter the arrow is like to come, it shall be easier to hold up the shield against it."

"Well," said he, "they come to church, and communicate, and pay all their dues; they may be honest folks: but this can I tell you, Mr. Rookwood is brother to a Papist, and is hand in glove with divers Popish perverts. Wherefore, my Lady Louvaine, I would not have you suffer your young folks to be too intimate with theirs; for though these Rookwoods may be safe and true—I trust they are—yet have they near kinsmen which assuredly are not, who should very like be met at their house. So let me advise you to have a care."

"That will I, most surely," said she: "and I thank you, Sir, for putting me on my guard."

In May the King arrived from Scotland, and in June the Queen, with the Prince, Prince Charles, and the Lady Elizabeth. "Princess" at this time indicated the Princess of Wales alone, and the first of our King's daughters to whom the term was applied, except as heiress of England, were the daughters of Charles I. Henry Prince of Wales was a boy of nine years old, his sister a child of seven, and the little Charles only three. The youthful Princess was placed in the charge of Lord Harrington, at Combe Abbey, near Coventry—a fact to which there will be occasion to refer again. The Princes remained with their

E

parents, to the great satisfaction of the Queen, who had struggled as ceaselessly as vainly against the rigid Scottish custom of educating the heir-apparent away from Court. Queen Anne of Denmark was a graceful, elegant woman, with extremely fair complexion and abundant fair hair. The King was plain even to ungainliness—a strange thing for the son of one of the most beautiful women that ever lived. The wisdom of James I. has been by different writers highly extolled and contemptuously derided. It seems to me to have partaken, like everything else, of the uncertainty of its author. He did give utterance to some apothegms of unquestionable wisdom, and also to some speeches of egregious folly. His subjects did not err far when they nicknamed their Scottish master and their "dear dead Queen," his predecessor, "King Elizabeth and Queen James." Yet justice requires the admission that the chief root of James's many failings was his intense, unreasoning, constitutional timidity, which would have been ludicrous if it had been less pitiful. He could not see a drawn sword without shuddering, even if drawn for his own defence; and when knighting a man, it was necessary for the Lord Chamberlain to come to his Majesty's help, and guide the blade, lest the recipient of the honour should be wounded by the unsteadiness of the King's hand under the strong shuddering which seized him. So afraid was he of possible assassins that he always wore a thickly-padded cotton garment under his clothes, to turn aside bullet or dagger.

Lord Oxford came to Town in May, and Aubrey at once began his duties as a squire in his household. During June and July, he ran into the White Bear some half-dozen times in an evening, he said, to assure them that he was still alive. In August and September he was more remiss: and after October had set in, they scarcely saw him once a month. It was noticeable, when he did come, that the young gentleman was becoming more fashionable and courtly than of old. Lettice asked him once if he had bidden the tailor to make his garments of snips, since the brown suit which had been his Sunday best was breaking out all over into slashes whence puffs of pink were visible. Aubrey drew himself up with a laugh, and told his cousin that she knew nothing of the fashions. Lettice fancied she caught the gleam of a gold chain beneath his doublet, but it was carefully buttoned inside so as not to show.

Meanwhile, Hans—whose brown suit did not break out like Aubrey's—was very busy in the garden, which he diligently dug and stocked. When this was done, he applied to a neighbouring notary, and brought home bundles of copying, at which he worked industriously in an evening. In the afternoon he was generally from home; what he did with himself on these occasions he did not say, and he was so commonly and thoroughly trusted that no one thought it necessary to ask him.

Edith and Temperance, coming in together one evening, were informed that Mrs. Rookwood had called during their absence, bringing with her Dorothy, Aubrey's beauty.

"And didst thou think her beauteous, Lettice?" asked her Aunt Edith, with an amused smile.

"Truly, Aunt Edith, I marvel what Aubrey would be at. His fancies must be very diverse from mine. I would liever a deal have our Rachel."

Temperance laughed, for Rachel had few claims of this nature.

"What like is she, Lettice?"

"She hath jet-black hair, Aunt, and thick black brows, with great shining eyes—black likewise; and a big nose-end, and pouting big red lips."

"Humph! I reckon folks see beauty with differing eyes," said Temperance.

The coronation did not take place before July. It was followed by severe pestilence, supposed to arise from the numbers who crowded into Town to witness the ceremony. Temperance kept fires of sweet herbs burning in the garden, and insisted on every body swallowing liberal doses of brick and wormwood, fasting, in the morning — her sovereign remedy against infection. Mrs. Abbott said that her doctor ordered her powder of bezoar stone for the same purpose, while the Rookwoods held firmly by a mixture of unicorn's horn and salt of gold. In consequence or in spite of these invaluable applications, no one suffered in the three houses in King Street. His Majesty was terribly afraid of the pestilence; all officials not on duty were ordered home, and all suitors —namely, petitioners—were commanded to avoid the Court till winter. A solemn fast for this visitation was held in August; the statutes against vagabonds and "masterless men" were confirmed, whereat Temperance greatly rejoiced; and "dangerous rogues" were to be banished.

This last item was variously understood, some supposing it aimed at the Jesuits, and some at the Puritans. It was popularly reported that the King "loved no Puritans," as it was now usual to term those Churchmen who declined to walk in the Ritualistic ways of the High Church party. To restrict the term Puritan to Nonconformists is a modern mistake. When, therefore, James began his reign by large remittances of fines to his Romish subjects, issued a declaration against toleration, revived the Star Chamber, and appointed Lord Henry Howard, a Roman Catholic, to the Privy Council, the Papists were encouraged, and the Puritans took alarm. The latter prepared to emigrate on a large scale to the American plantations, where no man could control them in religious matters; the former raised their heads and

ventured on greater liberties than they had dared to take
during the reign of the dead Queen. The French Ambassador, however, curled his lip contemptuously, and informed his master that James was a hypocrite.

The position of the English Roman Catholics at this
time was peculiar and not agreeable. But in order to
understand it, we must go back for thirty-five years—to
the close of that halcyon period, the earliest ten years of
Elizabeth, when the few Romanists then left in England
generally came to church like other good citizens, and if
they chose to practise the rites of their own faith in
private, no notice was taken of it. It was not the Protestant Government, but the Papal See, which was responsible for the violent ending of this satisfactory state of
things, when it was perceived at Rome that the Reformation was so thoroughly settled, and the nation so completely severed from Latin control, that (in the words of
one of those who attempted the Queen's life) " unless
Mistress Elizabeth were suddenly taken away, all the
devils in Hell should not be able to shake it." In 1568,
therefore, Pope Pius V. put forth a Bull which excommunicated Queen Elizabeth, deposed her, absolved her subjects from their allegiance, and solemnly cursed them if
they continued to obey her. To her Protestant subjects,
of course, this act of usurpation was mere waste paper—
the private spleen of an Italian priest who had no juris-
diction in this realm of England. But to the Romanists
it was the solemn decree of Christ by His appointed Vicar,
to be obeyed at the peril of their salvation. The first
visible effect of the Bull was that they all " did forthwith
refrain the church," and joined no more with their fellow-
subjects in public prayer. The Queen contented herself
in answer with forbidding the bringing in of Bulls—which
was no more than Edward I. had done before her. Had
the Pope and the Jesuits been then content to let matters

rest, no difficulty might have arisen : but they would not. First Mayne, then Campion, the first Jesuit who entered England, were sent to " move sedition," and to " make a party in execution of the former Bull." To this followed an influx of treasonable books. It had now become evident that the Papal Bull was to be no mere *brutum fulmen* which might be safely left alone to die out, but a deliberate attempt to stir up rebellion against the Queen. For the Government to have kept silence would have been practically to throw their influence into the scale against the reign and the life of their Sovereign Lady.

It is now fashionable with a certain section to stigmatise Elizabeth as a persecutor, and to represent the penal laws against the Papists enacted in her reign as cruel oppressions of innocent and harmless persons, enforced simply because they believed certain religious doctrines. Those who will carefully follow the facts can hardly avoid seeing that the disloyalty preceded the coercion, and that if the Romanists were maddened into plotting against the Government by oppressive laws, those laws were not due to groundless fear or malice, but were simply the just reward of their own deeds. During the five years of Queen Mary, three hundred men, women, and children, were put to death for their religious opinions only. During the forty-four years of Queen Elizabeth, less than thirty priests, and five harbourers of priests, were executed, not for their opinions nor their religion, but for distinctly treasonable practices.[1]

When matters had come to this pass, in 1580, the first penal laws were issued, against recusancy and seditious publications. The penalty for recusancy—by which was meant a legal conviction for absence from public worship on religious grounds—" was not loss of life or limb, or

---

[1] This is the computation of Sir Edward Coke in his opening speech at the trial of the Gunpowder conspirators.

whole estate, but only a pecuniary mulct and penalty; and that also only until they would submit and conform themselves and again come to church, as they had done for ten years before the Pope's Bull." Twenty pounds per lunar month was the fine imposed; but this referred only to adult males, "not being let by sickness." Compared with the laws of Queen Mary, and even of her predecessors, this penalty was gentleness itself; and those modern writers who see in it cruelty and rigour must have little knowledge of comparative history. Yet so far was this from stopping the flow of treason, that a Jesuit mission entered England with the special purpose of teaching the people that under the Bull of Pope Pius the Queen stood excommunicated, and that it was a positive sin to obey her. Their success was only too manifest. Men of all sorts and conditions, from peers to peasants, were " reconciled " in numbers by their teaching. If this were to go on, not only would Elizabeth's life be the forfeit, but the Reformation settlement would be uprooted and undone, and the blood of the Marian martyrs would have been shed for nought.

The laws were now made more stringent. By the Act of 1580 it had been provided that every priest saying mass should be liable to a fine of two hundred marks (£133), with half that sum for every hearer, and both to imprisonment for a year, or in the priest's case until the fine was paid. Now, all Jesuits and priests ordained since the Queen's accession were banished the kingdom, being allowed forty days after the close of the session; and none were to enter it, on penalty of death. All persons receiving or assisting such priests were held guilty of felony. Recusants were to be imprisoned until they should conform, and if they remained obstinate for three months, they must be banished.

These penal laws, however, were rarely enforced. They

were kept as a sword of Damocles, suspended over the heads of the unhappy Romanists, and capable of being brought down on them at any moment. In the hands of an unscrupulous Minister of the Crown they might be made an agency of considerable vexation: yet no reasonable remonstrance could be offered to the reminder that these penalties were inflicted by law, and it was only of the Queen's clemency that they had not been earlier exacted. It must also be admitted that the penal laws bore in reality much harder on the Romanists than they seem to do in Protestant eyes. To deprive a Protestant of the services of a clergyman is at most to incommode him; to deprive a Papist of his priest is equivalent in his eyes to depriving him of his salvation. To them, therefore, it was a matter of life and death. And yet, it must not be forgotten, they had brought it on themselves.

With the death of Elizabeth came a serious change. Revile her as they might, under her the Romanists had been on the whole gently and justly used. But it was in reality, though they could not see it, after her the deluge.

Who was to be Elizabeth's successor had been for years at once a serious and an unsettled question. There were three persons living when she died, each of whom could have put forward a claim to the Crown on various grounds.

Humanly speaking, the decision was made by two groups of persons—the Careys and Cecils, and the Romanists of England—both of whom were determined that James of Scotland should succeed. The latter had been working for some time past, and had secured promises from James that he would extend special toleration to them. He was expected to look kindly on the party which had adhered to his mother—it would be difficult to say why, since in Scotland his adherents had always been at war with hers—and it was remembered that he had been born and baptized in the Church of Rome. The Roman party, therefore, wrought earnestly in his favour. Sir Thomas Tresham proclaimed him at Northampton, at considerable personal risk; his sons and Lord Monteagle assisted the Earl of Southampton to hold the Tower for James. The Pope, Clement VIII., was entirely on James's side, of whose conversion he entertained the warmest hopes. To the French Ambassador, Monsieur de Beaumont, James asserted that "he was no heretic, that is, refusing to recognise the truth; neither was he a Puritan, nor separated from the Church: he held episcopacy as necessary, and the Pope as the chief bishop, namely, the president and moderator of councils, but not the head nor superior."

We in this nineteenth century, accustomed to ideas of complete and perpetual toleration, and alas! also to Gallio-like apathy and indifference, can scarcely form a conception of what was at that time the popular estimate of a Papist. A fair view of it is given by the following sarcastic description, written on the fly-leaf of a volume of manuscript sermons of this date.

"The Blazon of a Papist ["priest" is erased] contriued prettily by som Herault of Armes in yᵉ compasse of Armory.

"1st. There is papist Rampant, a furious beast: 'tis written that the Diuell goes about like a roaring Lion, but the Diuell himselfe is not more fierce and rigorous then is papist where [he] is of force and ability to shew his tyranny: wittnes yᵉ murthers, yᵉ massacres, yᵉ slaughters, yᵉ poysoning, yᵉ stabbing, yᵉ burning, yᵉ broyling, yᵉ torturing, yᵉ tormenting, yᵉ persecuting, with other their bloody execu'ons, euery [sic] fresh in example, infinite to be told, and horrible to be rememberd.

"2. A papist Passant: he's an instrument of sedition, of insurrection, of treason, of Rebellion, a priest, a Jesuite, a seminary, and such other as find so many friends in England and Ireland both to receaue and harbor them, that it is to be feard we shall smart for it one day.

"3. A papist Volant; of all the rest, these I take to do the least harme: yet they will say they fly for their consciences, when its apparently known they both practice and conspire.

"4. A pap: Regardant; he obserus times, occasions, places, and persons, and though he be one of the Popes intelligencers, yet he walks with such circumspection and heed, y^t he is not known but to his own faction.

"5. A pa: Dormant: he's a sly companion, subtill as a ffox: he sleeps with open eyes, yet somtymes seeming to winke, he looks and pries into opportunity, still feeding himselfe with those hopes that I am in hope shall never do him good.

"6. A pa: Couchant: this is a daungerous fellow, and much to be feard; he creeps into the bosom of ye state, and will not stick to look into ye Court, nay, if he can, into Court counsells: he will shew himselfe tractable to ye co[mm]on wealthe prescriptions, and with this shew of obedience to Law, he doth ye Pope more seruice then 20 others y^t are more resisting.

"7. A pa: Pendant: indeed a papist pendant is in his prime p'fection: a papist pendant is so fitting a piece of Armory for ye time present, as all Herauds in England are not able better to display him: a papist is then in chiefe when he is a Pendant, and he neuer coms to so high p'ferment, but by ye Popes especiall blessing." [1]

James's first act, when his succession was peaceably ensured, was to remit the fines for recusancy. For the

---

[1] The little MS. volume wherein this is inscribed, which is in my own possession, consists of sermons—not very legible, and mostly very dry— by the Rev. Thomas Stone, their dates ranging from 1622 to 1666, with a few occasional memoranda interspersed.

first and second years of his reign, they were not enforced at all. The sum paid into the Exchequer on this account, in the last year of Elizabeth, was £10,333; in the first and second years of James it was about £300 and £200 respectively. But in his third year, the fines were suddenly revived, and the Romanists took alarm. The King was evidently playing them false. He had been heard to say that "the Pope was the true Antichrist," that "he would lose his crown and his life before he would alter religion;" that "he never had any thought of granting toleration to the Catholics, and that if he thought that his son would condescend to any such course, he would wish the kingdom translated to his daughter;" and lastly, that "he had given them a year of probation, to conform themselves, which, seeing it had not wrought that effect, he had fortified all the laws against them, and commanded them to be put in execution to the uttermost."

Early in 1604, all Jesuits and seminary priests were banished; the recusancy fines and arrears were soon after stringently exacted, and many Roman Catholic families almost reduced to beggary. Sudden domiciliary visits were made in search of concealed priests, usually in the dead of night: empty beds were examined, walls struck with mallets, rapiers thrust into the chinks of wainscots. The Jesuit missionaries were in especial danger; they went about disguised, hid themselves under secular callings and travelled from one house to another, using a different name at each, to avoid discovery. One priest, named Moatford, passed as the footman of Lord Sandys' daughter, wore his livery, and said mass in secret when it seemed safe to do so. Serious difficulties were thrown in the way of educating children; if they were sent abroad, the parents were subject to a fine of £100; if taught at home by a recusant tutor, both he and his employer were mulcted in forty shillings per day.

It was in these circumstances that the Gunpowder Plot originated,—not from some sudden ebullition of groundless malice: and it was due, not to the Romanists at large, but to that section of them only which constituted the Jesuit party.

It is not generally understood that the Roman Church, which boasts so loudly of her perfect unity, is really divided in two parties, one siding with, and the other against, that powerful and mysterious body calling itself the Society of Jesus. It is with this body, "the power behind the Pope,"—which Popes have ere this striven to put down, and have only fallen a sacrifice themselves—that political plots have most commonly originated, and the Gunpowder Plot was no exception to the general rule. It was entirely got up by the Jesuit faction, the ordinary Roman Catholics not merely having nothing to do with it, but placing themselves, when interrogated, in positive opposition to it.

There are certain peculiarities concerning the conspirators which distinguish this enterprise from others of its class. They were mostly young men; they were nearly all connected by ties of blood or marriage; two-thirds of them, if not more, were perverts from Protestantism; and so far from being the vulgar, brutal miscreants usually supposed, they were—with one exception—gentlemen of name and family, and some of good fortune; educated and accomplished men, who honestly believed themselves to be doing God service. It is instructive to read their profound conviction that they were saving their country's honour, furthering their own salvation, and promoting the glory of God. The slaughter of the innocents which necessarily attended their project was lamentable indeed, but inevitable, and gave rise to as little real compunction as the eating of beef and mutton. These men were by no means heartless; they were only blind from ignorance of Scripture, and excess of zeal in a false cause.

The original propounder of the plot was unquestionably Robert Catesby, of Ashby St. Ledgers, a Northampton-shire gentleman of ancient ancestry and fair estate. He first whispered it in secret to John Wright, a Lincoln-shire squire, and soon afterwards to Thomas Winter, a younger brother of the owner of Huddington Hall in Worcestershire, and a distant cousin of an old friend of some of my readers—Edward Underhill, the "Hot Gospeller." Thomas Winter communicated it in Flanders to Guy Fawkes, a young officer of Yorkshire birth, and these four met with a fifth, Thomas Percy, cousin and steward of the Earl of Northumberland. The object of the meeting was to consider the condition of the Roman Catholics, with a view to taking action for its relief. There was also a priest in the company, but who he was did not transpire, though it is almost certain to have been one of the three Jesuits chiefly concerned in the plot—John Gerard, Oswald Greenway, or Henry Garnet. Percy, usually fertile in imagination and eager in action, was ready with a proposition at once. He said,—

"The only way left for us is to kill the King; and that will I undertake to do. From him we looked for bread, and have received nought save stones. Let him be prayed to visit my Lord Mordaunt at Turvey, where a masque may be had for him ; and he once there, in the house of one of us (though my Lord be not known so to be), he is at our mercy. How say you, gentlemen ? "

"Nay, my son," replied the priest. "There is a better course in hand—even to cut up the very roots, and remove all impediments whatsoever."

"That were to run great risk and accomplish little," added Catesby. "No, Tom: thou shalt not adventure thyself to so small purpose. If thou wilt be a traitor, I have in mine head a much further design than that,—to greater advantage, and that can never be discovered."

Every body wished to know his meaning.

"I have bethought me," continued Catesby, "of a way at one instant to deliver us from all our bonds, and without any foreign help to replant again the Catholic religion. In a word, it is to blow up the Parliament House with gunpowder, for in that place have they done us all the mischief, and perchance God hath designed that place for their punishment."

"Truly, a strange proposal!" said Thomas Winter. "The scandal would be so great that the Catholic religion might sustain thereby."

"The nature of the disease requires so sharp a remedy," was Catesby's reply.

"But were it lawful?" objected John Wright.

"Ask your ghostly father," said Catesby, who was pretty sure of the answer in that case.

"But remember," said Winter, "there are many of our friends and Catholic brethren amongst the Lords: shall we destroy them with the rest?"

Catesby's answer was in principle that of Caiaphas. "Ay: 'tis expedient the few die for the good of the many."

The next step was to obtain a house convenient for their operations,—namely, so close to the Houses of Parliament that they could carry a mine from its cellar right under the House. Percy was deputed to attend to this matter, as his circumstances offered an excuse for his seeking such a house. He was one of the band of gentlemen pensioners, whose duty it was to be in daily attendance on the King; a position into which he had been smuggled by his cousin Lord Northumberland, without having taken the oath requisite for it. This oath Percy could not conscientiously have taken, since by it he renounced the authority of the Pope. A little study of the topography induced him to fix on two contiguous houses, which stood close to the House of Lords. On investigation, it was found that these two houses belonged to the Parliament, and were held by Mr. Wyniard, Keeper of the King's Wardrobe, "an ancient and honest servant of Queen Elizabeth." Both, however, had been sub-let by him—the nearer to Mr. Henry Ferris; the further to Gideon Gibbons, a public porter, subsequently utilised by the plotters, to his danger and discomfort. Percy, therefore, in March, 1604, "began to labour earnestly" with Mr. Wyniard and his wife to obtain these houses. Mrs. Wyniard seems chiefly to have attended to this business; her husband was not improbably incapacitated by age or ill-health. Percy's efforts proved successful. He was accepted as tenant by the Wyniards at a rent of £12 per annum, Mr. Ferris being bought out with £30 for his good-will and £5 more "in consideration of the charges of the house." The agreement was signed on the 24th of May.

The next united act of these five exemplary gentlemen was to meet at a house "in the fields behind St. Clement's Church, near the arch, near the well called St. Clement's Well." This seems to have been the residence of the Jesuit priest Gerard; but it is uncertain whether it was identical with that of Percy, or with that of Mrs. Herbert, where Fawkes had apartments, both which are also described as "beyond St. Clement's." Gerard, who was in the company, was with delicate consideration left in an upper room, where he was provided with all necessaries for the celebration of mass, while the conspirators proceeded to business alone in the lower apartment. Taking a primer in his hand, Catesby administered to his four accomplices this oath, which he also took himself :—

" You swear by the blessed Trinity, and by the Sacrament which you now propose to receive, never to disclose directly or indirectly, by word or circumstance, the matter that shall be proposed to you to keep secret, nor desist from the execution thereof till the rest shall give you leave."

Then they passed into the upper room, where Gerard stood ready robed, and received the host from his hands —with what "intention" being unknown to him, if the assertion of the conspirators may be believed.

I have gone rather too far, chronologically speaking, in order to tell this part of the story straight through; and now we must go back a little. About four months before this oath was taken, in January, 1604, was held the famous conference of bishops at Hampton Court. The King, who, though baptized a Roman Catholic, had been educated as a Presbyterian, propounded various queries to the hierarchy concerning practices which puzzled him in the Church of England, of which he was now the supreme head upon earth. In the first place, he desired to know the meaning of the rite of confirmation : "if they held the sacrament of baptism invalidous without it, then was it in his judgment blasphemous ; yet if it were only that children might themselves profess and be blessed, then very good." The absolution of the Church he had heard compared to the Pope's pardons. Private baptism, he would have administered only by a lawful minister ; and concerning excommunications he had also something to say. On all these points the bishops fully satisfied his Majesty, "whose exquisite expositions did breed wonder and astonishment in that learned and noble audience." Modern readers of the proceedings have been much less inclined to astonishment, except indeed that the bishops should have been so easily astonished. On the second day, a deputation was received from the Puritan ministers, who petitioned for four points—which had they gained, the nineteenth century would have found its burdens considerably lightened. They requested that the doctrine of the Church might be preserved pure, according to God's Word; that good pastors might be planted in all churches, to preach in the same; that the Book of Common Prayer might be fitted to more increase of piety; and that Church government might be sincerely ministered according to God's Word.

King James made the deputation explain themselves; and after a day's debate, he angrily told them that they were aiming at a Scottish presbytery, which agreed with monarchy as well as God and the Devil. "No bishop, no king!" added his Majesty. Some few members of the Conference maintained that the Puritans had been crushed and insulted; but Chancellor Egerton said he had never seen king and priest so fully united in one person as in that of his sacred Majesty, and Bancroft (afterwards Archbishop) fell upon his knees, unctuously exclaiming that his heart melted for joy to think that England was blessed with such a ruler. The bishops and privy-councillors then conferred alone, altered a few expressions in the Liturgy, and summoned the Puritans to hear their decision. Dr. Raynolds, the Puritan spokesman, entreated that the use of the surplice and the sign of the cross in baptism might be laid aside, or at least not made compulsory, but the King sternly told him that they preferred the credit of a few private men to the peace of the Church; that he would have none of this arguing; "wherefore let them conform, and quickly too, or they shall hear of it." By this short-sighted policy, the opportunity for really securing peace to the Church was lost for sixty years, and many of the troubles of the next reign were sown. The next step was to arrest ten of the Puritan

F

leaders ; and then to eject from their benefices three
hundred clergy of that school. Among these was Mr.
Marshall, the pastor of our friends. Lady Louvaine was
sorely troubled. She said they were now as sheep without a shepherd, and were but too likely to have a shepherd set over them who would fleece and devour the
sheep. Of these clergy some joined the Presbyterians,
some the Brownists—whom people now began to call
Independents : others remained in the Church, ceasing to
minister, and following such callings as they deemed not
unbecoming the position of a Christian minister—chiefly
tutorship and literature. Mr. Marshall was in the last
class. He said better times might come, and he could
not see his way to desert the Church, though her ways to
him at this present were somewhat stepmotherly.

"But how, Mr. Marshall, if the Church cast you forth?"
asked Temperance.

"Then must I needs go," he answered with a smile.
"But that, look you, were not my deed, nor should I be
responsible for it before God. So long as I break not her
laws, she hath no right to eject me; and so long as she
abideth in the truth, I have no right to desert her."

"But the bishops abide not in the truth, as I take it."

"The bishops be not the Church," replied he. "Let
the Articles and Homilies be changed, with evil tendency,
and then that is to change the Church. I go forth of her
then at once ; for she should be no longer the Church of
my faith, to which I sware obedience, and she hath not
that right over me to require me to change with her. But
so long as these are left unaltered, what matter though
bishops change? They are not immortal : and very sure
am I they are not infallible."

"What think you, Mother?" said Edith.

"Children," replied Lady Louvaine, laying down her
knitting in her lap, "I can get no further at this present

than one line of Saint John : 'He Himself knew what He would do.' I do not know what He will do. It may be, as it then was, something that none of all His disciples can guess. One step at a time is all He allows us to see, and all He bids us take. 'He calleth His own sheep by name, and leadeth them out'; but also, 'He goeth before them.' At times He leads them, I think, outside the fold; and if He is outside, and we hear His voice, we must needs go to Him. Yet is this rare, and we should make very sure that it is from without we hear the familiar voice, and not rush forth in haste when He may be calling from within. Let us know that He is on the road before us, and then we need have no fear to run fast, no doubt whither the road will lead. There be some sheep in such haste to run that they must needs go past the Shepherd; and then have they no longer a leader, and are very like to miss the right way."

"You have the right, Lady Louvaine," said Mr. Marshall. "'He that believeth shall not make haste.' Yet there be sheep—to follow your imagery, or truly that of our Lord —that will lag behind, and never keep pace with the Shepherd."

"Ay," she answered: "and I know not if that be not the commoner fault of the twain. He calls, and calls, and they come not; and such sheep find many a sharp tap from the rod ere they will walk, never say run. Our Shepherd is human, therefore He can feel for us; He is Divine, therefore can He have patience with us. Let us thank God for both."

CHAPTER IV.

WE GET INTO BAD COMPANY.

*" Will you walk into my parlour ? ' said the Spider to the Fly :
' 'Tis the prettiest little parlour that ever you did spy.' "*

NE afternoon during that winter, as Lettice was coming down-stairs, her sense of smell was all at once saluted by a strange odour, which did not strike her as having any probable connection with Araby the blest, mixed with slight curls of smoke suggestive of the idea that something was on fire. But before she had done more than wonder what might be the matter, a sound reached her from below, arguing equal astonishment and disapproval on the part of Aunt Temperance.

"Northumberland, Cumberland, Westmoreland, and Durham!" was the ejaculation of that lady. "Lad, art thou afire, or what ails thee?"

The answering laugh was in Aubrey's voice.

"Why, Aunt!" said he, "is this the first time you did ever see a man to drink Uppówoc?"

"'Drink up a work!'" exclaimed she. "What on earth——"

"Picielt," said he.

"Lettice, is that thou?" inquired Aunt Temperance. "Call Charity quickly, and bid her run for the apothecary: this boy's gone mad."

A ringing peal of laughter from Aubrey was the answer. Lettice had come far enough to see him now, and there he stood in the hall (his coat more slashed and puffed than ever), and in his hand a long narrow tube of silver, with a little bowl at the end, in which was something that sent forth a great smoke and smell.

"Come, Aunt Temperance!" cried he. "Every gentleman in the land, well-nigh, doth now drink the Indian weed. 'Tis called uppówoc, picielt, petum,[1] or tobago, and is sold for its weight in silver; men pick out their biggest shillings to lay against it, and 'tis held a favour for a gentlewoman to fill the pipe for her servant.[2] I have heard say some will spend three or four hundred a year after this manner, drinking it even at the table; and they that refuse be thought peevish and ill company."

"And whither must we flee to get quit of it?" quoth she grimly.

"That cannot I say, Aunt. In France they have it, calling it Nicotine, from one Nicot, that did first fetch it thither; 'twas one Ralph Lane that brought it to England. Why, what think you? there are over six thousand shops in and about London, where they deal in it now."

"Six thousand shops for that stinking stuff!"

"Oh, not for this alone. The apothecaries, grocers, and chandlers have it, and in every tavern you shall find the pipe handed round, even where, as in the meaner sort, it be made but of a walnut shell and a straw. Why, Aunt, 'tis wondrous wholesome and healing for divers diseases."

"Let's hear which of them."

"Well—migraines,[3] colics, toothache, ague, colds, obstructions through wind, and fits of the mother:[4] gout, epilepsy, and hydropsy.[5] The brain, look you, being

---

[1] Whence comes petunia.   [2] Suitor.   [3] Headaches.
[4] Hysterics.   [5] Dropsy.

naturally cold and wet, all hot and dry things must be good for it."

"I'd as soon have any of those divers distempers as *that*," solemnly announced Aunt Temperance. "'Brain cold and wet!' when didst thou handle thy brains, that thou shouldst know whether they be cold or not?"

"I do ensure you, Aunt, thus saith Dr. Barclay, one of the first physicians in London town, which useth this tobago for all these diseases. He only saith 'tis not to be touched with food, or after it, but must be took fasting. Moreover, it helps the digestion."

"It'll not help mine. And prithee, Mr. Aubrey Louvaine, which of all this list of disorders hast thou?"

"I, Aunt? Oh, I'm well enough."

"Dear heart! When I am well enough, I warrant you, I take no physic."

"Oh, but, Aunt, 'tis not physic only. 'Tis rare comforting and soothing."

Aunt Temperance's face was a sight to see. She looked Aubrey over from the crown of his head to his boots, till his face flushed red, though he tried to laugh it away.

"Soothing!" said she in a long-drawn indescribable tone. "Lettice, prithee tell me what year we be now in?"

"In the year of our Lord 1603, Aunt," said Lettice, trying not to laugh.

"Nay," answered she, "that cannot be: for my nephew, Aubrey Louvaine, was born in the year of our Lord 1583, and he is yet, poor babe, in the cradle, and needs rocking and hushing a-by-bye. S-o-o-t-h-i-n-g!" and Aunt Temperance drew out the word in a long cry, for all the world like a whining baby. "Lad, if you desire not the finest thrashing ever you had yet, cast down that drivelling folly of a silver toy, and turn up your sleeves and go to work like a man! When you lie abed ill of the smallpox you may say you want soothing, and no sooner: and if I hear such another word out of your mouth, I'll leather you while I can stand over you."

Aunt Temperance marched to the parlour door, and flung it wide open.

"Madam," said she, "give me leave to introduce to your Ladyship the King of Fools. I go forth to buy a cradle for him; and Edith, prithee run to the kitchen and dress him some pap. He lacks soothing, Madam; and having been brought so low as to seek it, poor fool, at the hands of the evillest-smelling weed ever was plucked off a dunghill, I am moved to crave your Ladyship's kindliness for him. Here's his rattle"—and Aunt Temperance held forth the silver pipe,—"which lacks but the bells to be as rare a fool's staff as I have seen of a summer day.—Get thee in, thou poor dizard dolt![1] to think that I should have to call such a patch[1] *my* cousin!"

Lady Louvaine sat, looking first at Aubrey and then at Temperance, as though she marvelled what it all meant. Edith said, laughingly—

"Why, Aubrey, what hast thou done, my boy, so to vex thine aunt?" and Faith, throwing down her work, rose and came to Aubrey.

"My darling! my poor little boy!" she cried, as a nurse might to a child; but Faith's blandishment was real, while Temperance's was mockery.

All Aunt Temperance's mocking, nevertheless, provoked Aubrey less than his mother's reality. He flushed red again, and looked ready to weep, had it been less unmanly. Temperance took care not to lose her chance.

"Ay, poor little boy!" said she. "Prithee, Faith, take him on thy lap and cuddle him, and dandle him well, and

---

[1] All these are old terms signifying a fool or idiot. Patch was the favourite jester of Henry VIII., whose name was used as synonymous with fool.

sing him a song o' sixpence. Oh, my little rogue, my
pretty bird! well, then, it shall have a new coral, it shall.
—Now, Madam, pray you look on this piece of wastry!
(Dear heart, but a fool and his money be soon parted!)
What think you 'tis like?"

"Truly, my dear, that cannot I say," replied Lady
Louvaine, looking at the pipe as Temperance held it out:
"but either that or somewhat else, it strikes me, hath a
marvellous ill savour."

"Ill savour, Madam!" cried Temperance. "Would you
even such mean scents as roses and lilies to this celestial
odour? Truly, this must it be the angels put in their
pouncet-boxes. I am informed of my Lord of Tobago here
that all the gentlemen of the Court do use to perfume
their velvets with it."

"Well, I can tell you of two which so do," said Aubrey
in a nettled fashion—"my Lord of Northumberland and
Sir Walter Raleigh: and you'll not call them fools, Aunt
Temperance."

"I'll give you a bit of advice, Mr. Louvaine: and that
is, not to lay your week's wages out in wagers what I
shall do. I call any man fool that is given to folly: and
as to this filthy business, I should scarce stick at the
King's Majesty himself."

"Nay, the King is clean contrary thereto," saith Aubrey,
with a rather unwilling air: "I hear of my Lord that he
saith it soils the inward parts of men with oily soot, and
is loathsome to the eye, hateful to the nose, harmful to
the brain, dangerous to the lungs, counted effeminate
among the Indians themselves, and by the Spanish slaves
called sauce for Lutheran curs."

"Well, on my word!" cried Aunt Temperance. "And
knowing this, thou Lutheran cur, thou wilt yet soil thine
inward parts with this oily soot?"

"Oh, Aunt, every one so doth."

Lady Louvaine and Edith exchanged sorrowful looks, and the former said—

"Aubrey, my boy, no true man accounts that a worthy reason for his deeds. It was true of the Israelites when they fell to worship the golden calf, and of the scribes and priests when they cried, 'Crucify Him!' Hadst thou been in that crowd before Pontius Pilate, wouldst thou have joined that cry?"

Edith went up to her mother, and said in a low voice, "May I tell him?"

Evidently it cost Lady Louvaine some pain to say "Yes," yet she said it. Edith went back to her seat.

"Aubrey," she said, "four-and-twenty years gone, thine uncle, my brother Walter, was what thou art now, in the very same office and household. His wages were then sixteen pound by the year——"

"But mine are thirty-five, Aunt," responded Aubrey quickly, as though he guessed what she was about to say.

"In order to be like every one else, Aubrey, and not come in bad odour with his fellows, he spent well-nigh four hundred pound by the year, and——"

"Uncle Walter!" cried Aubrey in amazement, and Lettice could have been his echo.

"Ay!" said Edith, sadly. "And for over ten years thereafter was my father so crippled with his debts, that I mind it being a fine treat when I and my sisters had a new gown a-piece, though of the commonest serge, and all but bare necessaries were cut off from our board. Walter laid it so to heart that of a spendthrift he became a miser. I would not have thee so to do, but I bid thee mind that we have very little to live on, owing all we yet have, and have brought withal, to the goodness of my dear Aunt Joyce; and if thou fall in such ways, Aubrey——"

"Dear heart, Aunt! Think you I have no wit?"

"Thou hast not an ill wit, my lad," said Aunt Temperance, "if a wise man had the keeping of it."

"Temperance, you are so unfeeling!" exclaimed Faith. "Must I needs stand up for my fatherless boy?"

"You'd ruin any lad you were mother to," answered her sister.

Hans now coming in, she set on him.

"Look here, Hans Floriszoon! Didst ever see any thing like this?"

Hans smiled. "Oh ay, Mistress Murthwaite, I have seen men to use them."

"Hast one of these fiddle-faddles thyself? or dost thou desire to have one?"

"Neither, in good sooth," was his reply.

"There, Mr. Louvaine! hearken, prithee."

"Hans is only a boy; I am a man," said Aubrey, loftily: though Hans was but a year younger than himself.

"Lancaster and Derby! and are you then content, my Lord Man, that a contemptible boy should have better wit than your magnifical self? Truly, I think Hans was a man before thou hadst ended sucking of thy thumb."

Just then Charity brought in the Rector.

"See you here, Mr. Marshall!" cried Temperance, brandishing her pipe. "Be you wont to solace your studies with this trumpery?"

Mr. Marshall smiled. "Truly, nay, Mistress Murthwaite; 'tis accounted scandalous for divines to use that tobago, not to name the high cost thereof."

"Pray you, how many pence by the ounce hath any man the face to ask for this stinking stuff?"

"Three shillings or more, and that the poorest sort."

"Mercy me! And can you tell me how folks use it that account it physical?"

"Ay, I have heard tell that the manner of using it as physic is to fill the patient's mouth with a ball of the leaves, when he must incline the face downward, and keep his mouth open, not moving his tongue : then doth it draw a flood of water from all parts of the body. Some physicians will not use it, saying it causeth over-quick digestion, and fills the stomach full of crudities. For a cold or headache the fumes of the pipe only are taken. His Majesty greatly loathes this new fashion, saying that the smoke thereof resembles nothing so much as the Stygian fume of the bottomless pit, and likewise that 'tis a branch of drunkenness, which he terms the root of all sins."

Aubrey laughed rather significantly.

"Why," asked his mother, "is the King's Majesty somewhat given that way ? "

"Well, I have heard it said that when the King of Denmark was here, their two Majesties went not to bed sober every night of the week : marry, 'tis whispered all the Court ladies kept not so steady feet as they might have done."

" Alack the day ! not the Queen, I hope ? "

" Nay, I heard no word touching her."

" Ah, friends ! " said Mr. Marshall with a sigh, " let me ensure you that England's mourning is not yet over for Queen Elizabeth, and we may live to lament our loss of her far sorer than now we do. Folks say she was something stingy with money, loving not to part with it sooner than she saw good reason : but some folks will fling their money right and left with no reason at all. The present Court much affecteth masques, plays, and such like, so that now there be twenty where her late Majesty would see one."

"Mr. Marshall," asked Edith, "is it true, as I have heard say, that King James is somewhat Papistically given ? "

" Ay and no," said he. " He is not at all thus, in the

signification of obeying the Pope, or suffering himself to
be ridden of priests: in no wise.   But he hates a Puritan
worse than a Papist.   Mind you not that in his speech
when he opened his first Parliament, he said that he did
acknowledge the Roman Church to be our mother Church,
though defiled with some infirmities and corruptions?"

"Yet he said also, if I err not, that he sucked in God's
truth with his nurse's milk."

"Ay.   But what one calls God's truth is not what an
other doth.   All the Papistry in the world is not in the
Roman Church; and assuredly she is in no sense our
mother."

"Truly, I thought Saint Austin brought the Gospel
hither from Rome."

"Saint Austin brought a deal from Rome beside the
Gospel, and he was not the first to bring that.   The
Gallican Church had before him brought it to Kent; and
long ere that time had the ancient British Church been
evangelised from no sister Church at all, but right from
the Holy Land itself, and as her own unchanging voice
did assert, by the beloved Apostle Saint John."

"That heard I never afore," said Lady Louvaine, who
seemed greatly interested.   "Pray you, Mr. Marshall, is
this true?"

"I do ensure you it is," replied he; "that is, so far as
the wit of man at this distance of time may discern the
same."

"Was the French Church, then, lesser corrupted than
that of Rome?" queried Edith.

"Certainly so," he said: "and it hath resisted the
Pope's usurpations nigh as much as our own Church of
England.   I mean not in respect of the Reformation, but
rather the time before the Reformation, when our kings
were ever striving with the Pope concerning his right to
appoint unto dignities and livings.   Yet the Reformation

itself began first in France, and had they in authority been willing to aid it as in England, France had been a Protestant country at this day."

That evening, as they sat round the fire, Hans astonished them all.

"Lady Lettice," said he, "were you willing that I should embark in trade?"

"Hans, my dear boy!" was the astonished response.

"I will not do it without your good-will thereto," said he; "nor would I at all have done it, could I have seen any better way. But I feel that I ought to be a-work on some matter, and not tarry a burden on your hands: and all this time have I been essaying two matters—to look out for a service, and to make a little money for you. The second I have in some sense accomplished, though not to the extent I did desire, and here be the proceeds" —and rising from his seat, Hans opened his purse, and poured several gold pieces into his friend's lap. "The former, howbeit, is not——"

He was interrupted by a little cry from Lady Louvaine.

"Hans! thou surely thinkest not, dear lad, that I shall strip thee of thy first earnings, won by hard work?"

"You will, Lady Lettice, without you mean to disappoint and dishearten me very sore," he answered.

"But all this!" she exclaimed.

"'Tis much less than I would have had it; and it hath taken me three-quarters of a year to scrape so much together. But—nay, Lady Lettice, forgive me, but never a penny will I take back. You sure forget that I owe all unto you. What should have come of me but for you and Sir Aubrey? But I was about to say, I have essayed in every direction to take service with a gentleman, and cannot compass it in any wise. So I see no other way but to go into trade."

"But, Hans, thou art a gentleman's son!"

"I am a King's son, Madam," said Hans with feeling: "and if I tarnish not the escocheon of my heavenly birth by honest craft, then shall I have no fear for that of mine earthly father."

"Yet if so were, dear lad—though I should be verily sorry to see thee come down so low—yet bethink thee, thine apprenticeship may not be compassed without a good payment in money."

"Your pardon, Madam. There is one craftsman in London that is willing to receive me without a penny. Truly, I did nothing to demerit it, since I did but catch up his little maid of two years, that could scarce toddle, from being run over by an horse that had brake loose from the rein. Howbeit, it pleaseth him to think him under an obligation to me, and his good wife likewise. And having made inquiries diligently, I find him to be a man of good repute, one that feareth God and dealeth justly and kindly by men: also of his wife the neighbours speak well. Seeing, then, all doors shut upon me save this one, whereat I may freely enter, it seems to me, under your Ladyship's leave, that this is the way which God hath prepared for me to walk in : yet if you refuse permission, then I shall know that I have erred therein."

"Hans, I would give my best rebato Aubrey had one half thy wit and goodness !" cried Temperance.

"I thank you for the compliment, Mistress Murthwaite," said Hans, laughingly. "But truly, as for my wit, I should be very ill-set to spare half of it; and as for my goodness, I wish him far more of his own."

"Where dwells this friend of thine, Hans ? " inquired Lady Louvaine. "What is his name? and what craft doth he follow ? "

"He dwells near, Madam, in Broad Saint Giles' ; his name, Andrew Leigh, and is a silkman."

"We shall miss thee, my boy," said Edith.

"Mrs. Edith, that was the only one point that made me to doubt if I should take Master Leigh's offer or no. If my personal service be of more value to you than my maintenance is a burden, I pray you tell it me: but if not——"

"We never yet reckoned thy maintenance a burden, my dear," answered Lady Louvaine, lovingly. "And indeed we shall miss thee more than a little. Nevertheless, Hans, I think thou hast wisely judged. There is thine own future to look to: and though, in very deed, I am sorry that life offer thee no fairer opening, yet the Lord wot best that which shall be best for thee. Ay, Hans: thou wilt do well to take the offer."

But there were tears in her eyes as she spoke.

The old feudal estimate was still strong in men's minds, by which the most honourable of all callings was held to be domestic service; then, trade and handicraft; and, lowest and meanest of all, those occupations by which men were not fed, clothed, nor instructed, but merely amused. Musicians, painters, poetasters, and above all, actors, were looked on as the very dregs of mankind. The views of the old Lollards, who held that art, not having existed in Paradise, was a product of the serpent, had descended to the Puritans in a modified form. Was it surprising, when on every side they saw the serpent pressing the arts and sciences into his service? It was only in the general chaos of the Restoration that this estimate was reversed. The view of the world at present is exactly opposite: and the view taken by the Church is too often that of the world. Surely the dignity of labour is lost when men labour to produce folly, and call it work. There can be no greater waste either of time, money, or toil, than to expend them on that which satisfieth not.

When Hans came home, a day or two afterwards, he went straight to Lady Louvaine and kissed her hand.

"Madam," said he, in a low voice of much satisfaction, "I bring good news. I have covenanted with Mr. Leigh, who has most nobly granted me, at my request, a rare favour unto a 'prentice—leave to come home when the shop is closed, and to lie here, so long as I am every morrow at my work by six of the clock. I can yet do many little things that may save you pain and toil, and I shall hear every even of your welfare."

"My dear lad, God bless thee!" replied Lady Louvaine, and laid her hand upon his head.

Somewhat later in the evening came Aubrey, to whom all this concerning Hans was news.

"Master Floriszoon, silkman, at the Black Boy in Holborn!" cried he, laughingly. "Pray you, my worthy Master, how much is the best velvet by the yard? and is green stamyn now in fashion? Whereto cometh galowne lace the ounce? Let us hear thee cry, 'What do you lack?' that we may see if thou hast the true tone. Hans Floriszoon, I thought thou hadst more of the feeling of a gentleman in thee."

The blood flushed to Hans' forehead, yet he answered quietly enough.

"Can a gentleman not measure velvet? and what harm shall it work him to know the cost of it?"

"That is a quibble," answered Aubrey, loftily. "For any gentleman to soil his fingers with craft is a blot on his escocheon, and that you know as well as I."

"For any man, gentle or simple, to soil his fingers with sin, or his tongue with falsehood, is a foul blot on his escocheon," replied Hans, looking Aubrey in the face.

Once more the blood mounted to Aubrey's brow, and he answered with some warmth, "What mean you?"

"I did but respond to your words. Be mine other than truth?"

"Be not scurrilous, boy!" said Aubrey, angrily.

"Hans, I am astonished at you!" said Faith. "I know not how it is, but since we came to London, you are for ever picking quarrels with Aubrey, and seeking occasion against him. Are you envious of his better fortune, or what is it moves you?"

It was a minute before Hans answered, and when he did so, his voice was very quiet and low.

"I am sorry to have vexed you, Mrs. Louvaine. If I know myself, I do not envy Aubrey at all; and indeed I desire to pick no quarrel with any man, and him least of any."

Then, turning to Aubrey, he held out his hand. "Forgive me, if I said aught I should not."

Aubrey took the offered hand, much in the manner of an insulted monarch to a penitent rebel. Lettice glanced just then at her Aunt Edith, and saw her gazing from one to the other of the two, with a perplexed and possibly displeased look on her face, but whether it were with Aubrey or with Hans, Lettice could not tell. What made Aubrey so angry did not appear.

Lettice's eyes went to her grandmother. On her face was a very sorrowful look, as if she perceived and recognised some miserable possibility which she had known in the past, and now saw advancing with distress. But she did not speak either to Hans or Aubrey.

The full moon of a spring evening, almost as mild as summer, lighted up the Strand, throwing into bold relief the figure of a young man, fashionably dressed, who stood at the private door of a tailor's shop, the signboard of which exhibited a very wild-looking object of human species, clad in a loose frock, with bare legs and streaming hair, known to the initiated as the sign of the Irish Boy.

Fashionably dressed meant a good deal at that date. It implied a doublet of velvet or satin, puffed and slashed exceedingly, and often covered with costly embroidery or

G

gold lace; trunk hose, padded to an enormous width, matching the doublet in cost, and often in pattern; light-coloured silk stockings, broad-toed shoes, with extremely high heels, and silver buckles, or gold-edged shoe-strings; garters of broad silk ribbons, often spangled with gold, and almost thick enough for sashes; a low hat with a feather and silk hatband, the latter sometimes studded with precious stones; a suspicion of stays in the region of the waist, but too likely to be justified by fact; fringed and perfumed gloves of thick white Spanish leather; lace ruffs about the neck and wrists, the open ones of immense size, the small ones closer than in the previous reign; ear-rings and love-locks: and over all, a gaudy cloak, or rather cape, reaching little below the elbow. In the youth's hand was an article of the first necessity in the estimation of a gentleman of fashion,—namely, a tobacco-box, in this instance of chased silver, with a mirror in the lid, whereby its owner might assure himself that his ruff sat correctly, and that his love-locks were not out of curl. A long slender cane was in the other hand, which the youth twirled with busy idleness, as he carelessly hummed a song.

> "Let's cast away care, and merrily sing,
> For there's a time for every thing:
> He that plays at his work, and works at his play,
> Doth neither keep working nor holy day."

A second youth came down the street westwards, walking not with an air of haste, but of one whose time was too valuable to be thrown away. He was rather shorter and younger than the first, and was very differently attired. He wore a fustian doublet, without either lace or embroidery; a pair of unstuffed cloth hose, dark worsted stockings, shoes with narrow toes and plain shoe-strings of black ribbon; a flat cap; cloth gloves, unadorned and unscented, and a cloak of black cloth, of a more rational length than the other. As he came to the tailor's shop he halted suddenly.

"Aubrey!" The tone was one of surprise and pain.

"Spy!" was the angry response.

"I am no spy, and you know it. But I would ask what you do here and now?"

"Are you my gaoler, that I must needs give account to you?"

"I am your brother, Aubrey; and I, as well as you, am my brother's keeper in so far as concerns his welfare. It is over a month since you visited us, and your mother and Lady Lettice believe you to be with your Lord in Essex. How come you hither, so late at night, and at another door than your own?"

"No business of yours! May a man not call to see his tailor?"

"Men do not commonly go to their tailors after shops be shut."

"Oh, of course, you wot all touching shop matters. Be off to your grograne and cambric! I'm not your apprentice."

"My master's shop is shut with the rest. Aubrey, I saw you last night—though till now I tried to persuade myself it was not you—in Holborn, leaving the door of the Green Dragon. What do you there?"

The answer came blazing with wrath.

"You saw—you mean, sneaking, blackguardly traitor of a Dutch shopkeeper! I'll have no rascal spies dogging my steps, and——"

"Aubrey," said the quiet voice that made reply, "you know me better than that. I never played the spy on you yet, and I trust you will never give me cause. Yet what am I to think when as I pass along the street I behold you standing at the door of a Pa——"

"Hold your tongue!"

The closing word was cut sharply in two by that fierce response. It might be a pavior, a pearmonger, or a Papist. Hans was silent until Aubrey had again spoken, which he did in a hard, constrained tone.

"I sLall go where I please, without asking your leave or any body's else! I am of age, and I have been tied quite long enough to the apron-strings of a parcel of women: but I mean not to cut myself loose from them, only to pass under guidance of a silly lad that hath never a spark of spirit in him, and would make an old woman of me if I gave him leave." Then, in a voice more like his own, he added, "Get you in to your knitting, old Mistress Floriszoon, and tie your cap well o'er your ears, lest the cold wind give you a rheum."

"I will go in when you come with me," said Hans calmly.

"I will not."

"To-night, Aubrey—only just to-night!"

"And what for to-night, prithee? I have other business afloat. To-morrow I will maybe look in."

Perhaps Aubrey was growing a little ashamed of his warmth, for his voice had cooled down.

"We can never do right either to-morrow or yesterday," answered Hans. "To-night is all we have at this present."

"I tell you I will not!" The anger mounted again. "I will not be at the beck and call of a beggarly trades-fellow!"

"You love better to be at Satan's?"

"Take that for your impudence!"

There was the sound of a sharp, heavy blow—so heavy that the recipient almost staggered under it. Then came an instant's dead silence: and then a voice, very low, very sorrowful, yet with no anger in it—

"Good night, Aubrey. I hope you will come to-morrow."
And Hans's steps died away in the distance.

Left to himself, Aubrey's feelings were far from enviable. He was compelled to recognise the folly of his conduct, as more calculated to fan than deter suspicion ; and it sorely nettled him also to perceive that Hans, shopkeeper though he might be, had shown himself much the truer gentleman of the two. But little time was left him to indulge in these unpleasant reflections, for the door behind him was opened by a girl.

"Mr. Catesby at home ?"

"Ay, Sir, and Mr. Winter is here. Pray you, walk up."

Aubrey did as he was requested, adding an unnecessary compliment on the good looks of the portress, to which she responded by a simper of gratified vanity—thereby showing that neither belonged to the wisest class of mankind—and he was ushered up-stairs, into a small but pleasant parlour, where three gentlemen sat conversing. A decanter stood on the table, half full of wine, and each gentleman was furnished with a glass. The long silver pipe was passing round from one to another, and its smoker looked up as Aubrey was announced.

"Ah! welcome, Mr. Louvaine. Mr. Winter, you know this gentleman. Sir, this is my very good friend Mr Darcy,"—indicating the third person by a motion of the hand. "Mr. Darcy, suffer me to make you acquainted with Mr. Louvaine, my good Lord Oxford's gentleman and a right pleasant companion.—Pray you, help yourself to Rhenish, and take a pipe."

Aubrey accepted the double invitation, and was soon puffing at the pipe which Catesby handed to him.

He had not taken much notice of the stranger, and none at all of a gesture on the part of Mr. Catesby as he introduced him—a momentary stroking upwards of his forehead, intended as a sign not to Aubrey, but to the other. The stranger, however, perfectly understood it. To him it said, "Here is a simpleton: mind what you say."

Mr. Catesby, the occupant of the furnished apartments, was a man of unusually lofty height, being over six feet, and of slender build, though well-proportioned; he had a handsome and expressive face, and, while not eloquent, was possessed of the most fascinating and attractive manners by which man ever dragged his fellow-man to evil. Mr. Winter, on the other hand, was as short as his friend was tall. His rather handsome features were of the Grecian type, and he had the power of infusing into them at will a look of the most touching child-like innocence. He spoke five languages, and was a well-read man for his time.

The stranger, to whom Aubrey had been introduced as Mr. Darcy, was an older man than either of the others. Mr. Catesby was aged thirty-two, and Mr. Winter about thirty-five; but Mr. Darcy was at least fifty. He was a well-proportioned man, and dressed with studied plainness. A long, narrow face, with very large, heavy eyelids, and a long but not hooked nose, were relieved by a moustache, and a beard square and slightly forked in the midst. This moustache hid a mouth which was 'the characteristic feature of the face. No physiognomist would have placed the slightest confidence in the owner of that mouth. It was at once sanctimonious and unstable. The manners of its possessor might be suave or severe; his reputation might be excellent or execrable; but with that mouth, a Pharisee and a hypocrite at heart he must be. This gentleman found it convenient not to be too invariably known by a single name, and that whereby he had been introduced to Aubrey was one of five aliases—his real one making a sixth. Different persons, in various parts of the country, were acquainted

with him as Mr. Mease, Mr. Phillips, Mr. Farmer, and—
his best-known alias—Mr. Walley. But his real name
was Henry Garnet, and he was a Jesuit priest.

To do justice to Aubrey Louvaine, who, though weak
and foolish, being mainly led astray by his own self-
sufficiency, was far from being deliberately wicked, it
must be added that he entertained not the least idea of
the real characters of his new friends. At the house of
Mr. Thomas Rookwood, whither he was attracted by the
fair Dorothy—who, had he but known it, regarded him
with cleverly concealed contempt—he had made the acquaintance of Mr. Ambrose Rookwood, the elder of the
brothers, and the owner of Coldham Hall. This gentleman, to Aubrey's taste, was not attractive; but by him
he was introduced to Mr. Percy, and later, to Mr. Thomas
Winter, in whose society the foolish youth took great
pleasure. For Mr. Catesby he did not so much care; the
fact being that he was too clever to suit Aubrey's fancy.

Neither had Aubrey any conception of the use which
was being made of him by his new friends. He was very
useful; he had just brains enough, and not too much,
to serve their purpose. It delighted Aubrey to air his
familiarity with the Court and nobility, and it was convenient to them to know some one whom they could
pump without his ever suspecting that he was being
pumped. They often required information concerning
the movements and present whereabouts of various
eminent persons; and nothing was easier than to obtain
it from Aubrey as they sat and smoked. A few glasses
of Rhenish wine, and a few ounces of tobacco, were well
worth expending for the purpose.

Aubrey's anger with Hans, therefore, was not based
on any fear of discovery, arising from suspicion of his
associates. He was only aiming at independence, com-
bined with a little secret unwillingness to acknowledge

his close connection with Mr. Leigh's apprentice. Of the real end of the road on which he was journeying, he had not the least idea. Satan held out to him with a smile a fruit pleasant to the eyes and good for food, saying, "Thou shalt be as a god," and Aubrey liked the prospect, and accepted the apple.

Having enjoyed himself for about an hour in this manner, and—quite unconsciously on his part—given some valuable information to his associates, he bade them good evening, and returned to Lord Oxford's mansion, in a state of the most delicately-balanced uncertainty whether to appear or not at the White Bear on the following evening. If only he could know how much Hans would tell the ladies!

In the room which he had left, he formed for some minutes the subject of conversation.

"Where picked you up that jewel?" asked Garnet of Winter.

"He lives—or rather his friends do—next door to Tom Rookwood," answered Winter.

"A pigeon worth plucking?" was the next question.

"As poor as a church-mouse, but he knows things we need to know, and in point of wits he is a very pigeon. He no more guesseth what time of day it is with us than my Lord Secretary doth."

The trio laughed complacently, but a rather doubtful expression succeeded that of amusement in Garnet's face.

"Now, good gentlemen, be quiet," said he, piously. Was there a faint twinkle in his eyes? "God will do all for the best. We must get it by prayer at God's hands, in whose hands are the hearts of princes."

"You pray, by all means, and we'll work," said Catesby, removing the pipe from his lips for an instant.

At that moment the door opened, and a fourth gentleman made his appearance. He was as tall and as hand-

some as Catesby; but the considerable amount of white
in his dark hair, and more slightly in his broad beard,
made him look older than his real age, which was forty-
six. He stooped a little in the shoulders. His manners
were usually gentle and grave; but a pair of large and
very lively eyes and an occasional impulsive eagerness of
speech, wherein he was ready and fluent at all times,
showed that there was more fire and life in his character
than appeared on the surface. Those who knew him well
were aware that his temper was impetuous and pre-
cipitate, and on given occasions might be termed quarrel-
some without calumny.

"Shall we always talk, gentlemen, and never do anything?" demanded the new-comer, without previous
greeting.

"Come in, Mr. Percy, and with a right good welcome!
The talk is well-nigh at an end, and the doing beginneth."

"Our Lady be thanked!" was Percy's response. "We
have dallied and delayed long enough. This morning have
I been with Mr. Fawkes over the house; and I tell you,
the mining through that wall shall be no child's play."

Winter lifted his eyebrows and pursed his lips. Catesby
only remarked, "We must buy strong pickaxes, then," and
resumed his puffing in the calmest manner.

"The seventh of February, is it not, Parliament meets?"

"Ay. I trust the Bulls will come from Rome before
that."

"They will be here in time," said Garnet, rising.
"Well, I wish you good night, gentlemen. 'Tis time I
was on my way to Wandsworth. I lie to-night at Mrs.
Anne's, whither she looks for her cousin Tresham to
come."

"My commendations to my cousins," said Catesby.
"Good night. We meet at White Webbs on Tuesday."

"*Pax vobiscum,*" said Garnet softly, as he left the room.

CHAPTER V.

BEGINS WITH TEMPERANCE, AND ENDS WITH TREACHERY.

> " Whate'er we do, we all are doing this—
> Reaping the harvest of our yesterdays,
> Sowing for our to-morrows."
>
> S. W. PARTRIDGE.

N the following evening, Aubrey put in an appearance at the White Bear. As soon as he entered, he gave a quick, troubled look round the parlour, before he went up to kiss his grandmother's hand. His Aunt Temperance greeted him with, "Give you good even, my Lord Chamberlain! Lancaster and Derby! do but look on him! Blue feather in his hat—lace ruff and ruffles—doublet of white satin with gold aglets—trunk hose o' blue velvet, paned with silver taffeta—garters of blue and white silk—and I vow, a pair o' white silken hose, and shoes o' Spanish leather. Pray you, my Lord, is your allowance from the King's Majesty five hundred pounds or a thousand by the year?"

"Now, Aunt, you know," said Aubrey, laughing.

"That thou art a spendthrift?" answered she. "Ay, I do: and if thou run not into debt this side o' Christmas, my name is not Temperance Murthwaite."

"I'm not in debt a penny," retorted he

"Then somebody must have given thee thy pantofles,"
replied she. "Be they a cast-off pair of his Majesty's, or
did my Lord Oxford so much alms to thee?"

Aubrey laughed again, as merrily as if he had not a
care nor a fault in the world.

"They cost not so much as you reckon," he said.

"Four yards of velvet," calculated Aunt Temperance
—"you'll not do it under, stuffed that wise of bombast,
nor buy that quality, neither, under eighteen shillings
the yard—let's see,—that is three pounds twelve shillings :
silver taffeta, a yard and an half, twenty-two and sixpence—that's four pounds fourteen and six; then the
lining, dowlas, I suppose, at fourteen pence——"

"They are lined with perpetuana, Aunt," answered
Aubrey, who seemed greatly amused by this reckoning.

"Perpetuana—*lining?* Thou reckless knave! Three-
and-fourpence the yard at the least—well, we'll say ten
shillings—five pounds four and six: and the lace, at four
shillings by the ounce, and there'll be two ounces there,
good : five pounds twelve shillings and sixpence, as I'm a
living woman! 'Tis sinful waste, lad: that's what it is.
Your father never wore such Babylonian raiment, nor
your grandfather neither, and there was ten times the
wisdom and manliness in either of them that there'll ever
be in you, except you mean to turn your coat ere you
are a month elder."

As Aubrey turned to reply, his eyes fell on Hans, coming home from the mercer's. His face changed in a
minute: but Hans came forward with his hand held out
as cordially as usual, and a look of real pleasure in his
eyes.

"Good even, Aubrey; I am glad to see you," said he.

"Ay, see him, do!" cried Temperance, before Aubrey
could answer; and he only gave his hand in silence.
"Look at him, Hans! Didst ever behold such a pair

of pantofles? Five pounds twelve shillings and sixpence!
How much cost thine?"

"Mine be not so brave as these," replied Hans, smiling.
"My Lord Oxford's squire must needs wear better raiment
than a silkman's apprentice, Mrs. Murthwaite."

"Five pounds twelve shillings and sixpence!" persisted
she.

"Come, now, Aunt Temperance! They cost not the
half," said Aubrey.

"Who didst thou cheat out of them, then?" asked she.

"I bought them," he answered, laughing, "of a young
noble that had borne them but twice, and was ill content
with the cut and colour of them."

"He'll come to no good," sternly pronounced Aunt
Temperance.

"You made a good bargain," said Hans. "That velvet
cost full a pound the yard, I should say."

"Aubrey," inquired Temperance, "I do marvel, and I
would fain know, what thou dost all the day long? Doth
thy Lord keep thee standing by his chair, first o' one leg,
and then o' tother, while he hath an errand for thee?"

"Why, no, Aunt! I am not an errand-lad," said Aubrey,
and laughed more merrily than ever. "Of late is his
Lordship greatly incommoded, and hath kept his chamber
during many days of this last month; but when he hath
his health, I will specify unto you what I do."

"Prithee specify, and I shall be fain to hearken."

"Well, of a morning I aid his Lordship at his *lever*, and
after breakfast I commonly ride with him, if it be my
turn: then will he read an hour or twain in the law,
without the Parliament be sitting, when he is much
busied, being not only a morning man, but at committees
also; in the afternoon he is often at Court, or practising
of music—just now he exerciseth himself in broken music [1]

---

[1] The use of stringed instruments.

and brachigraphy :[1] then in the evening we join my Lady and her gentlewomen in the withdrawing chamber, and divers gestes and conceits be used—such as singing, making of anagrams, guessing of riddles, and so forth. There is my day."

"Forsooth, and a useless one it is," commented she. " The law-books and the Parliament business seem the only decent things in it."

" Ah, 'tis full little changed," remarked Lady Louvaine, "these sixty years since I dwelt at Surrey Place." And she sighed.

"Temperance, I am astonished at you," interposed Faith. "You do nought save fault-find poor Aubrey."

"Poor Aubrey! ay, that he is," returned his Aunt, "and like to be a sight poorer, for all that I can see. If you'll fault-find him a bit more, Faith, there'll not be so much left for me to do."

" What is the matter ? " asked Edith, coming softly in.

"There's a pair of velvet pantofles and an other of silken hose the matter, my dear," answered Temperance, "and a beaver hat with a brave blue feather in it. I trust you admire them as they deserve, and him likewise that weareth them."

" They are brave, indeed," said Edith, in her quiet voice. " I would fain hope it is as fair within as without, my boy."

She looked up in his face as she spoke with yearning love in her eyes; and as Aubrey bent his head to kiss her, he said, in the softest tone which he had yet employed since his entrance, "I am afraid not, Aunt Edith."

And Edith answered, in that low, tender voice—

" 'Thy beauty was perfect through My comeliness which I had put upon thee.' Dear Aubrey, let us seek that."

Aubrey made no answer beyond a smile, and quickly

---

[1] Shorthand.

turned the conversation, on his mother asking if he brought any news.

"But little," said he. "There be new laws against witchcraft, which is grown greater and more used than of old, and the King is mightily set against it—folks say he is afraid of it. None should think, I ensure you, how easily frightened is his Majesty, and of matters that should never fright any save a child."

"But that is not news, Aubrey," said his mother plaintively. "I want to hear something new."

"There isn't an artichoke in the market this morrow, ' suddenly remarked her sister.

"Temperance, what do you mean?"

"Why, that's news, isn't it? I am sure you did not know it, till I told you."

Mrs. Louvaine closed her eyes with an air of deeply-tried forbearance.

"Come, lad, out with thy news," added Temperance. "Wherewith hath my Lady guarded her new spring gowns? That shall serve, I reckon."

Aubrey laughed. "I have not seen them yet, Aunt. But I heard say of one of the young gentlewomen that silk is now for the first to be woven in England, so 'tis like to be cheaper than of old."

"There's a comfort!" said Mrs. Louvaine, rather less languidly than usual.

"I heard tell likewise of a fresh colewort, from Cyprus in the East—they call it brocoli or kale-flower. Methinks there is nought else, without you would hear of a new fashion of building of churches, late come up—but his Lordship saith 'tis a right ancient fashion, wherein the old Greeks were wont to build their houses and temples."

"Methinks it scarce meet to go to the heathen for the pattern of a church," said Lady Louvaine; "are not our old churches fair enough, and suitable for their purpose?"

" In this new fashion be no chancels," said Aubrey.

" Well, and I should hold with that," cried Temperance :
" they give rise to vain superstitions. If there be no
mass, what lack we of a chancel ? "

" If men list, my dear, to bring in the superstitions,"
quietly remarked Lady Louvaine, " they shall scarce stick
at the want of a chancel."

" True, Madam : yet would I fain make it as hard to
bring them as ever I could."

Aubrey left his friends about six o'clock, and Hans
followed him to the door. On the steps there was a short,
low-toned conversation.

" Hans, after all, thou art a good lad. Did I hurt thee ? "

" 'Tis all o'er now, Aubrey : no matter."

" Then I did. Well, I am sorry. Shall I give thee a
silver chain to make up, old comrade ? "

" All is made up. Prithee, give me nothing—save—my
brother Aubrey."

Aubrey's tone was glib and light, though with a slight
sub-accent of regret. Hans's voice was more hesitating
and husky. It cost Hans much to allow any one a glimpse
into his heart; it cost Aubrey nothing. But, as is often
the case, the guarded chamber contained rare treasure,
while in the open one there was nothing to guard.

" Thou art a good lad ! " said Aubrey again, in a slightly
ashamed tone, as he took the offered hand. " Truly, Hans,
I was after none ill, only—well, I hate to be watched and
dogged, or aught like thereto."

" Who does not ? " replied Hans. " And in truth likewise, I was but coming home, and spake my astonishment
at seeing you."

" We are friends, then ? "

" God forbid we should ever be any thing else ! Good
night, and God keep you in His way ! "

Not many days afterwards, an event happened, of some

consequence to our friends at the White Bear. Their one powerful friend, Edward de Vere, Earl of Oxford, died in June, 1604.

A strange study for a student of human nature is this Earl of Oxford—a curious compound, like his late royal lady, of greatness and littleness. He began life as a youthful exquisite. His costumes were more extravagant, his perfumes more choice, his Italian more pure and fluent, than those of the other dilettante nobles of his time. He was a minor poet of some note in his day, and was esteemed to be the first writer of comedy then living—though Shakespeare was living too. In middle life he blossomed out into a military patriot. He ended his days as a hard, cold, morose old man. His life-lamp was used up: it had been made so to flare in early youth, that there was no oil left to light him at the end, when light and warmth were most needed. Having quarrelled with his father-in-law, the great Earl of Burleigh, he registered a savage and senseless vow to "ruin his daughter," which he could do only by ruining himself. In pursuance of this insane resolution, he spent right and left, until his estate was wrecked, and the innocent Countess Anne was hunted into her grave.

The son who succeeded to his father's title, and to the few acres which this mad folly had not flung away, was a mere boy of twelve years old. It became a serious question in Lady Louvaine's mind whether Aubrey should remain in the household after the decease of the old Earl. She found, however, that the widowed Countess Elizabeth kept a very orderly house, and a strict hand over her son and his youthful companions, so that Lady Louvaine, who saw no other door open, thought it best to leave Aubrey where he was. The Countess, who had been Maid of Honour to Queen Elizabeth, had been well drilled by that redoubtable lady into proper and submissive behaviour;

and she now required similar good conduct from her dependants, with excellent reasons for absence or dereliction from duty. That she was never deceived would be too much to say.

Meanwhile, matters progressed busily in the house by the river-side. The conspirators took in a sixth accomplice—Christopher Wright, the younger brother of John—and the six began their mine, about the eleventh of December, 1604.

The wall of the House of Lords was three yards in thickness; the cellar of Percy's house was extremely damp, being close to the river, and the water continually oozed through into the mine. Finding their task more difficult than they had anticipated, a seventh was now taken into the number—a pervert, Robert Keyes, the son of a Protestant clergyman in Derbyshire. A second house was hired at Lambeth, of which Keyes was placed in charge, while to Fawkes was committed the chief business of laying in the combustibles, first in the Lambeth house, and afterwards of removing them to that at Westminster. Fawkes went cautiously about his business, purchasing his materials in various parts of the City, so as not to excite suspicion. He provided in all, three thousand billets of wood, five hundred faggots, thirty-six barrels of gunpowder, with stones and bars of iron, in order that the explosion might be more destructive. From the Bankside, or south bank of the Thames, where it lay in hampers, twenty barrels of the powder was first brought in boats, by night, to the house at Westminster, where it was stored in the cellar to await the finishing of the mine. By Christmas they had penetrated the wall of Percy's house, and had reached that of the House of Lords. They thought it desirable now to rest for the Christmas holidays; Keyes was left in charge of the house at Lambeth, and the others departed in various directions.

"Well, upon my word! Prithee, good my master, who's your tailor?"

The speaker was Temperance Murthwaite, who was clad in the plainest of brownish drab serges, without an unnecessary tag or scrap of fringe, and carried on her arm an unmistakable market-basket, from which protruded the legs of a couple of chickens and sundry fish-tails, notwithstanding the clean cloth which should have hidden such ignoble articles from public view. The person addressed was Mr. Aubrey Louvaine, and his costume was a marvel of art and a feast of colour.

"My tailor is Adrian Sewell, Aunt, in Thieving Lane——"

"Like enough!" was the response. "Well, Gentleman?"

"Shall I——" The words died on Aubrey's lips. His aunt, who read his thoughts exactly, stood wickedly enjoying the situation.

"Shall you carry the basket? By all means, if it please your Highness. Have a care, though, lest the tails of those whitings sully yon brave crimson velvet, and see the fowls thrust not their talons into that Spanish lace. Methinks, Master Aubrey, considering your bravery of array, you were best pocket your civility this morrow. It'll be lesser like to harm the lace and velvet than the chicks' legs and the fish-tails. You may keep me company an' you will, if I be good enough to trudge alongside so fine a Whitsuntide show as you are. That's two of 'em."

"Of what, Aunt?" said Aubrey, feeling about as unhappy as a mixture of humiliation and apprehension could make him. If they were to meet one of Lord Oxford's gentlemen, or one of his wealthy acquaintances, he felt as though he should want the earth to open and swallow him.

"Suits, Gentleman," was the reply. "Blue and white the

first; crimson and silver the second. Haven't seen the
green and gold yet, nor the yellow, nor purple. Suppose
they're in the wardrobe. Rather early times, to be thus
bedizened, or seems so to working folks—the Abbey clock
went eight but a few minutes since. But quality is
donned early, I know."

As Mistress Temperance emitted this tingling small-
shot of words, she was marching with some rapidity up
Old Palace Yard and the Abbey Close, her magnificent
nephew keeping pace with her, right sore against his will.
At last Aubrey could bear no longer. The windows of
the Golden Fish were in sight, and his soul was perturbed
by a vision of the fair Dorothy, who might be looking
out, and whose eyes might light on the jewel of himself
in this extremely incongruous setting of Aunt Temperance
and the fish-tails.

"Aunt Temperance, couldn't——" Aubrey's words did
not come so readily as usual, that morning.

"Couldn't I walk slower?" suggested the aggravating
person who was the cause of his misery. "Well, belike
I could.—There's Mrs. Gertrude up at the window yonder
—without 'tis Mrs. Dorothy.—There's no hurry in especial,
only I hate to waste time."

And suiting the action to the word, Aunt Temperance
checked her steps, so as to give the young lady, whether
it were Gertrude or Dorothy, a more leisurely view of the
fish-tails.

"Couldn't Rachel go marketing instead of you?"
sputtered out Aubrey.

"Rachel has her own work; and so has Charity.
And so have I, Mr. Louvaine. I suppose you haven't, as
you seem to be gallivanting about Westminster in crimson
and silver at eight o'clock of a morning. Now then——"

"Aunt, 'tis not my turn this morrow to wait on my
Lord's *lever*. I shall be at his *coucher* this even."

"You may open the door, my master, if it demean not so fine a gentleman.—Good maid! Take my basket, Rachel. The fish for dinner, and the chicken for to-morrow."

"There's nobut four whitings here, Mistress: shouldn't there be five?"

"Hush thee, good maid. They're twopence a-piece."

"Eh, yo' never sen[1] so!"

"Ay, but I do. Let be; I'll have a bit of green stuff, or something."

And as Rachel, looking but half satisfied, went off with the basket, Temperance threw open the parlour door.

"Madam, suffer me to announce the Duke of Damask, the Prince of Plush, the Viscount of Velvet, and the Baron of Bombast. Pray you, look not for four nobles; there is but one."

"Aubrey!" was the response, in diverse tones, from the three ladies.

The object of this attention did not look happy; but he walked in and offered due greeting to his relatives. Temperance sat down, untied her plain black hood, and laid it aside.

"And whither might your Lordship be going when I captivated you?" asked she. "Not to this house, for you had passed it by."

"In good sooth, Aunt, I did not—I meant, indeed—I should maybe have looked in," stammered the young man.

"Tell no lies, my lad, for thou dost it very ill," was Aunt Temperance's most inconsiderate reply.

"You might come to see us oftener, I'm sure, Aubrey, if you would," said his mother in a plaintive voice. "It is hard, when I have only one child, that he should never care to come. I wish you had been a girl like Lettice, and then we could have had some comfort out of you."

[1] Say.

"My dear," said Aunt Temperance, "he is devoutly thankful he's not. He doesn't want to be tied at the aprons of a parcel of women, trust me. Have you had your pipe of open-work, or what you are pleased to call it, Gentleman, this morrow? Only think of hanging that filthy stench about those velvet fal-lals! With whom spent you last even, lad?"

The question came so suddenly that Aubrey was startled into truth. "With some friends of mine in the Strand, Aunt." The next instant he was sorry.

"Let's have their names," said Aunt Temperance.

"Well, Tom Rookwood was one."

"Folks generally put the best atop. Hope *he* wasn't the best. Who else?"

"Some gentlemen to whom Rookwood introduced me."

"I want their names," said the female examiner.

"Well—one of them is a Mr. Winter." Aubrey spoke with great reluctance, as his aunt saw well. He selected Winter's name as being least uncommon of the group. But he soon found that Destiny, in the person of Aunt Temperance, did not mean to let him off so lightly as this.

"What sort of an icicle is he?"

"He isn't an icicle at all, Aunt, but a very good fellow and right pleasant company."

"Prithee bring him to see us. Where lodgeth he?—is he a London man?"

"He is a Worcestershire gentleman, on a visit hither."

"Pass him. Who else?"

"Well—a man named Darcy."

"A man, and *not* a gentleman? Whence comes he?"

"I don't know. Scarcely a gentleman, seeing he deals in horses."

"Horses are good fellows enough, mostly: but folks who deal in horses are apt to be worser,—why, can

I never tell. Is the horse-dealer pleasant company be-like?"

"Not so much to my liking as Mr. Winter."

"I'm fain to hear it. Who else?"

"There is a Mr. Percy, kin to my Lord Northumberland."

Aunt Temperance drew in her breath with an inverted whistle. "Lo' you now, we are in select society!"

But Edith turned suddenly round. "Aubrey, is he a true Protestant?" She knew that Lord Northumberland was reckoned "the head of the recusants."

"I really don't know, Aunt," replied Aubrey, to whom the idea had never before occurred. "I never heard him say aught whence I could guess it. He is a very agreeable man."

"The more agreeable, maybe, the more dangerous. My boy, do have a care! 'He that is not with Me is against Me.'"

"Oh, he's all right, I am sure," said Aubrey, carelessly.

"You seem sure on small grounds," said Aunt Temperance. "Well, have we made an end?—is he the last?"

"No, there is one other—Mr. Catesby."

Aubrey had deliberately left Catesby to the last, yet he could not have explained for what reason. Lady Louvaine spoke for the first time.

"Catesby?—a Catesby of Ashby Ledgers?"

"I have not heard, further than that his home is in Northamptonshire, and his mother the Lady Anne Catesby."

"I think it is. They are a Popish family, or were, not many years ago. Aubrey, come here."

The young man obeyed, in some surprise. His gentle grandmother was not wont to speak in tones of such stern determination as these.

"My boy!" she said, "I charge thee on my benison,

and by the dear memory of him from whom thou hast thy name, that thou endeavour thyself to thine utmost to discover whether these men be Papists or no. Ask not of themselves—they may deceive thee; and a Papist oft counts deceit no wrong when it is done in the interests of his Church. Make my compliments to my cousin, my Lady Oxford, and give her the names of these gentlemen, and where they lodge; saying also that I do most earnestly beseech that she will make inquiry by her chaplain, and give me to know, how they stand concerned in this matter. Aubrey, you know not the danger of such friendship: I do. Obey me, at your peril."

Never in his life had Aubrey heard such words from the usually soft, sweet lips of the Lady Lettice. He was thoroughly frightened, all the more because the dangers to be feared were so vague and unknown. A few minutes before, he had been feeling vexed with his Aunt Temperance for catechising him so strictly about his riends. Now, this sensation had quite given way before astonishment and vague apprehension.

"Yes, Madam, I will," he answered gravely.

And he meant it. But——

What a number of excellent people, and what a multiplicity of good deeds, there would be in this naughty world, if only that little conjunction could be left out!

Aubrey quitted the White Bear with the full intention of carrying out his grandmother's behest. But not just now. He must do it, of course, before he saw her again. Lady Oxford might take it into her head to pay a visit to Lady Louvaine, in which case it would surely be discovered if the question had not been passed on. Of course it must be done: only, not just now. He might surely spend a few more pleasant evenings at Winter's lodgings, before he set on foot those disagreeable inquiries which might end in his being deprived of the pleasure. Lady Oxford, therefore, was not troubled that evening,— nor the next, nor indeed for a goodly number to follow. But within a week of his visit to the White Bear, when the sharp edge of his grandmother's words had been a little blunted by time, and the cares of other things had entered in, Aubrey again made his way to the lodgings occupied by Winter at the sign of the Duck, in the Strand, " hard by Temple Bar."

There were various reasons for this action. In the first place, Aubrey was entirely convinced that the judgment of a man of twenty-one was to be preferred before that of a woman of seventy-seven. Secondly, he enjoyed Winter's society. Thirdly, he liked Winter's tobacco. Fourthly, he admired Betty, who usually let him in, and who, being even more foolish than himself, was not at all averse to a few empty compliments and a little frothy banter, which he was very ready to bestow. For Aubrey was not of that sterling metal of which his grandfather had been made, " who loved one only and who clave to her," and to whom it would have been a moral impossibility to flirt with one woman while he was making serious love to another. Lastly, the society of his friends had acquired an added zest by the probability of its being a dangerous luxury. He loved dearly to poise himself on the edge of peril, though of course, like all who do so, he had not the slightest intention of falling in.

On the evening in question, Betty made no appearance, and Aubrey was let in by her mistress, a plain-featured middle-aged woman, on whom he had no temptation to waste his perfumes. He made his way up the stairs to Winter's door, and his hand was on the latch when he heard Percy's voice.

"Through by the seventh of February! You'll be nothing of the sort."

"I cry you mercy. I think we shall," answered Catesby.

Aubrey lifted the latch, and entered.

Four gentlemen sat round the fire—Winter and Catesby; Percy, whom Aubrey knew, and in whose hand was the pipe; and a fourth, a tall, dark, and rather fine-looking man, with brown hair, auburn beard, and a moustache the ends of which curled upwards.

"Ha! Mr. Louvaine? You are right welcome," said Winter, rising to greet his young friend, while Percy took his pipe from his lips, and offered it to the latter. Nobody introduced the stranger, and Aubrey took but little notice of him, especially as thenceforth he sat in silence. He might have paid more if he could have known that after three hundred years had rolled by, and the names of all then known as eminent men should have faded from common knowledge, the name of that man should be fresh in the memory of every Englishman, and deeply interesting to every English boy. He was in the company of Guy Fawkes.

To appear as a nameless stranger, and indeed to appear at all as little as possible, was Fawkes's policy at this moment. He was just about to present himself on the stage as John Johnson, "Mr. Percy's man," and for any persons in London to know him by his own name would be a serious drawback, for it was to a great extent because he was unknown in Town that he had been selected to play this part. Yet matters were not quite ready for the assumption of his new character. He therefore sat silent, and was not introduced.

They smoked, sipped Rhenish wine, and chatted on indifferent subjects, for an hour or more; discussed the "sleeping preacher," Richard Haydock, then just rising into notoriety—who professed to deliver his sermons in his sleep, and was afterwards discovered to be an impostor; the last benefaction in the parish church, for two poor Irish gentlewomen on their journey home, recommended by letters from the Council; the last new ballad.

"But have you beheld," asked Winter, when these topics were exhausted, "the King's new caroche of the German fashion, with a roof to fall asunder at his Majesty's pleasure?"

"I have," said Catesby; "and methinks it shall take with many, gentlewomen more in especial."

"Wherefore, now?" inquired Percy, laughing. "Think you gentlewomen lack air rather than gentlemen, or that they shall think better to show their dainty array and their fair faces?"

"A little of both," was the answer.

"There is truly great increase in coaches of late years," remarked Winter.

"Why, the saddlers are crying out they are like to be ruined," said Percy; "the roads are cloyed and pestered, and the horses lamed."

"Ay, and that is not the worst of it," added Catesby. "Evil-disposed persons, who dare not show themselves openly for fear of correction, shadow and securely convey themselves in coaches, and so are not to be distinguished from persons of honour."

The whole company agreed that this was extremely shocking, and piously denounced all evil-disposed persons in a style which Aubrey thought most edifying. As he walked back later, he meditated whether he should make those inquiries of Lady Oxford that night, and decided not to do so. No real Papist or traitor, thought the innocent youth, would be likely to denounce evil-disposed persons! The airs they had been singing, before parting, recurred to his mind, and he hummed fragments of them as he went along. "Row well, ye mariners," "All in a garden green," "Phillida flouts me," and the catch of

"Whoop, Barnaby!" finishing up with "Greensleeves" and one or two madrigals—these had been their evening entertainment: but madrigals were becoming unfashionable, and were not heard now so often as formerly. The music of Elizabeth's day, which was mainly harmony with little melody, containing "scarcely any tune that the uncultivated ear could carry away," was giving way to a less learned but more melodious style. Along with this, there was a rapid increase in the cultivation of instrumental music, while vocal music continued to be exceedingly popular. It was usual enough for tradesmen and artisans to take part in antiphons, glees, and part-songs of all kinds, while ballads were in such general favour that ballad-mongers could earn twenty shillings a day. A bass viol generally hung in a drawing-room for the visitors to play; but the few ladies who used this instrument were thought masculine. The education of girls at this time admitted of scarcely any accomplishment but music: they were taught to read, write, sew, and cook, to play the virginals, lute, and cithern, and to read prick-song at sight,—namely, to sing from the score, without accompaniment. Those who were acquainted with any language beside their own were the few and highly-cultured; and a girl who knew French or Italian was still more certain to have learned Latin, if not Greek. German and Spanish were scarcely ever taught; indeed, the former was regarded as quite outside the list of learnable tongues.

It was a sore trouble to Aubrey that the White Bear and the Golden Fish were next door to each other. Had he had the ordering of their topography, they would have been so situated that he could have dropped into the latter, to sun himself in the eyes of the fair Dorothy, without the least fear of being seen from the former. He stood in wholesome fear of his Aunt Temperance's sharp speeches, and had a less wholesome, because more selfish, dislike of his mother's ceaseless complaints. Moreover, Aunt Edith was wont to disturb his equanimity by a few quiet occasional words which would ring in his ears for days afterwards, and make him very uncomfortable. Her speeches were never long, but they were often weighty, and were adapted to make their hearers consider their ways, and think what they would do in the end thereof— a style of consideration always unwelcome to Aubrey, and especially so since his view of the world had been enlarged by coming to London.

He was just now in an awkward position, and the centre and knot of the awkwardness was Dorothy Rookwood. He was making no way with Dorothy. Her brother he met frequently at Winter's rooms, but if he wished to see her, he must go to her home. If he went there, he must call at the White Bear. If he did that, he must first deliver his grandmother's message to Lady Oxford. And only suppose that Lady Oxford's inquiries should lead to discoveries which would end in a rupture between the Golden Fish and the White Bear—in Aubrey's receiving an order to drop all acquaintance with the Rookwoods! For Aubrey's training, while very kindly conducted, had been one of decided piety; and unchanged as was his heart, the habits and tone of eighteen years were not readily shaken off. He could not feel easy in doing many things that he saw others do; he could not take upon his lips with impunity words which he heard freely used around him. His conscience was unseared as yet, and it tormented him sorely. The result of these reflections was that Aubrey turned into Oxford House, without visiting King Street at all, and sought his bed without making any attempt to convey the message.

Before the conspirators resumed their work after the Christmas holidays, they took two more into their number.

These were Robert Winter of Huddington, the elder brother of Thomas, and John Grant of Norbrook, who had married Dorothy, sister of the Wrights. Catesby and Thomas Winter went down to the Catherine Wheel at Oxford, whence they sent for their friends to come to them, and having first pledged them to secrecy, they were then initiated into the plot.

It was about this Christmas that Catesby also took into his confidence the only one of the conspirators who was not a gentleman—his own servant, Thomas Bates, partly because he had "great opinion of him for his long-tried fidelity," and partly also because, having been employed in carrying messages, he suspected that he had some inkling of the secret, and wished that, like the rest, he should be bound to keep it by oath. Bates is described as a yeoman, and "a man of mean station, who had been much persecuted on account of religion." Having been desired to confirm his oath by receiving the Sacrament "with intention," and as a pre-requisite of this was confession, Bates went to Greenway, whom he acquainted with the particulars, "which he was not desirous to hear," and asked if he might lawfully join in such work. Greenway directed him to keep the secret, "because it was for a good cause," and forbade him to name the subject to any other priest. This is Bates's account; Greenway asserts that Bates never named the subject to him, either in or out of confession; but the Jesuit code of morality required his denial, if he had heard it in confession only. Poor Bates was the most innocent of the conspirators, and the most truly penitent: he was rather a tool and a victim than a miscreant. He lost his life through neglect of a much-forgotten precept—"If sinners entice thee, consent thou not."

The conspirators now set to work again on their mine, and wrought till Candlemas Day, by which time they were half through the wall of the House. Fawkes was on all occasions the sentinel. They had provided themselves with "baktmeats," pasties, and hard-boiled eggs, sufficient for twenty days, in order to avoid exciting the suspicions of their neighbours by constantly bringing fresh provisions to a house supposed to be occupied by one person alone. The labour was very severe, especially to Catesby and Percy, on account of their unusual height. The oozing in of the water was a perpetual annoyance. But one day, something terrible occurred.

As the amateur miners plied their picks with diligence, the toll of a bell was suddenly heard. John Wright, who was furthest in the mine, stopped with uplifted tool.

"Blessed saints! what can that be?"

Work was unanimously suspended.

"It comes from the very midst of the wall!" said Catesby, growing a shade paler.

"*Refugium peccatorum, ora pro nobis!*" piously entreated Percy, crossing himself.

"Call Mr. Fawkes," suggested Christopher.

Mr. Fawkes was summoned, by his official name of Johnson; and coming down into the cellar, declared that he also distinctly heard the uncanny sound.

"'Tis the Devil that seeketh to make stay of our work," pronounced Percy—a most improbable suggestion, for Satan surely had no cause to interfere with his servants when engaged in his own business.

"Have we here any holy water?" asked Catesby.

"Ay, there is in the bedchamber," said Fawkes.

"Pray you, fetch it quickly."

The holy water was at once brought, and the wall was sprinkled with it. At that moment the tolling ceased.

"Blessed be our Lady! the holy water hath stayed it," said Percy.

After a few minutes' pause, the work was recommenced : but it had gone on for barely an hour when again the unearthly bell began its work. Once more the bénitier was brought, and the wall sprinkled; whereupon the diabolical noise stopped at once. For several days these processes were repeated, the bell invariably being silenced by the sprinkling of the blessed element. At least, so said the conspirators.

About the second of February, there was another scare. A strange rushing noise was heard on the other side of the wall, from what cause was unknown; and Catesby, as usual the chief director, whispered to Fawkes to go out and ascertain what it was.

Fawkes accordingly went upstairs, and out into the street. A waggon stood before the door of the House of Lords, and men were busy carrying sacks and tubs from the cellar to the waggon. Charcoal only was then sold by the sack; sea-coal being disposed of in tubs.

"Good-morrow, Master," said Roger Neck, the servant who was superintending the transaction, as Fawkes paused a moment, apparently to look on, after the fashion of an idle man. Roger had seen him more than once, passing in and out of Percy's house; but he was the only one of the plotters ever visible in the daytime.

"Good-morrow, friend. Selling your coals off?"

"Ay, we're doing a middling stroke of business this morrow."

"How much a load? We shall want some ere long."

"Charcoal, fourteen shillings; cannel, sixpence to ninepence, according to quality."

Fawkes walked down the street, to avoid suspicion, into King Street, where he turned into the first shop to which he came. It happened to be a cutler's, and he bought the first thing he saw—a dozen knives of Sheffield make. Had they been London-made, they would have cost four

times as much as the modest shilling demanded for them.
He then returned to Percy's house, carrying the knives in
his hand.   Fawkes had now fully blossomed out in his
new rôle of "Mr. Percy's man," and was clad in blue
camlet accordingly, blue being then the usual wear of
servants out of livery.

"What is it, Johnson?" asked Percy, addressing Fawkes
by his assumed name, when he came down into the cellar.

"It is a dozen of Sheffield knives, Master," replied
Fawkes a little drily: "and by the same token, our next
neighbour is selling his coals, and looks not unlike to clear
out his cellar."

"Is that all?"

"That is all."

Two of the conspirators looked at each other.

"If you could hire the cellar——" suggested Catesby.

"Done!" said Percy.   "It should save us a peck of
trouble."

"Who owns it?—or who hath it?" asked Catesby.

"Why, for who owns it, I guess the Parliament
House," answered Fawkes; "but for who hath it, that
must we discover."

"Pray you, make haste and discover it, then."

Fawkes went out again to make inquiries.   He found
without difficulty that the cellar, like the houses adjoining, was held by the Wyniards, and it was agreed that
Percy should call on them and endeavour to obtain it.

He accordingly went to see his landlady, to whom he
represented that he wished to bring his wife up to live
with him in London—she was in the country at present,
and he missed her sorely—but if that were done, he must
have more stowage for wood and coals.

Mrs. Wyniard's interest was aroused at once in a man
who cared for his wife, and felt a want of her society.

"Well, now, I am sorry!" said she.   "You see, we've

let that vault to Mrs. Skinner—leastwise, Mrs. Bright, she is now—o' King Street, to store her coals. Her new husband's a coal-seller, see you. You should have had it, as sure as can be, if I hadn't."

"It were very much to my commodity," said Percy, truthfully this time, "if I could hire that cellar, and "— the second half of the sentence was a falsehood—" I have already been to Mrs. Skinner, and hold her consent."

"Well, now, but that's a bit mean o' Skinner's wife," said Mrs. Wyniard in a vexed tone; "she shouldn't ha' done that and ne'er ha' let me know. I wouldn't ha' thought that of Ellen Skinner—no, I wouldn't."

"But," suggested Percy, insinuatingly, "if I gave you twenty shillings over for your good-will, and prayed you to say nought to Mrs. Skinner, and I will likewise content her?"

"Well, you know how to drive a bargain, forsooth," answered Mrs. Wyniard, laughing. "Come, I'll let Widow Skinner be—Mistress Bright, I mean. You shall have the vault for four pounds a quarter, if so be she's content."

Percy's next visit was to the coal-seller and his bride. Mr. Bright was not at home, but Mrs. Bright was; and though she could not write her name,[1] she could use her tongue to some purpose.

"To be sure we hold the cellar. Sixteen pound by the year, and that's plenty. Takes a many loads of coals to make that, I warrant you."

"I wondered," said Percy in a careless manner, as though he did not much care whether he got it or not, " whether you might let me the cellar for the same purpose? I think to lay in wood and coals for the winter, and my own cellar is scarce large enough, for I am a Northern man, and love a good fire. This cellar of yours, being so

[1] She signed her deposition by a mark, while her servant, Roger Neck, wrote his name.

close by, should be greatly to my convenience, if you were willing."

"Well, to be sure, and it would so!" assented innocent Mrs. Bright. "You see, I can't speak certain till my master comes in, but I'm sure you may take it as good: he mostly does as I bid him. So we'll say, if Mrs. Wyniard be content to accept the rent from you, you shall have it at four pound by the quarter, and give me forty shillings in my hand."[1]

"Done," said Percy, "if your husband consent."

"I'll see to it he doth," she answered with a capable nod.

The bargain was struck: Andrew Bright did as he was told, and Percy was to become the occupant of the cellar without delay.

[1] Exam. of Ellen Bright, Gunp. Plot Book, art. 24.

CHAPTER VI.

WAIT A MONTH.

"Alas, long-suffering and most patient God!
Thou needst be surelier God to bear with us
Than even to have made us."
ELIZABETH BARRETT BROWNING.

THE conspirators had just concluded their bargain, and decided that the cellar must be stored with materials in all haste, to be ready for the meeting of Parliament on the seventh of February, when like a bomb-shell in their midst fell a royal proclamation, proroguing Parliament again until the third of October. To go on now, especially in haste, was plainly a useless proceeding.

A short consultation was held, which ended in the decision that they should part and scatter themselves in different places. Fawkes particularly was enjoined to keep out of the way, since he was wanted to appear as a stranger when the moment arrived for action; he therefore determined to go abroad.

The rest dispersed in various directions: Percy was left alone at the house in Westminster, where he beguiled his leisure by having a door made through the wall, where the mine had been, so as to give him easier access to the vault under the House, and better opportunities of carrying in the combustibles unseen. They agreed to meet again, ready for work, on the second of September; and before parting, one other was admitted to their fellowship, to whom was confided the task of aiding Fawkes to accumulate the store of powder. This was Mr. Ambrose Rookwood, of Coldham Hall, Suffolk.

Before Fawkes left England, he accomplished one important piece of business, by carrying into the vault beneath the House all the wood and coals hitherto stored in Percy's cellar. Among it was carefully hidden the gunpowder also in waiting, billets of wood being heaped upon the barrels. The door was then locked, and Fawkes took the key, marking the door on the inside in such a manner that its having been opened could be detected thereafter. The wife of the porter, Gideon Gibbons, the next-door neighbour, was placed in charge of Percy's house, in which no tell-tale combustibles had now been left. Keyes was made again custodian of the house at Lambeth.

These arrangements being complete, Percy went to see his wife, whom he had left in the country, and Fawkes, embarking at Dover, took his journey to Brussels, where he resumed his own name.

When Aubrey applied next at the door of Winter's lodgings, he was informed that the gentlemen were gone into the country. He turned back disappointed—after a little frothy banter with Betty, which it would be a sad waste of paper and ink to detail—and began to consider what he should do next. A sensation of extreme relief came to his mind, as the idea occurred to him that there could be no need at all to make any inquiries during the absence of his friends. He might visit the fair Dorothy, and even venture into the jaws of the White Bear, without fear of any thing unpleasant. Merely to say that his friends had left Town, and he was not now cultivating their society, would surely satisfy his grandmother: and as for any thing else,—why, let fate take care of the future. Being usually the creature of impulse, no sooner was this said, or rather thought, than it was done. Aubrey turned away from the Duck, and retraced his steps to Charing Cross, left Whitehall behind him, and came out into King Street.

Now came the tug of war. Would he meet Aunt Temperance? or would that formidable and irresistible individual pounce upon him from the door? But all was still, and he reached the Golden Fish without any mishap.

Another disappointment! He was shown into the parlour, where Gertrude rose to meet him, and Mrs. Rookwood came in a few minutes later. Tom was spending the evening with friends, and Anne was with him. Aubrey cared nothing about Anne, whom he mentally dubbed a stupid idiot; for Tom's absence he was more sorry. But what was Dorothy doing that she did not shine on her worshipper?

"Had you honoured us with a visit last Tuesday, Mr. Louvaine," said Gertrude, glancing at him, as she was wont to do, out of the corners of her dark eyes, "we had enjoyed the happiness of bringing you acquainted with our uncle Rookwood of Coldham Hall. He left us, o' Wednesday in the morning, for his place in Suffolk."

"Doll is gone with him," placidly added Mrs. Rookwood.

The bright colours of Gertrude's embroidery took a sudden tarnish in the eyes of the visitor.

"Ay, for a month or two," said Gertrude, lightly. "She shall find a merry house at Coldham, you may be sure. Our cousins, and all the Burgesses, and the Collinsons—ever so many young gentlemen and gentlewomen —and," with a slight, significant laugh, "Mr. Roland Burgess in particular."

Aubrey felt as if he should exceedingly have enjoyed despatching Mr. Roland Burgess to the Caucasus, or Cochin-China, or any other inconceivably remote locality.

He did not stay long after that. There was nothing to keep him. Bows and courtesies were exchanged, and Aubrey, feeling as if life were flat and unsatisfying, turned into the White Bear.

It was nearly dusk, and he could not see whom he met by the parlour door.

"Is that your Lordship?" greeted him, in the voice of Aunt Temperance. "Blue or yellow this even? Truly, we scarce looked for so much honour as two visits in the twelvemonth. Why, without I err, 'tis not yet three months since we had leave to see your Lordship's crimson and silver. Pray you, walk in—you are as welcome as flowers in May, as wise as Waltom's calf, and as safe to mend as sour ale in summer."

"You are full of compliments, Aunt Temperance," said Aubrey, half vexed and half laughing.

"I'm like, with strangers, Gentleman."

Aubrey went past her into the parlour, to receive a warmer and less sarcastic welcome from the rest of his relatives—his mother excepted, who reminded him, in her usual plaintive tones, that she was a poor widow, and it was very hard if she might never see her only child.

"Well, I am here, Mother."

"Ay, but you scarce ever come. 'Tis ever so long that we have not seen you. 'Tis cruel of my Lord Oxford thus to keep you away from your poor mother."

"My Lord Oxford has less to do with it, my dear, than Mr. Aubrey Louvaine," said her sister. "Young men don't commonly reckon their mothers' company the sweetest. They never know on which side their bread's buttered."

"No butter will stick on my bread, Aunt," said Aubrey, answering one proverb by another.

Instead of replying, Aunt Temperance lighted a candle and calmly looked her nephew over.

"Well!" said she, as the result of her inspection, "if I were donned in grass-green velvet, guarded o' black, with silver tags, and a silver-bossed girdle, and gloves o' Spanish leather, I should fancy I'd got a bit o' butter on my bread. Maybe your honour likes it thick? Promotes effusing of bile, that doth. Pray you, how fare your Papistical friends this even?"

Lady Louvaine looked up and listened for the answer.

"You set it down they be Papistical somewhat too soon, Aunt," said Aubrey a little irritably. "Mr. Winter and his friends, if they be whom you hit at, be gone away into the country, and I have not seen them this some time."

The next question put to him was the one that Aubrey was expecting, with an expectation which caused his irritability.

"What said my Lady Oxford to the matter, Aubrey?"

"Truly, Madam, I have not yet made the inquiration. My Lady is at this time full of business, and seeing my friends were away, I thought you should not require haste."

Aubrey's conscience stirred a little uneasily, and he said to it, "Be quiet! I have not told any falsehood."

"I would not have you to chafe your Lady, if she have no time to listen," said Lady Louvaine, with a disappointed look: "but indeed, Aubrey, the matter must be seen to, and not done by halves, moreover."

A rap at the door preceded Charity, who came to announce Mrs. Abbott—a ceremony always used at the White Bear, but entirely unnecessary in the eyes of the lady of the Angel.

"Well, what think you?" she began, before her greetings were well over; for Mistress Abbott was a genuine Athenian, who spent all her leisure hours, and some hours when she should not have been at leisure, in first gathering information, and then retailing it, not having any special care to ascertain its accuracy. "Well, what think you?

Here be three of our neighbours to be presented by the
street wardens—Lewce, the baker, for that they cannot
keep his pigs out of the King's Street; Joan Cotton the
silkwoman as a sower of strife amongst her neighbours;
and Adrian Sewell for unlawfully following the trade of a
tailor."

"Why, that is thy tailor, Aubrey!" exclaimed Aunt
Temperance. "I trust thou art not deep in his books?"

"Never a whit, Aunt; I owe him ne'er a penny," said
Aubrey, flushing, and not adding that Mr. William Patrick's
books were separate volumes, nor that those of Nathan
Cohen, in Knightriders' Street, were not entirely guiltless
of his name.

"Ay, that's the way," said Mrs. Abbott, nodding her
head. "Pay as you go, and keep from small scores.
Truly I would, Mr. Louvaine, our Stephen were as wise
as you. Such a bill as came in this week past from a
silkman in Paternoster Row! White satin collars at
eight and ten shillings the piece, and a doublet of the
same at two pound; curled feathers, and velvet doublets,
and perfumed gloves at twenty pence or more. His
father's in a heavy taking, I can tell you, and saith he
shall be ruined. Look you, we've four lads, and here's
Stephen a-going this path—and if Seth and Caleb and
Ben just go along after Stephen, it'll be a fine kettle o'
fish, I can tell you. Oh dear, but you've a deal to be
thankful for, and only one to trouble you! The bicker
those lads do make!"

"We have all something wherefore we may be thankful, friend," said Lady Louvaine gently, when Mrs. Abbott
stopped to breathe.

"Well, then, there's the maids—Mall, and Silence, and
Prissy, and Dorcas, and Hester—and I can promise you,
they make such a racket amongst 'em, I'm very nigh
worn to a shadow."

Aubrey and Lettice were giving funny glances at each other, and doing their utmost not to disgrace the family by laughing. If Mrs. Abbott were worn to a shadow, shadows were very portly and substantial articles.

"I declare, that Prissy! she's such a rattle as never you saw! no getting a word in for her. I tell her many a time, I wonder her tongue does not ache. such a chatter-box as she is. I'm no talker, you see; nobody can say such a thing of me, but as to her——"

A curious sound in Aubrey's direction was rapidly followed by a cough.

"Eh now, don't you say you've a spring cough!" ejaculated Mrs. Abbott, turning her artillery on that young gentleman. "Horehound, and mallow, and coltsfoot, they're the best herbs; and put honey to 'em, and take it fasting of a morrow. There be that saith this new stuff of late come up—tobago, or what they call it—my husband says he never heard of aught with so many names. Talking o' names, have you seen that young maid, daughter of the baker new set up at back here? Whatever on earth possessed him to call her Penelope? Dear heart, but they say there's a jolly brunt betwixt my Lord Rich and his Lady—she that was my Lady Penelope Devereux, you know. My Lord he is a great Puritan, and a favourer of that way; and my Lady, she likes a pretty gown and a gay dance as well as e'er a one; so the wars have fallen out betwixt 'em——"

"If it like you, Mistress Abbott," said Charity, opening the door immediately after a knock, "here's your Ben, that says your master wants you."

"Ay," shouted Ben from the door in no dulcet tones, "and he said if you didn't come, he'd fetch you. You were safe to be gossiping somewhere, he said, and says he——"

"Take that for your imperence, Sir!" was his mother's

answer, hurrying to the door, with a gesture suited to the words. "Well, I do vow, if ever I come forth to have half a word with a neighbour, that man o' mine's sure for to call it gossiping.—Get away wi' thee! I'm coming in a wink.—Well, but you do look cheery and peaceful! I would I could ha' tarried a bit. Mrs. Lettice, my dear, you take warning by me, and don't you marry a man as gives you no liberty. Stand up for your rights, my dear, and get 'em—that's what I say. Good even! There's no end to the imperence of lads, and no more to the masterfulness of men. Don't you have nought to do with 'em! Good night."

"I could not have stood it another minute!" said Aubrey as soon as she was out of hearing, while he and Lettice made the walls echo.

On a calm June evening, three men met at a house in Thames Street, where Garnet lodged. They were Robert Catesby, the Rev. Oswald Greenway, and the Rev. Henry Garnet. They met to consult and decide on the last uncertainties, and as it were to finish off the scheme of the plot. The conclusions ended, Garnet let out his friends, who with hats drawn low down, and faces muffled in their cloaks, glided softly and darkly away.

As the month of August ran out, the conspirators gradually returned to London, with some exceptions, who joined their ghostly father, Garnet, in a pious pilgrimage to St. Winifred's Well, better known as Holywell, in Flintshire. The party numbered about thirty, and comprised Lady Digby, two daughters of Lord Vaux, Rookwood, and his wife. Thomas Winter wrote to Grant that "friends" would reach Norbrook on the second or third of September, begging him to "void his house of Morgan and his she-mate," as otherwise it "would hardly bear all the company." The route taken was from Goathurst, the home and inheritance of Lady Digby, by Daventry, Norbrook, the residence of Grant, Huddington, the house of Robert Winter, and Shrewsbury, to Holt, in Flintshire. In some uneasy nightmare during that pilgrimage, did a faint prescience of that which was to come ever flit before the eyes of Ambrose Rookwood, as to the circumstances wherein he should journey that road again? From Holt the ladies walked barefoot to the "holy well," which, according to tradition, had sprung up on the place where St. Winifred's head had rolled on being cut off : they remained at the well for the night. They returned the same way, mass being said by Garnet at Huddington and Norbrook. It is difficult to believe that those who went on this pilgrimage could be wholly innocent of "intention" respecting the plot so soon to be executed.

Fawkes arrived from abroad on the first of September, staying the first night at an inn outside Aldgate. The next day, he went down to the Tower Wharf, hailed a boat, and was ferried to Westminster, where, under his alias of John Johnson, and Percy's servant, he relieved Mrs. Gibbons of her charge, took possession of his master's house, and of the cellar where was stored his master's stock of winter fuel. A careful examination of the door of the vault showed that it had not been tampered with during the absence of the conspirators.

Winter now returned to London, taking up his abode in his old quarters at the Duck, where Keyes, Rookwood, and Christopher Wright, had apartments also. Catesby and Percy did not return till later. The latter had gone to Bath, where he found Lord Monteagle; and the two sent to Catesby, entreating "the dear Robin" to join them. Catesby obeyed, and came.

The Bath, as it was then usual to call the ancient city of hot springs, was a very different town from that which we now know. Like all of Roman origin, its design was cruciform, with four gates, and as usual a church at every gate. The only one of these churches now standing—and that has been rebuilt—is St. James's, at South Gate. The modern fashionable part of Bath, including Milsom Street, the Circus, and the Crescent, lies outside the walls of the ancient Aqua Solis.

Mr. Catesby found his friends in Cheap Street, which ran from Stawles Church, in the midst of the city, to East Gate. Here he vegetated for a week, resting after his toil, and applying himself to the business which had apparently brought him, by diligent attendance at the King's Bath, on the site of the present Pumproom. Here, at this time, ladies and gentlemen, in elaborate costumes and adorned by wonderful hair-dressing, bathed together under the eyes of the public, which contributed its quota of amusement and interest by pelting the bathers with dead dogs, cats, and pigs—a state of things not considered disgusting, but laughable.

On the morning after the arrival of Catesby, he and Percy went down to the East Gate, hailed a boat, which ferried them across the Avon, where Laura Place now stands, and leaving Bathwick Mill on the left hand, they began to ascend the hill on whose summit once stood the yet older British city of Caer Badon.

"Mr. Percy," said Catesby, as they walked slowly upwards, "since I have tarried here, I have had some time for thought; and I can tell you, I am nigh beat out of heart touching our matter."

"You, Mr. Catesby! Truly, I never thought to see you struck into your dumps. But what now, I beseech you?"

Gentlemen did not, at that time, speak to each other without the respectful prefix of "Mister," though they might now and then speak of an acquaintance without it When intimacy was so great as to warrant laying it aside, the Christian name took its place.

"Well, look you here," said Catesby. "We are all men of birth, but not one of us is a man of money. You, 'tis true, have my Lord Northumberland behind you, but how long time may he tarry? Were he to die, or to take pepper in the nose, where then are we? All is naught with us at once, being all but mean men of estate."

"My cousin of Northumberland is not like to play that prank, or I err," answered Percy, who well knew that Lord Northumberland was not in all cases cognisant of the use made of his name by this very worthy cousin: "as to death, of course that may hap,—we are all prone to be tumbled out of the world at short notice. But what then is your project? for without you have some motion in your mind, good Mr. Catesby, I read you not aright."

"To be sure I have," said Catesby with a smile. "But first—if I remember rightly, your friend young Louvaine is not he that can aid us in this juncture?"

"Hasn't a penny to bless himself with," replied Percy, "save his wage from my Lord Oxford, and that were but a drop in the sea for us. His old grandmother can do but little for him—so much have I picked out of his prattle. But, surely, Mr. Catesby, you would not think to take into our number a green lad such as he, and a simpleton, and a Protestant to boot?"

"Take into our number!" cried Catesby. "Good Mr. Percy, you miss the cushion.[1] A good tale, well tinkered, should serve that companion, and draw silver from his pockets any day. What we lack is two or three men of good estate, and of fit conditions and discreet years, that may safely be sworn—and I think I know where to find them."

"I'll lay my crown to pawn you do!" exclaimed Percy admiringly. "Pray you, who be they?"

[1] Make a mistake.

"Sir Everard Digby, of Tilton, in Rutland; and my cousin, Frank Tresham of Rushton."

"Good men and true? Both are strange to me."

"Ay; Digby is a staunch Catholic, but may lack some persuasion to join us. Tresham—well, I count he may be trusted. His money-bags be heavy, though his character is but light. I will make certain that he will not blab nor tattle—that is the thing most to be feared. Know you not Frank Tresham?—my cousin, and my Lord Monteagle's wife's brother."

"Oh ay! I have met him," said Percy. "I wist not it was he you meant."

"I had hope once that Mr. Fawkes should bring grist to our mill," said Catesby, thoughtfully: "but I see that is but a Will-o'-the-Wisp."

"Mr. Fawkes? Oh no! His father was but a younger son—Mr. Edward Fawkes of Farnley, a notary at York, and Registrar of the Consistory Court there. He left him but a farm of some thirty pound by the year, and Guy ran through it like a herring through the water. The only hope by his means would be the borrowing of money from his step-father, Mr. Foster, and methinks he hath a larger heart than purse."

They walked on for a few minutes in silence, when Percy said, "How will you get hold of these men?"

"Send Tom Winter to Sir Everard, and I will tackle Tresham. Then, when I return, will we go forth with the mine."

"Done!" said Percy.

And the pair of conspirators came down the hill.

Instead of returning direct to London, Catesby went to visit Robert Winter at Huddington, Percy going to his own house at the upper end of Holborn. Catesby remained for three days with Robert Winter, whom he induced to send for Stephen Littleton of Holbeach and his cousin

Humphrey Littleton. These gentlemen were not, however, initiated into the plot, but only desired to lend their assistance to "a matter of weight, and for the especial good of all Catholics."

The Christmas holidays being over, the mining was resumed, the conspirators having now added to their number Francis Tresham and Sir Everard Digby. It was not done without some difficulty. The oath was administered to both; but when they learned to what they had bound themselves, they recoiled in horror. Sir Everard was disposed of with comparative ease. His own good sense led him to demur, but no sooner was he told that three priests had approved of the scheme than, as in duty bound, the poor weak creature laid his good sense aside, told his conscience to be quiet, and united cordially and thoroughly in the project, finding horses, arms, and money, to the amount of £1500. If the Church approved, "the prerogative of the laity was to listen and to obey." Francis Tresham proved less pliable. He at once inquired if the Roman Catholic peers were to be warned, so as to keep away from Parliament on the doomed day.

"Generally, only," said Catesby. "We have let them understand that strict laws are to be passed against the Catholics, which they cannot prevent, and therefore they had best tarry away."

"My Lord Arundel, though he be not of age, is very desirous to be present," said Percy.

"My Lord Montague, on the contrary part, would fain be thence," returned Catesby, "and I have told him he can do no good there."

"I asked my Lord Mordaunt if he meant to come," said Winter, laughing, "and quoth he, 'Nay, for I was too much disgusted at the former session, being forced to sit there with my robes on, all the time the King was in church.'"[1]

"But surely," cried Tresham, looking from one to another, "you will take some further means to save our brethren than only these? Mr. Percy, you never will suffer your cousin the Earl of Northumberland to perish?"

"Indeed, Mr. Tresham, I should be loth so to do, because I am bounden to him."

"Gentlemen," said the voice of Fawkes, who had hitherto been silent in the conclave, "what we must principally respect is our own safety, and we will pray for the Catholic Lords."

"And how shall we set ourselves right with the Catholic commons?" demanded Keyes.

"Oh, we will satisfy the Catholics at large that the act is done for the restitution of religion," answered Catesby; "and the heretics, that it was to prevent the Union sought to be established at this Parliament."

"Sirs, I cannot brook this!" Tresham broke in eagerly. "My Lords Monteagle and Stourton, as you know, have wedded my sisters. I implore you to warn them: at the least, I do beseech you, save my Lord Monteagle!"

"What, to tell him what shall hap?" cried Catesby. "Never!"

"Impossible, Mr. Tresham!" replied Percy. "I regret it as much as you."

"They *shall* be warned!" cried Tresham vehemently.

"Remember your oath!" answered Catesby sternly.

"I shall not forget it. But something must be done to save my Lord Monteagle. I am beholden to him, and I love him dear."

---

[a] Lord Mordaunt was a trimmer, afraid of being known to be a Papist, and, like most half-hearted people, a great sufferer from the struggle between the conscience and the flesh.

" Well, well !" suggested Winter, making an endeavour to cast oil upon the troubled waters, " can you not be earnest with him to do something on that day, which shall carry him out of the way ? "

" I am afraid not ! " said Tresham, shaking his head. " He will reckon it his duty to be there, or I err."

" Time enough betwixt now and October," said Fawkes.

" Ay, time enough, indeed," echoed Winter. " My Lord Monteagle may be abroad, or what not, when the Parliament opens. Pray you, Mr. Tresham, trouble not yourself. I doubt not all shall go well."

Tresham murmured something to the effect that things left to drift as they would did not invariably drift into the right harbour : but he dropped the topic for the moment.

Hitherto the secret meetings of the conspirators had been in the house beyond Clement's Inn : but it was now deemed necessary to have a more secluded and secure retreat.

In the forest depths of Enfield Chase was an old hunting lodge, named White Webbs, never used except occasionally by sportsmen. This was selected as a non-suspicious place of meeting. The conspirators were now nearly ready : a few days would make them quite so. Satan was also ready, and probably required no time for preparation. And God was ready too.

They met at White Webbs on the 21st of September, just a fortnight before the day appointed for the meeting of Parliament: Catesby, the Winters, the Wrights, Digby, Keyes, Grant, and Bates. Tresham was not there ; he had ceased to attend the meetings, and said, if Lord Monteagle at least might not be saved he would neither find the money he had promised, nor assist any further with the plot.

They had not sat many minutes, when Percy and Fawkes joined them, the former impetuous person being

K

in an evident state of suppressed excitement, while the latter very cool individual showed no trace of emotion.

"Now, what think you?" cried Percy. "The Parliament is prorogued yet again."

"Sure, they have never wind of our project?" suggested one of the brothers Wright.

"Till when?" demanded Catesby, knitting his brows.

"For another month—till the fifth of November."

Catesby pondered for a moment in silence.

"Is there any stir thereabouts?—any search made of the house or the vault?"

"No—no semblance thereof."

"Then I think they have not got wind of it. But if so —Mr. Fawkes, is all the powder now in the cellar?"

"No, Mr. Catesby; there are five or six barrels to come, which I meant to move thither on Monday night next."

"Wait a little. You had best make sure that all is safe. Tarry for another fortnight, and move them then. Is this not your minds, gentlemen?"

The rest of the group, as usual, deferred to their leader. There was now another point requiring discussion, and it was introduced by Catesby.

"'Tis time, methinks, gentlemen, that we took thought on a question whereof we have not yet spoken. After the thing you wot of is done, what then shall follow? If not the King alone be present there, but the Queen also, and maybe the Prince——"

"If they be, we will not save them," interjected Fawkes.

"We need not," coolly responded Catesby: "but if all be gone, who then shall be published or elected king?"

"Why, we have never entered into that consideration," said Grant, dubiously.

"Had we not best enter into it? Our plans must be

ready at once, when the time comes, not all hanging betwixt the eyelids." [1]

"The Queen and Prince are safe to be there," said Percy. "And in any case, the Prince were best away; for if all be true that is said, or the half thereof, he were like to do us more mischief than his father. He is not of the King's humour, but more like old Bess—hath a will of his own, and was bred up strictly Protestant."

"Bad, that!" said Catesby. "Then the Prince must go."

"'Tis pity, though," observed Robert Winter. "A bright little lad."

Catesby laughed scornfully. "Come now, Robin, no sensibility,[2] I beg! We cannot afford to be punctual [3] in this affair. There are bright lads by the dozen everywhere, as cheap as blackberries. Now, what of the little Duke?"

The man who spoke thus was himself the father of two boys.

"He'll not be much of aught at five years old," said Winter. "Mr. Percy, you were the most like of any of us to win him into your hands."

Percy, as one of the band of gentleman pensioners, whose duty it was to wait on the King, had opportunities of access to the little Prince, beyond any of his accomplices.

"I will undertake that," said Percy eagerly.

"Do we concur, then, to elect him King?" asked Catesby.

"Hold, good gentlemen! by your leave, we go something too fast," said Fawkes. "How if Mr. Percy be unable—as may be—to win Duke Charles into his hands?"

"Why, then comes the Lady Elizabeth," said Winter.

---

[1] *i.e.*, in uncertainty.   [2] Susceptibility, sentimentality.   [3] Particular.

"What say you to the only English-born of the royal issue—the Lady Mary? She, at least, is uninfect with heresy."

There was a laugh at this suggestion: for the Princess Mary was not quite five months old.

"Very well, if we could win her," answered Catesby: "but she would be hard to come by. No—the one easiest had, and as likely as any to serve our turn, is the young lady at Combe. Let the memory of Elizabeth the heretic, so dear to the hearts of Englishmen, be extinguished in the brighter glories of Elizabeth the Catholic. Bring her up in the Catholic faith, and wed her to a Catholic Prince, and I will lay mine head to pawn that she shall make a right royal queen, and the star of England's glory shall suffer no tarnish in her hands. I have seen the little maid, and a bright, brave, bonnie lass she is."

"How old?" asked Robert Winter.

"Nine years. Just the right age. Old enough to queen it, and take a pleasure therein; and not old enough to have drunk in much heresy—no more than Fathers Garnet and Gerard can soon distil out again."

"Nay! Too old, Mr. Catesby," said Thomas Winter. "At five years, the little Duke might be so: but not his sister at nine. She'll have learned heresy enough by then; and women are more perverse than men. They ever hold error tighter, and truth likewise."

"Well, have the little Duke, if you can win him," replied Catesby. "I doubt thereof."

"Trust me for that," cried Percy.

"I'll trust you to break your neck in the attempt," said Catesby with a grim smile.

"But how look you to secure the Lady Elizabeth? My Lord Harrington's an old fox, and none so easy to beguile. He shall smell a rat, be sure, before you have half your words out, and then you may whistle for the rest of your hopes—and are like enough to do it in the Fleet or Newgate."

"Kit Wright," said Percy, addressing the last speaker, who was his wife's brother, "all the wit in the world is sure not in thine head. Thinkest we shall march up to the door at Combe, and sweetly demand of my Lord Harrington that he give us up the Lady Elizabeth? Why, man, we must compass the matter that he shall wit nought till all be done."

"You might make a hunting party," suggested Fawkes.

"Say you so, Mr. Fawkes? You have eyes in your head. We'll send Sir Everard Digby down to see to that business."

"How went your business, Mr. Catesby?" asked Grant.

"Why, right well, Mr. Grant. I gathered together a goodly number of friends to assist the Archduke Albert in Flanders: bought horses, and laid in powder. All shall be ready when the Archduke hath need of them."

The laugh went round.

"That was a jolly fantasy of yours, to levy troops for the Archduke," said Robert Winter. "Truly, these heretics are easy to beguile. Not one, methinks, hath the least suspicion."

"It were soon up with us if they had,' added his brother.

"Look out for yourself, Tom, and smoke not too many pipes with externs," responded Robert. "That young Louvaine that you affect—I scarce trust him."

"That affects me, you mean. Trust him! I never do. He's only a simpleton at best."

"Have you never heard of simpletons carrying tidings?' said Fawkes. "Mind you drop not any chance words, Mr. Winter, that might do mischief."

"Let me alone for that," was the answer.

"Gentlemen," said Catesby, who had been in a brown

study for some minutes, "methinks Mr. Fawkes's proposal to seize the Lady Elizabeth under cover of a hunting party is good.   Sir Everard, will you undertake this?"

"Willingly.   Where must they be gathered?"

"Gather them at Dunchurch," said Catesby, "for a hunt on Dunsmoor Heath, and for the day of the Parliament's meeting: you shall have notice of the blow struck, as quick as a horseman can reach you.   As soon as you hear it, then away to Combe, and carry off the young lady to my mother's at Ashby.   Proclaim her Queen, and bring her next day to London, proclaiming her in all the towns on your way."

"May there not be some awkwardness in the matter, if her brothers be alive?" suggested the most cautious of the party, Robert Winter.

"Pooh!" ejaculated the impetuous Percy.   "'Nothing venture, nothing have.'"

"'Faint heart never won fair lady' were more pertinent to the occasion," said Thomas Winter, raising a general laugh.

"We must see to that," grimly responded Catesby.

The conspirators then separated. Sir Everard Digby set out for Warwickshire, Percy went to see Lord Northumberland at Syon, Keyes returned to Lambeth, and Fawkes resumed his duties at the house on the riverbank. Mr. Marshall, on his way to call at the White Bear, little guessed that the apparently respectable, busy man-servant in blue camlet, who met him as he went down King Street, was engaged in an evil work which would hand down his name to everlasting infamy.

Mrs. Abbott was standing at her door as he went past.

"Well, to be sure! so 'tis you, Parson? How's Mrs. Agnes this even? I reckoned I saw her t'other day, a-passing through the Strand, but she saw not me—in

a green perpetuance gown, and a black camlet hood. I
trust it'll wear better than mine, for if ever a camlet
was no worth, 'tis that. Dear heart, the roguery of
wooldrapers, and mercers beside! I do hope Master
Floriszoon 'll not learn none of their tricks. If I see
my Lady Lettice this next day or twain, I'll drop a
word to her. Don't you think she's looking a bit pale
and poorly this last week or so? But mayhap you have
not seen her, not of late."

"I have not, but I am now on my way," answered
Mr. Marshall, turning into the White Bear, in the
hope of escaping Silence's tongue. It was the first word
he had been able to cast into the stream she poured
forth.

" Well, maybe you'll drop a word to her touching
Master Floriszoon? Dear heart, what queer names them
foreign folks do get! I never could abide no foreigners,
and if I—Bless us, the man's off—there's no having a
word with him. I say, Charity, I don't believe them eggs
you had of that——"

" You'll excuse me, Mistress Abbott, but I've no time
to waste i' talk. 'The talk of the lips tendeth only to
penury,'—and if you'll go in and look for that i' th' Good
Book, it'll happen do you a bit o' good—more than talking. Good even."

And Charity shut the door uncompromisingly.

Mr. Marshall was too much at home in the White Bear
to need announcement. He tapped softly at the parlour
door, and opened it.

" Mrs. Gertrude, I don't care who saith it! it's a wicked
heresy!" were the first words he heard, in the blunt tones
of Temperance Murthwaite. " And it's not true to say we
Puritans teach any such thing. It's a calumny and a
heresy both.—Mr. Marshall, I'm fain to see you. Do,
pray you, tell this young gentlewoman we hold not that

if a man but believe in the merits of Christ, he may live as he list, and look for Heaven in the end. 'Tis a calumny, I say—a wicked calumny!"

"A calumny as old as the Apostle James, Mrs. Murth-waite," answered Mr. Marshall, as he turned from greeting Lady Louvaine. "Some in those days had, it should seem, been abusing Paul's doctrine of justification by faith, and said that a man need but believe, and not live according thereto."

"Why, Mr. Marshall, I have heard you to say a man may believe and be saved!" cried Gertrude, who sat on a velvet-covered stool beside Lady Louvaine, having run in from the next door without hood or scarf.

"That I doubt not, Mrs. Gertrude, and yet may, since you have heard Paul, and John, and the Lord Himself, to say it in the Word. But, believe what? Believe that a man once lived whose name was Jesus, and who was marvellous good, and wrought many great works? That faith shall not save you,—no more than believing in King James's Majesty should. It is a living faith you must have, and that is a dead."

"Mr. Marshall, I thought Puritans made much of the doctrine of imputed righteousness?"

"You thought truth, Mrs. Gertrude."

"Well, but what is that save believing that Christ hath wrought all goodness for me, and I need not work any goodness for mine own salvation? Look you, there is no need, if all be done."

"No need of what? No need that you should attempt to do what you never can do, or no need that you should show your love to Him that did it for you at the cost of His own life?"

"Well!" said Gertrude in a slow, deprecating tone, "but——"

"Mrs. Gertrude, you mix up two things which be

utterly separate, and which cannot mix, no more than oil and water. The man whom Christ hath saved, it is most true, hath no need to save himself. But hath he no need to save others? hath he no need to honour Christ? hath he no need to show forth to angels and to men his unity with Christ, the oneness of his will with His, the love wherewith Christ's love constraineth him? You mix up justification and sanctification, as though they were but one. Justification is the washing of the soul from sin; sanctification is the dressing of the soul for Heaven. Sanctification is not a thing you do for God; 'tis a thing God doth in you. There is need for it, not that it should justify you before His tribunal, but that it should make you meet for His presence-chamber. It were not fit that you should enter the King's presence, though cleansed, yet dressed in your old soiled clothes. But you make a third minglement of things separate, when you bring in imputed righteousness. The righteousness of Christ imputed unto us justifieth us before the bar of God. It payeth our debt, it washeth our stains, it unlocketh our fetters. But this is not sanctification. Justification was wrought by Christ for us; sanctification is wrought by the Holy Ghost in us. Justification was completed on Calvary; sanctification is not finished so long as we be in this life. Justification is quick and lively; the moment my faith toucheth the work of Christ for me, that moment am I fully justified, and for ever. Sanctification is slow, and groweth like a plant. I am as entirely justified as I ever shall be, but I am not as sanctified as I ever shall be. I look to be more and more sanctified—' to grow up unto Him in all things,' to be like Him, to be purified even as He is pure. I pray you make no mingle-mangle of things that do so differ in themselves, though 'tis true they come all of one source—the union and the unity of Christ and the believer."

Gertrude was yawning behind her hand before the clergyman was half through his explanation.

"I thank you, Mr. Marshall," said Temperance, who had listened attentively. "Methinks I had some apprehension of the difference in myself, but I could not have expounded it thus clearly."

"To know it in yourself, my sister, is a far greater thing, and a better, than being able to expound it.—And how is it with you, Lady Lettice?"

"Well, Mr. Marshall," she said with her soft smile. "At times I think that a few more pins of the tabernacle are taken down, and then the passing wind causeth the curtains to shake. But at worst it shall be only the moving of the pillar of cloud—the 'Come up higher' into the very presence of the King."

"And in the interim 'the Lord sitteth between the cherubim, be the people never so unquiet.' And how is it, dear Sister, with your two young men?"

Lady Louvaine paused to accept Gertrude's offered hand and bid her good-night. That young woman did not enjoy Mr. Marshall's conversation, and suddenly discovered that it was time for her return home.

"Hans is all I could desire," said the old lady, returning to the subject: "he is a dear, good, sober-minded lad as need be. But I will not disguise from you, Mr. Marshall, that I am in some disease of mind touching Aubrey."

"May I ask wherefore?"

"You may ask, indeed, yet can I scarce tell. That is no wise-sounding thing to say: yet one may have cause for fear where he hath no evidence for demonstration."

"He may so, indeed. Then you reckon there is good cause for fear?"

"Mr. Marshall, you told us some time back that our neighbour Mr. Rookwood was brother to a Papist. Know you aught of a friend of his, one Mr. Winter, that is in London at times, and hath his lodging in the Strand?"

"A friend of this Mr. Rookwood, your neighbour?"

"I reckon so. At least, a friend of his son."

"Sons do at times make friends apart from their fathers," said Mr. Marshall with a smile. "I cannot say, Lady Lettice, that the name is quite unknown to me; yet cannot I, like you, lay a finger on any special thing I may have heard thereabout."

"What were the other names, Edith? I cannot call them to mind."

"Mr. Catesby, Mother, and Mr. Percy, and Mr. Darcy: those, I think, were what Aubrey told us."

"Mr. Percy!—what Percy is he?"

"I know not: some kin to my Lord Northumberland."

"Where dwells he?"

"That know I not."

"At the Green Dragon in Upper Holborn, in St. Giles's parish," said another voice.

"Ha!" echoed Mr. Marshall, turning to his new informant. "A recusant, Madam, and a dangerous fellow. And if this Mr. Catesby you name be Mr. Robert Catesby of Ashby Ledgers, he also is a recusant, and if I know him, a worser man than the other."

"Hans, art thou sure of this Mr. Percy?—that he whom Aubrey wist is the same man of whom Mr. Marshall speaks?"

"I have seen Aubrey leave his house, Madam."

Lady Louvaine looked very uneasy.

"And Mr. Darcy?" said Edith.

"Him I know not," answered Mr. Marshall: which was not surprising, since he knew him only as Mr. Walley.

"Hans, how much dost thou know?"

Hans knelt down by the large cushioned chair, and kissed the thin, blue-veined hand.

"Dear Lady Lettice, I know very little: and Aubrey would account me a sneak and a spy, were I to tell you what I do know.   But I would not care for that if it might save him."

" I do hope Mr. Louvaine is not drawn in among them," said Mr. Marshall, thoughtfully.

"They have been away of late," replied Hans, " and he hath not been there so often."

" Are they away now ? "

" No, lately returned."

" I would I could win Aubrey for a talk," said Edith.

"Shall I call at my Lord Oxford's and leave a message that you would have him call here ? "

"Truly, Mr. Marshall, you should do me a great kindness."

"Then I so will.   Good-night."

Aubrey was playing billiards with his young master and several of the younger gentlemen of his household, when he was told that Mr. Marshall requested a word with him. The information alarmed him, for he thought it meant bad news.   Having obtained the young Earl's leave to go and ascertain why he was wanted, Aubrey ran hastily down the stairs, and found Mr. Marshall awaiting him in the hall.

" Good even, Mr. Louvaine," said he, rising: " I had the honour this evening to wait on my Lady your grandmother, and was desired to drop a word to you as I went home, to the effect that your friends have a mind to speak with you on some matter of import.   Her Ladyship bids you, the first opportunity you can make, to visit the White Bear."

" I will do so," said Aubrey, recovering from his alarm. " I cry you mercy for my short greeting, but truly I was afraid, not knowing if you had ill news for me."

"That I have not at this time, God be thanked!   Yet if I may, I would fain ask you, Mr. Louvaine, whether some time hath not run since you saw your friends in King Street?"

"Oh no! not very long — at least not more than common—only about——" Aubrey hesitated and flushed, as he realised that it was now the middle of October, and his last visit had been paid early in June. "You see, Sir, I am close tied by my duties here," he added in haste.

"So close tied that you may not even be away for an hour? Well, you know your own duty; do it, and all shall be well. But I would beseech you not to neglect this call any longer than till your earliest opportunity shall give leave."

Mr. Marshall bowed, and with an official "May God bless you!" passed out of the hall door. Aubrey returned to his urgent duties in the billiard-room.

"Who is your visitor, Louvaine?" asked the youthful Earl.

"If it please your Lordship, 'tis but a messenger from my grandmother."

"What would the ancient dame?" inquired one of the irreverent young gentlemen-in-waiting.

"She would have me go and wait on her: what else I know not. I shall find out, I reckon, when I go."

"When saw you her Ladyship, Mr. Louvaine?" said an unexpected voice behind him, and Aubrey turned to meet the Countess.

"Madam, in June last, under your Ladyship's pleasure."

"It scarcely is to my pleasure. Son Henry, cannot you allow this young gentlemen to visit his friends more often?"

"Under your leave, Madam, he can visit them every day if he will. I tarry him not."

"Then how comes it, Mr. Louvaine, that you have not waited on my Lady Lettice for four months?"

Aubrey mentally wished Mr. Marshall in America, and himself anywhere but in Oxford House. There was no escape. The wise Countess added no unnecessary words to help him out, but having put her question in plain terms, quietly awaited his reply. He muttered something not very intelligible, in which " business " was the chiefly audible word.

"Methinks your duty to your mother and Lady Lettice should be your first business after God," said the Countess gravely. "I pray you, Mr. Louvaine, that you wait on her Ladyship to-morrow even. The Earl will give you leave."

Aubrey bowed, and as the Countess took her departure, for she had merely paused in passing through the room, gave a vicious blow to the nearest billiard ball.

"You are in for it now, Louvaine!" said his next neighbour.

"Poor lad! will his gra'mmer beat him?" suggested another in mock compassion.

"He's been stealing apples, and the parson has told of him," added a third.

"Will you hold your stupid tongues?" said Aubrey, stung beyond endurance.

"Take a pinch of sneezing tobago," said one of his companions, holding out his snuff-box. "Never mind it, lad! put on a bold face, and use ruffling language, and you'll get over this brunt."

Aubrey flung down his cue and escaped, pursued by his companions' laughter.

"We were somewhere near the truth," said the young Earl.

"He looks for a scolding, take my word for it."

Very like it Aubrey felt, as he went down King Street on the following evening. He, too, met a man, not in blue camlet, but in a porter's frock, trundling a truck with two or three barrels on it, in whom he did not in the least recognise the dark, tall stranger to whom he had not been introduced in Catesby's rooms. He received a warm welcome at the White Bear.

"Aubrey, hast thou of late seen thine acquaintance Mr. Percy?"

"Not since his return out of the country, Madam."

He had seen Winter, but he did not think it necessary to mention it.

"Nor Mr. Catesby?"

"Nay, save to meet him in the street, Madam."

"My son, should it give thee great compunction[1] if I bade thee have no more ado with either of these gentlemen?"

"What mean you, Madam?"

"I mean not that if thou meet them in the street thou shalt not give them greeting; but no more to visit them in their lodgings. My boy, Mr. Percy is a Popish recusant, and there is much fear of Mr. Catesby likewise."

"Not all recusants are bad men, I hope," answered Aubrey evasively, as if he were unwilling to respond by a direct promise to that effect.

"I hope likewise: but some are, as we know. And when innocent men be drawn in with bad men, 'tis often found that the bad slip forth unhurt, and leave the innocent to abide the hazard. Promise me, Aubrey, that thou wilt haunt[2] these men's company no longer."

"Truly, Madam, I know not what I should say to my friends. Bethink you also, I pray, that I am of age."

"Of what age?" demanded his Aunt Temperance in her usual style. "Not of the age of discretion, I being witness."

"Of the age at which a man commonly takes care of himself," answered Aubrey, loftily.

---

[1] Grief, annoyance.　　　　[2] Visit.

"'Bate me an ace, quoth Bolton.' At the age at which a man commonly takes no care of himself, nor of any other belike. Nor you are not the wisest man of your age in this world, my master : don't go for to think it. You don't need to look at me in that way, my fine young gentleman : you'll not get sugarplums from Temperance Murthwaite when you need rhubarb."

"I know that, Aunt Temperance," said Aubrey, trying to laugh.

"And you may as well open your mouth and take your physic with a good grace. If not, there'll be another dose to follow."

"What ? " demanded Aubrey with drawn brows, and a flash in his eyes.

"'Three can keep a secret if twain be away,'" was the enigmatical answer. "Now then, answer Lady Lettice."

"He has no mind to promise—that can I see," said Lady Louvaine, sorrowfully.

"He shall, afore he go," was the cool reply of Temperance.

"Aunt Temperance, I am not a babe ! " exclaimed Aubrey rather angrily.

"That you are, and in sore need of leading-strings."

"Aubrey here ? " asked his mother, coming in. "Well now, I do think one of you might have told me. But you never think of me. Why, Aubrey, it must be six months since we saw you ! "

"Four, Mother, under your pleasure."

"I am sure 'tis six. Why come you no oftener ? "

"I have my duties," said Aubrey in a rather constrained voice.

"Closer than to thy mother, my boy ? " asked Edith softly.

"Prithee harry not him," retorted Aunt Temperance. "Hast thou not heard, he hath his duties ? To hold skeins of silk whilst my Lady winds them, maybe, and to ride the great horse, and play tennis and shuttlecock with his Lord, and to make up his mind to which of all his Lady's damsels he'll make love o' the lightest make."

"Aubrey, I do hope you are ne'er thinking of marriage!" said his mother's querulous voice. "Thou shouldst be put out of thine office, most like, and not a penny to keep her, and she saddled upon us that——"

"That'll kick and throw her, as like as not," said Aunt Temperance by way of interjection.

"I ensure you, Mother, I have no expectations of the kind. 'Tis but Aunt Temperance that—that——"

"That sometimes hits the white, Sir, if she do now and then shoot aside o' the mark. Howbeit, hold thou there. And if thou want leave to carry on thine acquaintance with these gentlemen, bring them to see us. I'll lay mine head to an orange I see in ten minutes if they be true men or no."

"What business have they?" asked Edith.

Aubrey hesitated. He knew of none except Garnet's pretended profession of horse-dealing.

"Is there any woman amongst them?" said Temperance.

"I never saw one."

"Not even at Mr. Percy's house?"

"I went there but once, to ask for him. I have heard that he hath a wife, but she lives very privately, and teaches children. He dwelleth not with her, but hath his lodging at my Lord Northumberland's. I never saw her."

"That's an ill hearing. 'Tis meet for men to come together by themselves for business: but to dwell in their own homes, and never a woman with them, wife, mother, sister, nor daughter,—that means mischief, lad. It means some business of an evil sort, that they don't want a woman to see through. If there had been one, I went

L

about to say, take me with thee some even to visit her. I'd have known all about it under an hour, trust me."

"You should have seen nought, Aunt."

"Tell that to the cowcumbers. You see nought, very like."

Lady Louvaine laid her hand on her grandson's.

"Aubrey, promise me at least this: that for a month to come thou wilt not visit any of these gentlemen."

After an instant's pause, Aubrey replied, "Very well, Madam; I am ready to promise that."

"That's not much to promise," commented Temperance.

"It is enough," said Lady Louvaine, quietly.

An hour later, when Aubrey was gone, Faith asked rather complainingly what had induced Lady Louvaine to limit the promise to a month.

"I cannot tell thee, Faith," was the answer. "Something seemed to whisper within me that if the lad would promise that, he would be safe. It may be no more than an old woman's fantasy; and even so, no harm is done. Or it might be that God spake to me—and if thus, let us obey His voice. He knows what He will do, and what men will do."

"I've as great a mind as ever I had to eat——"

"What to do, Temperance?"

"Get to see those fellows, somehow."

"Wait the month, Temperance," suggested Edith, quietly.

"Wait! you're always for waiting. I want to work."

"Waiting is often the hardest work," said Edith.

The middle of the month was nearly come. The six last barrels of powder were in the vault; the whole thirty-six were covered with stones and iron bars: Gideon Gibbons, the porter, was delivering at the door three thousand billets and five hundred faggots of wood and another man in a porter's frock was stacking the wood in the vault.

"There, that's the last lot !" said Gibbons, throwing in a packet of tied-up billets. "Count right, Johnson ? "

" All right, Gibbons."

" Your master likes a good fire, I should say," observed Gibbons, with a grin of amusement, as he looked into the vault. "There's fuel there to last most folks a couple of winters."

" Ay, he doth so : he's a northern man, you see—comes from where sea-coal's cheaper than here, and they are wont to pile their fires big."

"Shouldn't ha' thought them billets wouldn't hardly ha' taken all that there room," said Gibbons, looking into the vault, while he scratched his head with one hand, and hitched up his porter's frock to put the other in his pocket.

" Oh, I didn't stack 'em so tight," said Mr. Percy's man, carelessly, tying up a bit of string which he picked from the floor.

"Ah ! well, but tight or loose, shouldn't hardly ha' thought it. Master coming soon, eh ?"

" Haven't heard what day. Afore long, very like."

" Has he e'er a wife that he'll bring ? "

" She's in the country," said the disguised man-servant, who knew that she was then at the Green Dragon, teaching sundry little girls the mysteries of felling and whipping cambric.

"Well, 'tis dry work. Come and have a pint at the Maid's Head."

"No, thank you, I don't care for it. There's a penny for yours."

As this was the price of a quart of the best ale, Mr. Gibbons pocketed the penny with satisfaction, and forbore to remark censoriously on what he deemed the very

singular taste of Mr. Percy's man. He shambled awk-
wardly off with his waggon, meaning first to put up his
horses, and then go and expend his penny in the beverage
wherein his soul delighted. His companion gave a low
laugh as he turned the key in the door of the cellar.

"No, thank you, Gideon Gibbons," said he to himself.
"It may suit you to sit boozing at the Maid's Head, telling
all you know and guessing much that you don't: here's
wishing your early muddlement before you get on the
subject of this wood! But it won't do for Guy Fawkes,
my fine fellow!"

CHAPTER VII.

AN APPLE-CAST AND A LETTER.

"Better the blind faith of our youth
Than doubt, which all truth braves ;
Better to die, God's children dear,
Than live, the Devil's slaves."
—DINAH MULOCK.

OOD morrow, Lady Lettice! I am come to ask a favour."

"Ask it, I pray you, Mrs. Rookwood."

"Will you suffer Mrs. Lettice to come to our apple-cast on Tuesday next? We shall have divers young folks of our neighbours—Mrs. Abbott's Mary, Dorcas, and Hester, Mrs. Townsend's Rebecca, my Lady Woodward's Dulcibel and Grissel, and such like; and our Doll, I am in hopes, shall be back from Suffolk, and maybe her cousin Bessy with her. I have asked Mr. Louvaine to come, and twain more of my Lord Oxford's gentlemen; and Mr. Manners, Mr. Stone, and our Tom, shall be there. What say you?"

Lady Louvaine looked with a smile at her granddaughter, who sat in the window with a book. She was not altogether satisfied with the Rookwoods, yet less from anything they said or did than from what they omitted to say and do. They came regularly to church, they attended the Sacrament, they asked the Vicar to their dinner-parties, they were very affable and friendly to their neighbours. There was absolutely nothing on which it was possible to lay a reproving finger, and say, This is what I do not like. And yet, while she could no more give a reason for distrusting them than the schoolboy for objecting to the famous Dr. Fell, she did instinctively distrust them. Still, Lettice was a good girl, on the whole a discreet girl; she had very few pleasures, especially such as took her outside her home, and gave her the companionship of girls of her own age. Lettice had been taught, as all Puritan maidens were, that "life is, to do the will of God," and that pleasure was not to be sought at all, and scarcely to be accepted except in its simplest forms, and as coming naturally along with the duties of life. An admirable lesson—a lesson which girls sadly need to learn now, if only for the lowest reason—that pleasures thus taken are infinitely more pleasing than when sought, and the taste for them is keener and more enduring. To the moral taste, no less than the physical, plain fare with a good appetite is incomparably more enjoyable than the finest dainties with none : and the moral appetite can cloy and pall at least as soon as the physical. Lettice's healthy moral nature had been content with the plain fare, and had never cried out for dainties. But, like all young folks, she liked a pleasant change, and her grandmother, who had thought her looking pale and somewhat languid with the summer heat in town, was glad that she should have the enjoyment. She knew she might trust her.

Not even to herself did Lady Louvaine confess her deepest reason for allowing Lettice to go to the apple-cast —an assembly resembling in its nature the American "bee," and having an apple-gathering and storing for its object. It was derived from the fact that Aubrey had been invited. It occurred to her that something might transpire in Lettice's free and innocent narrative of her enjoyment, which would be of service in the difficult business of dealing with Aubrey at this juncture.

Lettice, as beseemed a maiden of her years, was silent, though her eyes said, "Please!" in very distinct language.

"I thank you, Mrs. Rookwood; Lettice may go."

Lettice's eyes lighted up.

"Then, Mrs. Lettice, will you step in about nine o'clock? My maids'll be fain to see you. And if any of you gentlewomen should have a liking to look in ——"

"Nay, the girls should count us spoil-sports," said Edith, laughingly.

"Now come, Mrs. Edith! 'tis not so long since you were a young maid."

"Twelve good years, Mrs. Rookwood: as long, pretty nigh, as Hester Abbott has been in the world."

"Eh, but years don't go for much, not with some folks."

"Not with them that keep the dew of their youth," said Lady Louvaine with a smile. "But to do that, friend, a woman should dwell very near to Him who only hath immortality."

It was something so unusual for one of this sober household to go out to a party, that a flutter arose, when Mrs. Rookwood had departed, concerning Lettice's costume.

"She had best go in a washing gown," was the decision of her practical Aunt Temperance. "If she's to be any good with the apples, she must not wear her Sunday best."

Lettice's Sunday best was not of an extravagant character, being a dark green perpetuana gown, trimmed with silver lace, a mantle of plum-coloured cloth, and a plum-coloured hood lined with dark green.

"But a washing gown, Temperance! It should look so mean," objected Mrs. Louvaine.

"Her best gown'll look meaner, if all the lace be hung

with cobwebs, and all the frilling lined with apple-parings," said Temperance.

"She'll take better care of it than so, I hope," said Edith. "And a lawn gown should be cold for this season."

"Well, let the child wear her brown kersey. That'll not spoil so much as some."

In her heart Lettice hoped she would not have to wear the brown kersey. Brown was such an ugly colour! and the kersey, already worn two seasons, was getting shabby —far too shabby to wear at a party. She would have liked to put on her best. But no girl of twenty, unmarried, at that date decided such matters for herself.

"Oh, never that ugly thing!" said Mrs. Louvaine. "I mean her to wear my pearls, and that brown stuff——"

Wear Aunt Faith's pearls! Lettice's heart beat.

"Faith, my dear, I would not have the child use ornaments," said Lady Louvaine quietly. "You wot, those of our way of thinking do commonly discard them. Let us not give occasion for scandal. I would have Lettice go neat and cleanly, and not under her station, but no more."

The palpitations of Lettice's heart sobered down. Of course she could not expect to wear pearls and such worldly vanities. Grandmother was always right.

"I can tell you, Mrs. Gertrude and Mrs. Anne shall not be in brown kersey," said Mrs. Louvaine, in her usual petulant tone. "And if Aubrey don him not in satin and velvet, my name is not Faith."

"It shouldn't have been, my dear, for it isn't your nature," was her sister's comment.

"We need not follow a multitude to do evil," quietly responded Lady Louvaine, as she sat and knitted peacefully.

"Well, Madam, what comes that to——the brown kersey, trow? Edith saith truth, lawn is cold this weather."

"I think, my dear, the green perpetuana were not too good, with clean apron, ruff, and cuffs, and a silver lace: but I would have nought more."

So Lettice made her appearance at the apple-cast in her Sunday gown, but decked with no pearls, and her own brown hair turned soberly back under her hood. She put no hat on over it, as she had only to slip into the next house. In the hall Tom Rookwood met her, and bowing, requested the honour of conducting her into the garden, where his sisters and cousin were already busy with the day's duties.

On the short ladder which rested against one of the apple-trees stood Dorothy, the tallest of the Rookwoods, clad in a long apron of white lawn edged with lace, over a dress of rich dark blue silk, gathering apples, and passing them to Anne at the foot of the ladder, by whom they were delivered to Gertrude, who packed them in sundry crates ready for the purpose. By Gertrude's side stood a dark, rosy, merry-looking child of six, whom she introduced to Lettice as her cousin Bessy. Lettice, who had expected Bessy to be much older, was disappointed, for she was curious to know what kind of a creature a female Papist might be.

"Now, Tom, do your duty!" cried Dorothy, as Tom was about to retire. "I am weary of gathering, and you having the longest legs and arms amongst us, should take my place. Here come Mr. Montague and Rebecca Townsend; I'm coming down. Up with you!"

Tom pulled a face and obeyed: but showing a disposition to pelt Dorothy and Bessy, instead of carefully delivering the apples unbruised to Anne, he was screamed at and set upon at once, Gertrude leading the opposition.

"Tom, you wicked wretch! Come down this minute, or else behave properly. I shall——"

The—accidental?—descent of an enormous apple on

the bridge of Gertrude's nose put her announcement of her intentions to speedy flight: and in laughing over the *fracas*, the ice rapidly melted between the young strangers.

The apple-gathering proceeded merrily, relieved by a few scenes of this sort, until the trees were stripped, the apples laid carefully in the crates for transportation to the garrets, and on their arrival, as carefully taken out and spread on sheets of grey paper on the floor. When all was done, the girls were marshalled into Gertrude's room to tidy themselves: after which they went down to the dining-room. Mrs. Rookwood had provided an excellent dinner for her youthful guests, including geese, venison, and pheasants, various pies and puddings, Muscadel and Canary wines. After dinner they played games in the hall and dining-room, hoodman blind, and hunt the slipper, and when tired of these, separated into little groups or formed *tête-à-têtes* for conversation. Lettice, who could not quite get rid of an outside feeling, as if she did not belong to the world in which she found herself, was taken possession of by her oldest acquaintance, Gertrude, and drawn into a window-seat for what that young lady termed " a proper chat."

" I thought my cousin was to be here," said Lettice, glancing over the company.

" Ay, Tom asked him, I believe," said Gertrude. " Maybe his Lord could not spare him. Do you miss him ? "

" I would like to have seen him," said Lettice innocently.

" Tom would not love to hear you say so much, I can tell you," laughed Gertrude. " He admires you very much, Lettice. Oh, do let us drop the ' Mistress '—it is so stiff and sober—I hate it."

" Me ! " was all that it occurred to Lettice to answer.

" You. Don't you like men to admire you ? "

"I don't know; they never did."

Gertrude went off into a soft explosion of silvery laughter.

"O Lettice, you are good! You have been brought up with all those sober, starched old gentlewomen, till you don't know what life is—why, my dear, you might as well be a nun!"

"Don't I know what life is?" said Lettice. "I've had twenty years of it."

"You haven't had twenty days of it—not *life*. You've been ruled like a copy-book ever since you were born. I have pitied you, poor little victim, you cannot guess how much! I begged Mother to try and win you for to-day. She said she did not believe Starch and Knitting-Pins would suffer it, but she would try. Wasn't I astonished when I heard you really were to come!"

"What do you mean by Starch and Knitting-Pins?" asked the bewildered Lettice.

"Oh, that awful aunt of yours who looks as if she had just come out of the wash, and your sweet-smiling grandmother who is always fiddling with knitting-pins——"

Gertrude stopped suddenly. She understood, better than Lettice did herself, the involuntary, unpremeditated gesture which put a greater distance between them on the window-seat, and knew in a moment that she had scandalised her guest.

"My dear creature!" she said with one of her soft laughs, "if you worship your starchy aunt, I won't say another word! And as to my Lady Louvaine, I am sure I never meant the least disrespect to her. Of course she is very sweet and good, and all that: but dear me! have you been bred up to think you must not label people with funny names? Everybody does, my dear—no offence meant at all, I assure you."

"I beg your pardon!" said Lettice stiffly—more so,

indeed, than she knew or meant. "If that be what you call 'life,' I am afraid I know little about it."

"And wish for no more!" said Gertrude, laughing. "Well, if I offended you, I ought to beg pardon. I did not intend it, I am sure. But, my dear, what a pity you do not crisp your hair, or curl it! That old-fashioned roll back is as ancient as my grandmother. And a partlet, I declare! They really ought to let you be a *little* more properly dressed. You never see girls with turned-back hair now."

Lettice did not know whether to blush for her deficiencies, or to be angry with Gertrude for pointing them out. She felt more inclined to the latter.

"Now, if I had you to dress," said Gertrude complacently, "I should just put you in a decent, neat corset, with a white satin gown, puffed with crimson velvet, a velvet hood lined with white satin, a girdle of gold and pearls, crimson stockings, white satin slippers, a lace rebato, and a pearl necklace. Oh, how charming you would look! You would not know yourself. Then I should put a gold bodkin in your hair, and a head-drop of pearls set round a diamond, and bracelets instead of these lawn cuffs, and a fan; and wash your face in distilled waters, and odoriferous oils for your hands."

"But I should not like my hands oily!" said Lettice in amazement.

Gertrude laughed. "Oh yes, you would, when you were accustomed to it. And then just the least touch on your forehead and cheeks, and—O Lettice, my dear, you would have half London at your feet!"

"The 'least touch' of what?" inquired Lettice.

"Oh, just to show the blue veins, you know."

"'Show the blue veins!' What can you show them with?"

"Oh, just a touch of blue," said Gertrude, who began to

fear she had gone further than Lettice would follow, and did not want to be too explicit.

"You never, surely, mean—*paint?*" asked Lettice in tones of horror.

"My dear little Puritan, be not so shocked! I do, really, mean paint; but not all over your face—nothing of the sort : only a touch here and there."

"I'll take care it does not touch me," said Lettice decidedly. "I don't want to get accustomed to such abominable things. And as to having half London at my feet, there isn't room for it, and I am sure I should not like it if there were."

"O Lettice, Lettice!" cried Gertrude amidst her laughter. "I never saw such a maid. Why, you are old before you are young."

"I have heard say," answered Lettice, laughing herself, "that such as so be are young when they are old."

"Oh, don't talk of being old—'tis horrid to think on. But, my dear, you should really have a little fine breeding, and not be bred up a musty, humdrum Puritan. I do hate those she-precise hypocrites, that go about in close stomachers and ruffles of Geneva print, and cannot so much as cudgel their maids without a Scripture to back them. Nobody likes them, you know. Don't grow into one of them. You'll never be married if you do."

Lettice was silent, but she sat with slightly raised eyebrows, and a puzzled expression about her lips.

"Well, why don't you speak?" said Gertrude briskly.

"Because I don't know what to say. I can't tell what you expect me to say : and you give such queer reasons for not doing things."

"Do I so?" said Gertrude, looking amused. "Why, what queer reasons have I given?"

"That nobody will like me, and I shall never be married!"

"Well! aren't they very good reasons?"

"They don't seem to me to be reasons at all. I may never be married, whether I do it or not; and that will be as God sees best for me, so why trouble myself about it? And as to people not liking me because I am a Puritan, don't you remember the Lord's words, 'If the world hate you, ye know that it hated Me before it hated you'?"

"Oh, you sucked in the Bible with your mother's milk, I suppose," said Gertrude pettishly, "and have had it knitted into you ever since by your grandmother's needles. I did not expect you to be a spoil-sport, Lettice. I thought you would be only too happy to come out of your convent for a few hours."

"Thank you, I don't want to be a spoil-sport, and I do not think the Bible is, unless the sports are bad ones, and they might as well be spoiled, might they not?"

"There's Mr. Stone!" cried Gertrude inconsequently, and in a relieved tone, for Lettice was leading in a direction whither she had no wish to follow. "Look! isn't he a fine young man? What a shame to have christened so comely a man by so ugly a name as Jeremy!"

"Do you think so? It is a beautiful name; it means 'him whom God hath appointed,'—Aunt Edith says so."

"Think you I care what it *means?*" was the answer, in a rather vexed tone, though it was accompanied by a laugh. "'Tis ugly and old-fashioned, child. Now your cousin, Mr. Louvaine, has a charming name. But fancy having a name with a sermon wrapped up in it!"

"I do not understand!" said Lettice a little blankly. "You seem to think little of those things whereof I have been taught to think much; and to think much of those things whereof I have been led to think little. It puzzles me. Excuse me."

Gertrude laughed more good-naturedly.

" My dear little innocence ! " said she. " I am sorry to let the cold, garish daylight in upon your pretty little stained-glass creed: it is never pleasant to have scales taken from your eyes. But really, you look on things in such false colours, that needs must. Why, my child, if you were to go out into the world, you would find all those fancies laughed to scorn. 'Tis only Puritans love sermons and Bibles and such things. No doubt they are all right, and good, and all that; quite proper for Sunday, and sick-beds, and so on. I am not an infidel, of course. But then—well ? "

Lettice's face of utter amazement arrested the flow of words on Gertrude's lips.

" Would your mother think you loved her, Gertrude, if you told her you never wanted to see her except on Sundays and when you were sick ? And if God hears all we say, is it not as good as telling Him that ? You puzzle me more and more. I have been taught that the world is the enemy of God, and refuses to guide its ways by His Word : but you speak as if it were something good, that we ought to look up to, and hearken what it bids us. It cannot be both. And what God says about it *must* be true."

" Lettice, whatever one says, you always come back to your Puritan stuff. I wish you would be natural, like other maids. See, I am about to turn you over to Dorothy. Let us see if she can make something of you— I cannot.—Here, Doll ! come and sit here, and talk with Lettice. I want to go and speak to Grissel yonder."

Dorothy sat down obediently in the window-seat.

" I thought Mr. Louvaine was to be here to-day," she said.

" So did I likewise. I cannot tell why he comes not."

" Have you seen him lately ? "

" No, not in some time. I suppose he is busy."

Dorothy looked amused. "What think you he doth all the day long?"

Lettice had not been present when Aubrey detailed his day's occupations, and she was under the impression that he led a busy life, with few idle hours.

"Truly, I know not what," she answered; "but the Earl, no doubt, hath his duties, and 'tis Aubrey's to wait on him."

"The Earl, belike, reads an hour or two with his tutor, seeing he is but a child: and the rest of the time is there music and dancing, riding the great horse, playing at billiards, tennis, bowls, and such like. That is your cousin's business, Mrs. Lettice."

"Only that?—but I reckon he cannot be let go, but must come after his master's heels?"

"He is on duty but three days of every week, save at the *lever* and *coucher*, and may go whither he list on the other four."

"Then I marvel he comes not oftener to visit us," said innocent Lettice.

"Do you so? I don't," answered Dorothy, with a little laugh.

"Why?"

"How old are you, Mrs. Lettice?"

The notion of discourtesy connected with this query is modern.

"I was twenty last June," said Lettice.

"Dear heart! I should have supposed you were about two," said Dorothy, with a little curl of her lip.

"But my grandmother thinks so likewise, and she is near eighty," said Lettice.

"Ah! Extremes meet," answered Dorothy, biting her lip.

Lettice tried to think out this obscure remark, but had not made much progress, when at the other end of the room she caught a glimpse of Aubrey. Though he stood with his back to her, she felt sure it was Aubrey. She knew him by the poise of his head and the soft golden gloss on his hair; and a moment later, his voice reached her ear. He came up towards them, stopping every minute to speak with some acquaintance, so that it took him a little time to reach them.

"There is Cousin Aubrey," said Lettice.

Dorothy answered by a nod. "You admire your cousin?"

"Yes, I think he looks very well," replied Lettice, in her simplicity.

Dorothy bit her lip again. "He is not so well-favoured as Mr. Jeremy Stone," said she, "though he hath the better name, and comes of an elder line by much."

By this time Aubrey had come up. "Ah, Lettice!" said he, kissing her. "Mrs. Dorothy, your most obedient, humble servant."

"Are you?" responded she.

"Surely I am. Lay your commands on me."

"Then bring Mr. Stone to speak with me."

Aubrey gave a little shrug of his shoulders, a laugh, and turned away as if to seek Mr. Stone: while Dorothy, the moment his back was turned, put her finger on her lip, and slipped out of sight behind a screen, with her black eyes full of mischievous fun.

"Why, my dear," said a voice beside Lettice, "is none with you? I thought I saw Doll by your side but now."

"She was, Gentlewoman," answered Lettice, looking up at Mrs. Rookwood, and beginning to wish herself at home again. Might she slip away? "May I pray you of the time?"

Mrs. Rookwood was neither of wealth nor rank to carry a watch, so she went to look at the clock before replying, and Aubrey came up with Mr. Stone.

"Why, where is gone Mrs. Dorothy?" asked the former, knitting his brows.

"All the beauty has not departed with her," responded Mr. Stone gallantly, bowing low to Lettice, who felt more and more uncomfortable every minute.

"'Tis on the stroke of four, my dear," said Mrs. Rookwood, returning: "but I beg you will not hurry away."

"Oh, but I must, if you please!" answered Lettice, feeling a sensation of instant and intense relief. "Grand-mother bade me not tarry beyond four o'clock. I thank you very much, Gentlewoman, and I wish you farewell.— Aubrey, you will come with me?"

Aubrey looked extremely indisposed to do so, and Lettice wondered for what reason he could possibly wish to stay: but Mrs. Rookwood, hearing of Lady Louvaine's order, made no further attempt to delay her young guest. She called her daughters to take their leave, and in another minute the Golden Fish was left behind, and Lettice ran into the door of the White Bear. She went straight upstairs, and in the chamber which they shared found her Aunt Edith.

Lettice had no idea how uneasy Edith had been all that day. She had a vague, general idea that she was rather a favourite with Aunt Edith—perhaps the one of her nieces whom on the whole she liked best: but of the deep pure well of mother-like love in Edith's heart for Dudley Murthwaite's daughter, Lettice had scarcely even a faint conception. She rather fancied herself preferred because, as she supposed, her mother had very likely been Aunt Edith's favourite sister. Little notion there-fore had Lettice of the network of feeling behind the earnest, wistful eyes, as the aunt laid a hand on each shoulder of the niece, and said,—

"Well, Lettice?"

"Aunt Edith," was the answer, " if that is the world I have been in to-day, I hope I shall never go again !"

" Thank God!" spoke Edith's heart in its innermost depths ; but her voice only said, quietly enough, " Ay so, dear heart ? and what misliked thee ? "

" It is all so queer ! Aunt Edith, they think the world is something good. And they want me to paint my face. And they call Aunt Temperance 'Starch.' And they say I am only two years old. And they purse up their faces, and look as if it were something strange, if I quote the Bible. And they talk about being married as if it must happen, whether you would or not, and as if it were the only thing worth thinking about. And they seemed to think it was quite delightful to have a lot of gentlemen bowing at you, and saying all sorts of silly things, and I thought it was horrid. And altogether, I didn't like it a bit, and I wanted to get home."

" Lettice, I prayed God to keep thee, and I think He has kept thee. My dear heart, mayest thou ever so look on the world which is His enemy, and His contrary ! "

Edith's voice was not quite under her control—a most unusual thing with her.

" Aunt Edith, I did think at first—when Mrs. Rook-wood came—that I should like it very well. I felt as if it would be such a pleasant change, you know, and— sometimes I have fancied for a minute that I should like to know how other maids did, and to taste their life, as it were, for a little while ; because, you see, I knew we were so quiet, and other people seemed to have more bright-ness and merriment, and—well, I wanted to see what it was like."

" Very natural, sweet heart, at thy years. I can well believe it."

" And so, when Mrs. Rookwood asked, I so hoped Grandmother would let me go. And I did enjoy the

apple gathering in the garden, and the games afterward
in the hall. But when we sat down, and girls came up
and talked to me, and I saw what they had inside their
hearts—for if it had not been in their hearts, it would not
have come on their tongues—Aunt Edith, I hope I shall
never, never, *never* have anything more to do with the
world! I'd rather peel onions and scrub tiles every day
of my life than live with people, and perhaps get like
them, who could call my dear old Grandmother 'Knitting-
pins' in scorn, and tell God Himself that they only
wanted to think of Him on Sundays. That world's
another world, and I don't belong to it, and please, I'll
keep out of it!"

"Amen, and Amen!" said Aunt Edith. "My Lettice,
let us abide in the world where God is King and Father,
and Sun, and Water of Life. May that other world
where Satan rules ever be another and a strange world to
thee, wherein thou shalt feel thyself a traveller and a
stranger. My child, there is very much merriment which
hath nought to do with happiness, and very much happiness which hath nought to do with mirth. 'Tis one thing
to shut ourselves from God's world which He made, and
quite another to keep our feet away from Satan's world
which he hath ruined. When God saith, 'Love not the
world,' He means not, Love not flowers, and song-birds,
and bright colours, and sunset skies, and the innocent
laughter of little children. Those belong to His world;
and 'tis only as we take them out thereof, and hand them
unto Satan, and they get into the Devil's world, that they
become evil and hurtful unto us. Satan hath ruined, and
will yet, so far as he may, all the good things of God;
and beware of the most innocent-seeming thing so soon
as thou shalt see his touch, upon it. Thank God, my
darling, that He suffered thee not to shut thine eyes
thereto! Was Aubrey there, Lettice?"

" He came but late, Aunt, and therefore it was, I suppose, that as it seemed, he had no list to come with me. He said he might look in, perchance, at after."

" And Mr. Tom Rookwood ? "

" Ay, he was there, though I saw scarce anything of him but just at first."

Edith was privately glad to hear it. She had been a little afraid of designs upon Lettice from that quarter.

" Aunt, was it not rude to give nicknames ? "

" Very rude, and very uncomely, Lettice."

" I thought it was horrid !" said Lettice.

" Louvaine," Tom Rookwood was saying, next door, " I met Mr. Tom Winter this afternoon, and he asked me if you had gone to the Low Countries to take service under the Archduke. He hath seen nought of you, saith he, these three weeks."

" I know it," said Aubrey, sulkily.

" Well, he told me to bid you to supper with him o Thursday even next. I shall be there, and Sir Josceline Percy, Sir Edward Bushell, and Mr. Kit Wright."

" I can't. Wish I could."

" Why, what's to hinder ? "

" Oh, I'm—ah—promised beforehand," said Aubrey, clumsily.

" Can't you get off? "

" No. But I've as great a mind to go—"

" You come, and never mind the other fellows. You'll find us much jollier grigs of the twain."

" I know that. Hang it, Tom, I'll go !"

" There's a brave lad ! Four o'clock sharp, at the Duck. I'll meet you there."

" Done !"

" Where was he promised, I marvel ?" asked Dorothy in a whisper, with a yawn behind her hand.

"Oh, didn't you see how he flushed and stammered?" said Gertrude, laughing. "I vow, I do believe old Knitting-pins had made him swear on her big Bible that he wouldn't speak another word to Mr. Winter. Had it been but another merry-making, he should never have looked thus."

There was no visit from Aubrey at the White Bear that evening. He felt as if he could not meet his grandmother's eyes. He was not yet sufficiently hardened in sin to be easy under an intention of deliberate disobedience and violation of a solemn promise; yet the sin was too sweet to give up. This once, he said to himself: only this once!—and then, no more till the month was over.

When the Saturday evening arrived, Aubrey made a very careful toilet, and set forth for the Strand. It was a long walk, for the Earl of Oxford lived in the City, near Bishopsgate. Aubrey was rather elated at the idea of making the acquaintance of Sir Josceline Percy and Sir Edward Bushell. He was concerned at the family disgrace, as he foolishly considered it, of Hans's connection with the mercer, and extremely desirous to attain knighthood for himself. The way to do that, he thought, was to get into society. Here was an opening which might conduct him to those Elysian fields—and at the gate stood his grandmother, trying to wave him away. He would not be deprived of his privileges by the foolish fancies of an old woman. What did old women know of the world? Aubrey was not aware that sixty years before, that very grandmother, then young Lettice Eden, had thought exactly the same thing of those who stood in her way to the same visionary Paradise.

Temple Bar was just left behind him, and the Duck was near, when to Aubrey's surprise, and not by any means to his satisfaction, a hand was laid upon his shoulder.

"Hans! you here?"

"Truly so. Where look you I should be an half-hour after closing time?"

This was a most awkward contretemps. How should Hans be got rid of before the Duck was reached?

"You are on your way to the White Bear," said Hans. in the tone of one who states an incontrovertible fact. "Have with you."

Aubrey privately wished Hans in the Arctic Sea or the torrid zone, or anywhere out of the Strand for that afternoon. And as if to render his discomfiture more complete, here came Mr. Winter and Tom Rookwood, arm in arm, just as they reached Mrs. More's door. What on earth was to be done?

Mr. Thomas Rookwood, whose brain was as sharp as a needle, guessed the situation in a moment, and with much amusement, from a glance at Aubrey's face. He, of course, at once recognised Hans, and was at least as well aware as either that Hans represented the forces of law and order, and subordination to lawful authority, while Aubrey stood as the representative of the grand principle that every man should do what is right in his own eyes. A few low-toned words to Mr. Winter preceded a doffing of both the plumed hats, and the greeting from Tom Rookwood as they passed, of—

"Good even to you both. Charming weather!"

A scarcely perceptible wink of Tom's left eye was designed to show Aubrey that his position was understood, and action taken upon it. Aubrey saw and comprehended the gesture. Hans saw it also, but did not comprehend it except as a sign of some private understanding between the two. They walked on together, Aubrey engaged in vexed meditation as to how he was to get rid of Hans. But Hans had no intention of allowing himself to be dismissed. He began to talk, and Aubrey had to answer, and could not satisfy himself what course to pursue, till he found himself at the door of the White Bear.

Charity was at the door, doing what every housemaid was then compelled to do, namely, pouring her slops into the gutter.

"Eh, Mestur Aubrey, is that yo'?" said she. "'Tis a month o' Sundays sin' we've seen you. You might come a bit oftener, I reckon, if you'd a mind. Stand out o' th' way a minute, do, while I teem these here slops out. There's no end to folks' idleness down this road. Here's Marg'et Rumboll, at th' back, been bidden by th' third-borough to get hersen into service presently, under pain of a whipping, and Mary Quinton, up yon, to do th' same within a month, at her peril.[1] I reckon, if I know aught of either Mall or Marg'et, they'll both look for a place where th' work's put forth. Dun ye know o' any such, Mestur Aubrey, up City way?"

Aubrey was not sufficiently sharp to notice the faint twinkle in Charity's eyes, and the slight accent of sarcasm in her tone. Hans perceived both.

"I do not, Charity, but I dare be bound there are plenty," said Aubrey, stepping delicately over the puddle which Charity had just created, so as to cause as little detriment as possible to his Spanish leather shoes and crimson silk stockings.

"Ay, very like there will. They'll none suit you, Mestur 'Ans; you're not one of yon sort. Have a care o' th' puddle, Mestur Aubrey, or you'll mire your brave hose, and there'll be wark for somebody."

With which Parthian dart, Charity bore off her pail, and Aubrey and Hans went forward into the parlour.

"Good even, my gracious Lord!" was the greeting with which the former was received. "Your Lordship's

---

[1] These exemplary women really resided at Southampton, a few years later.

visits be scarcer than the sun's, and he has not shown his face none wist when. Marry, but I do believe I've seen that suit afore!"

"Of course you have, Aunt Temperance," answered the nettled Aubrey. He was exceedingly put out. His evening was spoiled; he was deprived of his liberty, of his friends' company, of a good dinner—for Mr. Winter gave delightful little dinners, and Mrs. Elizabeth More, the housewife at the Duck, was an unusually good cook. Moreover, he was tied down to what he contemptuously designated in his lofty mind "a parcel of women," with the unacceptable and very unflattering sarcasms of Aunt Temperance by way of seasoning. It really was extraordinary, thought Mr. Aubrey, that when women passed their fortieth milestone or thereabouts, they seemed to lose their respect for the nobler sex, and actually presumed to criticise them, especially the younger specimens of that interesting genus. Such women ought to be kept in their places, and (theoretically) he would see that they were. But when he came in contact with the obnoxious article in the person of Aunt Temperance, in some inscrutable manner, the young lord of creation never saw it.

At the Duck, the company were making merry over Tom Rookwood's satirical account of Aubrey's discomfiture. For his company they cared little, and the only object they had for cultivating it was the consideration that he might be useful some day. Their conversation was all the freer without him, since all the rest were Papists.

Something, at that moment, was taking place elsewhere, with which the company at the Duck, and even Aubrey Louvaine, were not unconcerned. Lord Monteagle was entertaining friends to supper at his house at Hoxton, where he had not resided for some time previously. Just before the company sat down to table, a young footman left the house on an errand, returning a few minutes later. As he passed towards his master's door, a man of "indifferent stature," muffled in a cloak, and his face hidden by a slouched hat drawn down over the brow, suddenly presented himself from amongst the trees.

"Is your Lord within, and may a man have speech of him?" asked the apparition.

"His Lordship is now sitting down to supper," was the answer.

The stranger held out a letter.

"I pray you, deliver this into your Lord's own hand," said he, "seeing it holdeth matter of import."

The young man took the letter, and returned to the house. Lord Monteagle was just crossing the hall to the dining-room, when his servant delivered the letter. Grace having been said, and the business of supper begun, he unfolded the missive. His Lordship found it difficult to read, which implies that his education was not of the most perfect order, for the writing is not at all hard to make out. But gentlemen were much less versed in the three R.'s at that date than at the present time,[1] and Lord Monteagle, calling one of his servants, named Thomas Ward, desired him to read the letter.

Now, Mr. Thomas Ward was in the confidence of the conspirators,—a fact of which there is no doubt: and that Lord Monteagle was the same may not inaptly be described as a fact of which there is doubt—an extremely strong probability, which has been called in question without any disproof.[2] Both these gentlemen, however, conducted themselves with perfect decorum, and as if the subject were entirely new to them.

[1] A letter of Lord Chief-Justice Popham would be a suitable subject for a competitive examination.
[2] See Appendix.

This was what Mr. Ward read :—

" My Lord out of the loue i beare you [this word was crossed out, and instead of it was written] some of youere frends i haue a caer of youer preseruacion Therfor i would aduyse yowe as yowe tender youer lyf to deuyse some exscuse to shift of youer attendance at this parleament For god and man hathe concurred to punishe the wickednes of this tyme and thinke not slightlye of this aduertisment but retire youer self into youre contri wheare yowe maye expect the euent in safti for thowghe theare be no apparance of anni stir yet i saye they shall receyue a terrible blowe this Parleament and yet they shall not seie who hurts them This councel is not to be acontemned because it maye do yowe good and can do yowe no harm for the dangere is passed as soon as yowe have burnt the letter and I hope god will giue yowe the grace to mak good use of it to whose holy proteccion I commend yowe."

The writing was tall, cramped, and angular. There was neither signature nor date.

The hearers gazed on each other in perplexed astonishment, not unmixed with fear.

" What can it mean ? " asked one of the guests.

" Some fool's prating," replied Lord Monteagle. " How else could the danger be past so soon as I had burnt the letter ? "

This question no one could answer. Lord Monteagle took the letter from the reader, pocketed it, and turned the conversation to other topics. The thoughts of the company soon passed from the singular warning ; and occupied by their own fancies and amusements, they did not notice that their host quitted them as soon as they left the dining-room.

With the letter in his pocket, Lord Monteagle slipped out of his garden gate, mounted his horse, and rode to his house in the Strand. Leaving the horse here, he went down to the water-side, where he hailed a boat, and was rowed to Westminster Stairs. To hail a boat was as natural and common an incident to a Londoner of that day as it is now to call a cab or stop an omnibus. Lord Monteagle stepped lightly ashore, made his way to the Palace of Whitehall, and asked to speak at once with the Earl of Salisbury, Lord High Treasurer of England.

CHAPTER VIII.

THE FIFTH OF NOVEMBER.

"Better to have dwelt unlooked for in some forest's shadows dun,
Where the leaves are pierced in triumph by the javelins of the sun !
Better to be born and die in some calm nest, howe'er obscure,
With a vine about the casements, and a fig-tree at the door !"

THE Earl of Salisbury sat in his private cabinet in Whitehall Palace. He was Robert Cecil, younger son of the great Earl of Burleigh, and he had inherited his father's brains without his father's conscientiousness and integrity. The dead Queen had never trusted him thoroughly: she considered him, as he was, a schemer— a schemer who might pay to virtue the tribute of outward propriety, but would pursue the scheme no less. Yet if Robert Cecil cared for any thing on earth which was not Robert Cecil, that thing was the Protestant religion and the liberties of England.[1] The present Sovereign was under pre-eminent obligation to him, for had he not cast his great weight into the scale in his favour, the chances were that James might very possibly, if not probably, have been James VI. of Scotland still. Lord Salisbury was in person insignificant-looking. When she

---

[1] Sicklemore, one of the priests, said with a sigh, " The Divell is in that Lord of Salisbury ! All our undoing is his doing, and the execution of Garnet is his only deed." (Addit. MS. 6178, fol. 165.)

wished to put him down, his late mistress had been accustomed to address him as "Little man," and his present master termed him "my little beagle." His face was small, with wizened features, moustache, and pointed beard; and though only forty-five years of age, there were decided silver threads among the brown.

He looked up in surprise at the announcement that Lord Monteagle requested permission to speak with him quickly. What could this young Roman Catholic nobleman want with him at nine o'clock in the evening—a time which to his apprehension was much what midnight is to ours? Perhaps it was better to see him at once, and have done with the matter. He would take care to dismiss him quickly.

"Show my Lord Monteagle this way."

In another moment Lord Monteagle stood by the table where Salisbury was seated, his plumed hat in his hand.

"My Lord," said he, "I entreat your Lordship's pardon for my late coming, and knowing your weighty causes, will be as brief as I may. A letter has been sent me which, in truth, to my apprehension is but the prating of some fool; yet seeing that things are not alway what they seem, and that there may be more in it than appeareth, I crave your Lordship's leave to lay it before you, that your better judgment may pronounce thereupon. Truly, I am not able to understand it myself."

And the nameless, undated letter, on which the fate of King and Parliament hung, was laid down before Salisbury.

The Lord High Treasurer read it carefully through; scanned it, back and front, as if to discover any trace of origin: then leaned back in his chair, and thoughtfully stroked his moustache.

"Pray you, be seated, my Lord. Whence had you this?"

Lord Monteagle gave such details as he knew.

"You have no guess from whom it could come?"

" Never a whit."

" Nor you know not the writing ? "

" It resembleth none hand of any that I know."

There was another short pause, broken by Lord Monteagle's query, "Thinks your Lordship this of any moment?"

" That were not easy to answer. It may be of serious
import ; or it may be but a foolish jest."

" Truly, at first I thought it the latter ; for how could
the danger be past as soon as the letter were burnt ? "

" Ah, that might be but—— My Lord, I pray you leave
this letter with me. I will consider of it, and if I see
cause, may lay it before the King. Any way, you have
well done to bring it hither. If it be a foolish jest, there
is but a lost half-hour : and if, as might be, it is an honest
warning of some real peril that threatens us, you will then
have merited well of your King and country. I may tell
you that I have already received divers advices from
beyond seas to the same effect."

" I thank your Lordship heartily, and I commend you to
God." So saying, Lord Monteagle took his leave.

The Sunday passed peacefully. Thomas Winter, in his
chamber at the sign of the Duck, laid down a volume of
the writings of Thomas Aquinas, and began to think about
going to bed; when a hasty rap on the door, and the
sound of some one being let in, was succeeded by rapid
steps on the stairs. The next moment, Thomas Ward
entered the room.

" What is the matter ? " said Winter, the moment he
saw his face.

" The saints wot ! A warning letter is sent to my Lord
Monteagle, and whereto it may grow—— Hie you to
White Webbs when morning breaketh, with all the speed
you may, and tell Mr. Catesby of this. I fear—I very much
fear all shall be discovered."

" It's that rascal Tresham ! " cried Winter. " He was

earnest to have his sister's husband warned, and said he would not pluck forth not another stiver without our promise so to do."

"Be it who it may, it may be the ruin of us."

"God forbid! I will be at White Webbs with the dawn, or soon after."

Before it was light the next morning Winter was on horseback, and was soon galloping through the country villages of Islington, Holloway, and Hornsey, on his way to Enfield Chase. In the depths of that lonely forest land stood the solitary hunting-lodge, named White Webbs, which belonged to Dr. Hewick, and was let in the shooting season to sportsmen. This house had been taken by "Mr. Meaze" (who was Garnet) as a very quiet locality, where mass might be said without being overheard by Protestant ears, and no inconvenient neighbours were likely to gossip about the inmates. In London, Garnet was a horse-dealer; at White Webbs he was a gentleman farmer and a sportsman. Here he established himself and somebody else, who has not yet appeared on the scene, and whom it is time to introduce. And I introduce her with no feeling save one of intense pity, as one more sinned against than sinning—a frail, passion-swayed, impulsive woman, one of the thousands of women whose lives Rome has blighted by making that sin which was no sin, and so in many instances leading up to that which was sin—poor, loving, unhappy Anne Vaux.

The Hon. Anne Vaux was a younger daughter of William Lord Vaux of Harrowden, and Elizabeth Beaumont, his first wife. Like many another, she "loved one only, and she clave to him," whose happy and honourable wife she might have been, had he been a Protestant clergyman instead of a Jesuit priest. That Anne Vaux's passionate love for Garnet was for the man and not the priest, her own letters are sufficient witness, and Garnet returned the love. She took a solemn vow of obedience to the Superior of the Jesuit Mission in England, in order that she might be with him where he was, might follow his steps like a faithful dog, that his people should be her people, and his God her God. But where he died she could not die. To "live without the vanished light" was her sadder destiny.

At White Webbs, she passed as Mrs. Perkins or Parkyns, a widow lady, and the sister of Mr. Mease. She received numerous visitors, beside Mr. Mease himself,— Catesby, who does not appear to have assumed any alias, Mr. and Mrs. Brooksby (the latter of whom was Anne's sister Eleanor), Tresham, the Winters, and two dubious individuals, who passed under the names of Robert Skinner and Mr. Perkins. The former was accompanied by his wife, real or professed ; the latter professed to be a brother-in-law of "Mrs. Perkins," and is described as "of middle stature, long visage, and somewhat lean, of a brown hair, and his beard inclining to yellow,"—a description which suits none of the conspirators whose personal appearance is known.

At White Webbs, accordingly, Thomas Winter alighted, and broke in on the party there assembled, with the startling news that—

"All is discovered ! There is a letter sent to my Lord Monteagle, and our action is known."

The party consisted of Anne Vaux, Fawkes, the Brooksbys, and Catesby, who had presented himself there a few days before, with the avowed object of joining the royal hunting-party at Royston the next day, but in the morning resolving to "stay and be merry with his friends," he settled down comfortably, sent his man for venison, and took his ease.

The ease and comfort were broken up by this sudden and startling news.

"Pray you, flee, Mr. Catesby, while you have time!" said Winter, anxiously.

"Nay, I will be further as yet," was the resolute answer.

"What shall we now do? How say you?"

"Make sure how much is truth. Go you to Town, Mr. Fawkes, to-morrow, as soon as may be, and bring us word what time of day it shall be with us. Try the uttermost; for if the part belonged to myself I would try the same adventure."

Fawkes obeyed, on the Wednesday, returning at night, to the great relief of the conspirators, with reassuring news. There was no appearance of any attempt to meddle with the cellar; all seemed quiet in London: no excitement among the people, no signs of special precaution by the authorities. They might safely go on with the work.

On the following day, Thomas Winter returned to London, and Fawkes followed in the evening, arriving at the Chequers, in Holborn, just before it grew dark. He did not stay here, but proceeded to the house next to the House of Lords, where he slept that night in its solitary bed, turning out his supposed master, as the one bed would not accommodate both, and "when Mr. Percy lay there, his man lay abroad."

Percy, meanwhile, had not been idle. His vocation as gentleman pensioner gave him easy access to any part of the Palace; and the previous day had seen him making himself very agreeable in the apartments of the young Prince, playing with the child, and chatting in a very affable manner with his nurse.

The youthful Prince's nurse, happily for him, was a shrewd Scotchwoman, and Percy took little by his motion.

"Pray you, Mrs. Fordun, whither leads that door?"

"Out o' the chalmer, Sir," said Agnes Fordun.

"What time doth his Highness ride forth commonly?"

" When it likes the King's Majesty."

" How is his Highness attended ? "

" Atweel, 'tis maistly by them that gang wi' him."

" Is his Highness a brisk, lively child, or no ? "

" He's what a Prince suld be," stiffly said Agnes.

Percy gave her up as impracticable, and reported to his colleagues at White Webbs that the Duke could not be compassed.

" Comes the Prince, then, to the Parliament ? " asked Catesby.

Percy and Winter agreed that on this head rumour was assuming a negative aspect.

" Then must we have our horses beyond the water," said Catesby, " and more horses and company to surprise the Prince, and let the Duke alone."

The King returned from Royston on the 31st of October. The next morning, Salisbury requested a private audience, and in the Long Gallery of Whitehall Palace, laid before his Majesty the mysterious letter. The astute Salisbury, and also the Lord Chamberlain, had already fathomed the meaning of the " terrible blow," and the means by which it was to be effected ; but the former would scarcely have been a Cecil had he not also read his royal master. His Majesty must have the matter so communicated to him that he should be able to believe that his own supernatural sagacity had solved a mystery impenetrable to the commonplace brains of the Lords of the Council. It might be reasonably anticipated that such a warning should be no mystery to the son of Lord Darnley—that his thoughts would fly rapidly to that house in the Kirk o' Field, where his own father had received his death-blow, and had not seen who hurt him. That the one word " Gunpowder ! " should drop from white, stern lips was to be expected. But do people ever do what is expected of them by others ? In this case, at any rate, nothing half so dramatic took place.

" His Majesty made a short reply "—which it may be was then thought such, but which now would assuredly be set down as long, wordy, and sententious.

" The incertainty of the writer, and the generality of the advertisement," began the royal orator, " besides the small likelihood of any such conspiracy on the general body of any realm, gives me less cause to apprehend it as a thing certain to be put in execution. Considering that all conspiracies commonly distinguish of men and persons, yet seeing the words do rather seem (as far as they are to be regarded) to presage danger to the whole Court of Parliament (over whom my care is greater than over mine own life), and because the words describe such a form of doing as can be no otherwise interpreted than by some stratagem of fire and powder,—I wish that there may be special consideration had of the nature of all places yielding commodity for those kinds of attempts : and I will then deliver my further judgment."

The man who could deliver his judgment in this stilted style of pompous word-building, in such circumstances as were then existing, would have required a powdered footman in spotless plush to precede him out of a house on fire. I must confess to a little misgiving as to the authenticity of this speech. It looks much more likely to have been deliberately penned by my Lord Salisbury in the calm of his official study, when the smoke had cleared away from the battlefield, than to have been fired off by King James in haste and trepidation—which he was sure to feel—at the moment when the letter was laid before him. The evidence that the Government account of the circumstances was drawn up with due regard to what they might and should have been to produce the proper effect on the docile public, and not very much as to what they were, is irresistible. But as no other narrative exists, we can but have recourse to the stained-glass article before us.

His Sacred Majesty having thus exhibited his incomparable wisdom, and been properly complimented and adored on account thereof, my Lord Salisbury left the gallery with a grave face, and hastily summoning the Lords of the Council, went through the farce of laying the letter before them.

"Sire," said he, when he returned to the King, "the Lords of the Council, subject to your Majesty's gracious pleasure, advise that my Lord Chamberlain shall straitly view the Parliament House, and my Lord Monteagle beseecheth leave to be with him."

"Gude!" said his Majesty, who to the day of his death never lost his Scottish accent. "I wad ha'e ye likewise, my Lord Salisbury, ta'e note o' such as wad without apparent necessity seek absence frae the Parliament, because 'tis improbable that among a' the nobles, this warning should be only gi'en to ane."

"Sire, your Majesty's command shall be obeyed."

"Atweel, let the search be made, and report to me," said the King, as he left the gallery.

The following Monday, which was the day before the opening of Parliament, was appointed for the search.

On the Friday, Catesby, Thomas Winter, and Tresham met at Barnet, when Catesby angrily accused Tresham of having sent the warning to Lord Monteagle, and Tresham vehemently denied it.

"Marry, it must be you!" said Catesby. "The only ones that harried us touching the saving of persons were you and Mr. Keyes, who would fain have saved his master, my Lord Mordaunt ; all other were consenting to the general issue that the Catholic Lords should be counselled to tarry away on account of the new statutes."

"I never writ nor sent that letter, on my honour!" cried Tresham.

Did he speak the truth ? No man knows to this day.

On the Saturday, the conspirators had another scare. In Lincoln's Inn Walks, Thomas Winter met Tresham, who told him in a terrified whisper that Lord Salisbury had been to the King, and, there was grave reason to fear, had shown him the fatal letter. Winter hastened away to Catesby, to whom he communicated the news. For the first time Catesby's heart failed him.

"I will be gone!" said he. "Yet—nay, I will stay till Mr. Percy come, without whose consent will I do nothing."

But money was wanted; and one of the moneyed men, who had been drawn into the conspiracy for that purpose, could alone supply it. Tresham, that one who was at hand, took Winter to his apartments in Clerkenwell,[1] where he counted out a hundred pounds.

The same night a letter was brought to Salisbury which had been found dropped in the street. A few words of it were in cipher. It purported to be written by E. F. Mak to Richard Bankes: and in it these words occurred:— "The gallery with the passage thereto yieldeth the best of assurance, and a safety of the actors themselves." "I hope to behold the tyrannous heretic defeated in his cruel pleasures." These mysterious hints, coming so quickly after the Monteagle letter, still further alarmed and excited the Council.

The conspirators gathered on Sunday night in the house behind St. Clement's—Fawkes, Catesby, Thomas Winter, and the two Wrights. They were shortly joined by Percy. It was late when they parted—parted, to meet all together

---

[1] Clerkenwell was a suburb wherein many Roman Catholics dwelt. "There were divers houses of recusants in St. John's Street," among them those of Sir Henry James and Thomas Sleep, at the last of which Fawkes was a frequent visitor. Mrs. Wyniard bore witness that when Fawkes paid her the last quarter's rent, on Sunday, November 3rd, he had "good store of gould in his pocket."

ın this world never any more. Catesby had made up his mind to go down into the country the next day; Percy and the Wrights were preparing to follow; all were ready to escape the moment the necessity should arise, except Fawkes, who was to fire the powder, and Thomas Winter, who said he would tarry and see the end. Some had already departed—Sir Everard Digby to Coughton, the house of Mr. Throckmorton, which he had borrowed —where Garnet already was.

Percy spent the Monday in a visit to the Earl of Northumberland at Syon; Christopher Wright and Thomas Winter in buying articles needful for the coming journey. In the morning Rookwood accidentally met Catesby, whose spirits had risen. There was no need to fear things would go on well.

Three o'clock in the afternoon saw Lord Suffolk, the Lord Chamberlain of the Household, accompanied by Lord Monteagle, descending into the vaults of the House of Lords. They glanced into different parts, and coming to the cellar immediately under the House, the Lord Chamberlain noticed that it was apparently filled with stacked faggots.

" Whose are all these ? " said he.

A tall, dark man, who had unlocked the cellar for their Lordships' entrance, and was now standing by with the key in his hand, gave the answer, with an air of rustic simplicity.

" An't like your Lordships, 'tis my master's provision for the winter."

" Who is your master ? " asked the Lord Chamberlain.

" An't please you, Mr. Percy, one , of his Majesty's pensioners, that hath his lodging this next door."

" I thought none dwelt next door. How long hath your master had the house ? "

" Under your Lordships' leave, about a year and an

half; but hath deferred his lying there by reason of some occasions which caused him to be absent."

"Well, he has laid in a good stock of fuel," said the Chamberlain, as if carelessly; and their Lordships turned and remounted the stairs.

Arrived at a place where they might speak unheard, the noble searchers looked each into the other's face with the same question on the lips of both.

"What thinks your Lordship of all this stock of fuel below ? "

"Nay, what think you, my Lord ? "

"Truly, I am very suspicious thereof."

"My Lord, the more I do observe the letter," said Lord Monteagle, earnestly, "and meditate on the words thereof, the more jealous am I of the matter, and of this place. Look you, this Mr. Percy the pensioner and I had great dearness of friendship between us at one time; he is a near relative of my Lord Northumberland, and a Catholic. Were I you, that cellar should be thoroughly overhauled."

"Well, let us go to the King."

It was between five and six o'clock, and the short November daylight was over, when the searchers brought back their report to his Majesty, recounted their suspicions, and asked what they were to do.

"Gi'e me a man wi' his heid on his shoulders," said his Majesty, "and ye ha' that, my Lord Monteagle. Noo, I'll just tell ye, I aye held ane maxim, to wit, Either do naething, or do that quhilk shall make a' sure. So ye'll just gang your ways, and ha'e a glint ahint thae faggots in the bit cellar."

"If it please your Highness, is there no fear that so we may give room for murmurings and evil rumours ? If we search this cellar and find nothing, may not men say the Government is unduly suspicious ? "

"And, under your Highness' leave, shall it not place my Lord Northumberland in jeopardy?—he being akin to Mr. Percy, and his great friend."

"Ay, is there twa heids weel screwit on? I jalouse, my Lord Monteagle, ye're saying ae word for my Lord Northumberland and twa for yoursel'. Be it sae: a man hath but ane life. My Lord Chamberlain, can ye no raise a bit rumour that a wheen o' the hangings are missing that suld ha'e been in the Wardrobe in Wyniard's keeping? Then gang your ways, and turn out the faggots."

"And, if it might please your Majesty," suggested the Lord Chamberlain, "were it not best some other made the search—one of the gentlemen of your privy chamber,—so as to rouse less suspicion?"

"Ay, gang your ways, and send auld Knevet down, wi' a pair or twa o' younger hands to toss the faggots."

"Might it not be well also, Sire, to extend the search to the houses adjoining the Parliament House, and so make examination of the lodging where Mr. Percy lieth?"

"Do sae, do sae," responded the King. "I affy me in you: only heed this, What you do, do throughly."

Just as the Abbey clock struck eleven, Fawkes came out of Percy's rooms, and went down into the vault by the door which had been made the previous Easter. He carried in one hand a dark lantern, lighted, and in the other a piece of touchwood, and a match eight or nine inches in length. As he set the lantern down in the corner of the vault, he felt a touch upon his shoulder, and looked up in alarm until he met the eyes of Robert Keyes.

"Mr. Fawkes, take this watch, which Mr. Percy sends you, that you may the better know when to fire the train."

Keyes spoke in a very low tone, so that he might not be heard outside. Fawkes took the watch, and secreted it carefully. Watches were rare and precious things, not

carried by every gentleman even when wealthy; and
Percy had bought this one for its special purpose.

Keyes departed, and Fawkes opened the door of the
vault for a breath of fresh air. He had scarcely come
out, and closed it behind him, when another hand
grasped his shoulder, not with the light touch of his
confederate.

"Who are you?" asked the voice of an old man.

"My name is John Johnson, my master; I am Mr.
Percy's man."

"Make stay of him," said the voice; "and you, come
after me into the vault."

Into the vault went Sir Thomas Knevet, and with his
men began a search among the carefully-stacked wood.
It did not take long to lay bare the six-and-thirty barrels,
and by drilling a small hole into two of them to make sure
of the nature of their contents. Spread before them, in
the full magnitude of its horror, lay the "gunpowder
treason and plot," which through the coming ages of
English history, should "never be forgot."

A slight noise overhead alarmed the searchers, who
feared lest "Mr. Percy's man" might be endeavouring to
escape. Sir Thomas sent up one of his men, named
Doubleday, to make sure of him till his return. Fawkes,
however, was still in the hands of the watchman, but on
Doubleday's appearance, he requested permission to go to
his own room in the adjoining house. This Doubleday
allowed, posting himself as watchmen at the door. No
sooner was Fawkes alone than he took the opportunity to
rid himself of the chief evidences against him, by flinging
the match and tinder out of his window, which overlooked
the river. In another minute Sir Thomas Knevet and his
men entered the chamber.

"Know you what we have found in your master's
cellar?"

"You have found what was there, I suppose," was the cool reply.

"Search the man," was Sir Thomas Knevet's order.

But this indignity Fawkes resented, and opposed with all his strength. The struggle was severe, but short. He was overpowered, and bound with his own garters. They found on him the watch which Keyes had brought from Percy.

"How could you have put fire to the gunpowder," asked Knevet, "without danger to yourself?"

"I meant to fire it by a match, eight or nine inches long; as soon as I had set it I should have fled for mine own safety. If I had been in the cellar when you took me, I would at once have blown up all."

"Keep a strong guard on this caitiff," said Sir Thomas, "and you, Doubleday, see to the cellar. I will to his Majesty."

As he left Percy's house, midnight tolled out on the clock of the Abbey. The fifth of November had begun.

Sir Thomas Knevet left his prisoner under guard, and returned to the King. Late as it was, his Majesty had not retired. The members of the Council who were at hand—for some always slept in the Palace—were called in, the gates secured, a cordon of troops set across King Street, and another at Charing Cross. The remainder of the Council in Town had been sent for, and as soon as they arrived, about one o'clock A.M., the King sat at their head in his bedchamber, and Fawkes was brought in and placed before them.

Nothing quelled the spirit of Guy Fawkes. The councillors were eager, impatient, vehement: he was calm as a summer eve, cool as the midnight snow. To their hurried queries he returned straightforward, unabashed, imperturbable answers, still keeping up his character of an ignorant rustic.

"Tell us, fellow, why that store of gunpowder was laid in?"

"To blow up the Parliament House," said Fawkes.

"When should it have been executed?"

"To-morrow, when the King had come, and the Upper House was sitting."

"Of whom?"

"Of myself."

"How knew you that the King would come?"

"Only by report, and the making ready his barge."

"And for what cause?"

"For the advancement of the Catholic religion."

"You are a Papist?"

"Ay."

"And wherefore would you be a party to the destruction of so many of your own religion?"

"We meant principally to have respected our own safety, and would have prayed for them."

"Your name and calling?"

"John Johnson, and Mr. Percy's man."

"Was your master a party to this treason?"

"You can ask him when you see him."

"Who were your accomplices?"

Then the dark eyes shot forth fire.

"You would have me betray my friends!" said Guy Fawkes. "The giving warning to one hath overthrown us all."

It was found impossible to obtain any further information from Fawkes. Neither fear nor coaxing would induce him to name his accomplices. He was sent to the Tower, which he entered by Traitor's Gate.

"Well, to be sure! Whatten a thingcum's[1] this? Has

---

[1] What sort of a thing.

summat happened sin' we went to bed? Rachel! I say, Rachel, lass! come here."

Rachel heard the exclamation when Charity opened the front door, and came running with a wooden spoon in her hand.

"See thou, lass! dost thou see all them soldiers drawn right across th' street? Look, they're turning folks back 'at goes up, and willn't let 'em pass. There's summat up, for sure! What is it, thinkst thou?"

"Thou'd best ask somebry [1] as comes down from 'em," suggested Rachel: "or send in next door. Eh, Mistress Abbott will be some mad, [2] to think hoo's missed th' news by lying abed."

"Ah, hoo will. Here—I say, Master! What's up, can you tell us?"

The man addressed stopped. He had been up to the cordon, and had been turned back by them.

"Why, there's a plot discovered," he answered: "one of the worst ever was heard. The Parliament House should have been blown up this very morning, and you should have been in danger of your lives."

"Lord, have mercy!" cried Rachel.

"Thanks be, that 'tis found out!" said Charity. "Be the rogues catched, think you?"

"One of 'em—he that should have fired the mine. They have learned nought of the rest as yet."

"Well, for sure! Happen [3] he'll tell o' t'others."

"They'll make him, never fear," said the man, as he passed on.

"Why, my maids! are you both so warm this November morrow, that you stand at the street door?" said Edith's voice behind them. "Prithee shut it, Charity; my mother comes anon."

Charity obeyed, while Rachel hastily poured the aston-

---

[1] Somebody.   [2] Greatly vexed.   [3] Perhaps.

ishing news into Edith's ears. The latter grew a shade paler.

"What be these traitors?" she said.

"They're Papists, for sure!" said Rachel, decidedly. "Nobry else'd think of nought so wicked."

"Ah, I reckon they are," added Charity, clinching the nail. "They're right naught,[1] the whole boilin' of 'em."

The news was broken to Lady Louvaine more gently than it had been to Edith; but she clasped her hands with a faint cry of—"Aubrey! If these be they with whom he hath consorted, God keep the lad!"

"I trust, Mother dear, God will keep him," responded Edith, softly. "Would you have him hither?"

"Truly, I know not what to say, daughter. Maybe he is the safest with my Lady of Oxford. Nay, I think not."

Now came Temperance with her market-basket, and she had to be told. Her first thought was of a practical nature, but it was not Aubrey.

"Dear heart, you say not so? How ever am I to get to market? Lancaster and Derby! but I would those Papist companions were swept clean away out of the realm. I don't believe there's a loyal man amongst 'em!"

"Nay, Temperance, we know not yet if they be Papists."

"Know not if they be! Why, of course they are!" was the immediate decision of Temperance. "What else can they be? There's none other sort ill enough to hammer such naughty work out of their fantasy. 'Don't know,' indeed! don't tell *me!*"

And Temperance and her basket marched away in dudgeon.

The previous evening had been spent by Christopher Wright, Rookwood, and Keyes at the Duck; and they

---

[1] Modern writers are apt to confuse nought and naught. At this time they were quite distinct, the former signifying *nothing*, and the latter (whence naughty is derived) *wickedness.*

were the first among the conspirators to hear of the
discovery and arrest. At five o'clock in the morning,
Christopher Wright made a sudden appearance in Thomas
Winter's chamber, where that worthy was sleeping, certainly not the sleep of the just.

"Rise up, Mr. Winter!" he cried excitedly. "Rise and
come along to Essex House, for I am going to call upon
my Lord Northumberland. The matter is discovered, by
a letter to my Lord Monteagle."

Thomas Winter sat up in his bed.

"Go back, Mr. Wright," said he, "and learn what you
can about Essex Gate."

Off dashed Christopher, and Winter dressed hastily.
He was scarcely ready when his friend returned.

"Surely, all is lost!" cried Wright, "for Leyton is got
on horseback at Essex door, and as he 'parted, he asked
if their Lordships would have any more with him, and
being answered 'No,' is rode as fast up Fleet Street as
he can ride."

"Go you, then, to Mr. Percy," urged Winter, "for sure
it is for him they seek, and bid him be gone. I will stay
and see the uttermost."

Away went Wright again, and Winter followed more
slowly. He found the Court gates "straitly guarded," so
that he was not allowed to enter. Then he turned and
went down towards the Houses of Parliament, and in the
middle of King Street he found the guard standing, who
would not let him pass. As Winter passed up King
Street again, Silence Abbott came out of her door, having
just published herself for the day, and accosted Rachel,
who was busy with the doorsteps.

"Why, whatever's all this to-do?" said she, in considerable dismay. Had she been wasting daylight and precious
material for gossip, by lying in bed half-an-hour longer
than usual?

"Why, there's a treason discovered," said Rachel, wringing out her flannel.

"Lack-a-day! what manner of treason?"

"Biggest ever was heard on. The King and all th' Lords o' th' Parliament to be blown up."

Winter hesitated no more. Evidently all was known. To save himself—if it might be—was the only thing now possible. He went straight to the livery-stable where he kept his horse, mounted, and set forth for Dunchurch, where the hunting party was to meet. If all were lost in London, it was not certain that something might not be retrieved in the country.

It was a grievous blunder, and grievously they answered it. Had they instantly gone on board the vessel which lay moored in the river, ready to carry Fawkes away when the mine was fired, and set sail for Flanders, every one of them might have fulfilled the number of his days. It seems almost as if their eyes were holden, that they should go up and fall at the place appointed.

The first to fly had been Catesby and John Wright. Keyes followed at eight o'clock, going straight to Turvey; Rookwood at eleven, overtaking Keyes three miles beyond Highgate, and Catesby and Wright at Brickhill. As they rode together, Wright "cast their cloaks into a hedge to ride more speedily."

Percy had spent the night in the City, but Christopher Wright soon found him, and they galloped after their colleagues. At Hockliffe Percy's servant Story met them with fresh horses, and overtaking the others further on, they at last reached Ashby St. Ledgers in safety.

Robert Winter, the elder brother of Thomas, was then at Grafton, the residence of his father-in-law, stalwart old John Talbot, whither he and his wife had ridden on the last day of October. He was among the more innocent of the plotters, and had taken no active part in anything but the mining. Riding from Grafton, on the 4th, he spent the night at the Bull Inn, Coventry, and next day reached the Hall at Ashby St. Ledgers, where the widowed Lady Catesby held her solitary state. Lady Catesby (*née* Anne Throckmorton) and her worthy son were not on the best terms, having found it necessary or amusing to sue one another in his Majesty's Law Courts; and shortly before this, Lady Catesby had been to Huddington to request Robert Winter's assistance in making peace with her son. He was now on his way to advise her, and had heard nothing of the proceedings in London. But soon after his arrival at the Hall, four weary, bemired men arrived also. These were Percy, the Wrights, and Rookwood, Keyes having left them on the way.

"Lost, lost!" cried impetuous Percy, as he came, booted, spurred, and covered with mud, into the very neat drawing-room where Lady Catesby and her young daughter Elizabeth were engaged on their embroidery. "All is lost! the whole plot discovered. I cast no doubt proclamations shall be out by morning light to seize us all, with a full relation how short or how long we be."

Lady Catesby exerted herself to provide for the refreshment and comfort of her very unexpected guests, and they were soon on their way across the hall to supper, when one of the servants came up with a message that "one at the base door prayed speech of Mr. Winter." Robert Winter excused himself to his hostess, and going to the back door, he there found Martha Bates, wife of the Bates who was his fellow-conspirator and Catesby's servant.

"Pray you, Sir," said Martha with a bob of deprecation mingled with deference, "to come into the fields by the town's end, where is one would speak quickly with you."

"Who is it?"

Martha glanced round, as if afraid of the chestnuts overhearing her.

"Well, Sir, to tell truth, 'tis Mr. Catesby; but I pray you, let not my Lady Anne know of his being here."

Robert Winter took his way to the place appointed, and found a group of some twelve horsemen awaiting him.

"Good even! Well, what news?"

"The worst could be. Mr. Fawkes is taken, and the whole plot discovered."

"Ay, you have heard it, then? Here are come but now my cousins Wright, with Mr. Percy and Mr. Rookwood, bringing the same news. What now do we?"

"What say you?"

"Well, it seems to me best that each should submit himself."

"We've not yet come to that. Bid them every one follow me to Dunchurch without loss of time. Only—mind you let not my mother know of my being here."

"To Dunchurch—what, afore supper? We were but just come into the dining-chamber, and I smell somewhat uncommon good."

"You may tarry for jugged hare," said Catesby contemptuously. "I shall ride quickly to Dunchurch, and there consult."

"Well—if you must, have with you."

"Bring some pies in your pocket, Robin, and then you'll not fall to cannibalism on the way," called Catesby after him. "And—hark! ask if any wist the road to Dunchurch, for I know it not."

The question was put in vain to all the party. It appeared, when they came up with Catesby, that nobody knew the road to Dunchurch. Guide-posts were a mystery of the future.

"We must needs have a guide," said Catesby; "but I am fain at this moment not to show myself in Ashby.

Robin, wilt thou win us one? Go thou to Leeson, the
smith, at the entering in of the village as thou comest
from Ravensthorpe——"

"Ay, I know."

"Ask him if he will guide us to Dunchurch, and he
shall be well paid for it. He is safe, being a Catholic.
We will follow anon."

Bennet Leeson, the blacksmith at Ashby St. Ledgers,
had given up work for the day, and having gone through
some extensive ablutions and the subsequent supper, now
stood at his cottage door, looking out on the green and
taking his rest. He was not enjoying a pipe, for that
was as yet a vice of the city, which had not penetrated to
rustic and primitive places such as Ashby St. Ledgers. A
horseman came trotting up the street, and drew bridle at
his door.

"Give thee good den, smith! Dost know the road to
Dunchurch?"

Bennet Leeson took off his leather cap, and scratched
his head, as if it were necessary to clear a path to his
brains before the question could penetrate so far.

"Well, I reckon I do, when 'tis wanted. What o'
that?"

"Wilt guide me thither?"

"What, this even?"

"Ay, now."

Bennet's cap came off again, and he repeated the clear-
ing process on the other side of his head.

"I will content thee well for it," said the stranger:
"but make up thy mind, for time presseth."

A dulcet vision of silver shillings—of which no great
number usually came his way—floated before the charmed
eyes of the blacksmith.

"Well, I shouldn't mind if I did. Tarry while I get
my horse."

The stranger waited, though rather impatiently, till Bennet reappeared, leading a rough Dunsmoor pony, with a horsecloth tied round it, on which he mounted without saddle.

"Now then, my master. Nay, not that way! You're turning your back on Dunchurch so."

The horseman checked his hasty start with a smile, and followed his guide. As they reached the other end of the village, and came out into the open, Catesby and his companions emerged from the trees, and joined Robert Winter.

"Him's growed!" said Bennet Leeson to himself, as he glanced round at the increased sound of horses' hoofs. "First time I ever see one man split his self into thirteen. The beast's split his self too. Wonder if them'll ha' come to six-and-twenty by the time us gets at Dunchurch!"

The company, however, grew no further, and Bennet led them up to the door of the Lion at Dunchurch without any more marvels. It was now about "seven or eight o'clock in the night." Catesby, the only one whom he knew by sight, said to the smith as he dismounted,—

"Here, smith, wilt walk the horses a few moments? It shall not be forgot in the reckoning."

The whole party then went into the Lion, where Sir Everard Digby and others awaited them. A hurried, eager discussion of future plans took place here. The drawer was called to bring bottles of sack and glasses, and before he was well out of hearing, impetuous Percy cried, "We are all betrayed!"

"Softly, an't like you!" responded the cooler Catesby.

"We must go on now," cried Percy: "we shall die for it else."

"But what must we now do?" asked Rookwood. "Go, even yet, to Combe Abbey, and seize on the Lady Elizabeth?"

"We wait for you, Mr. Catesby," said Sir Everard. "You have been our leader from the beginning, and we of your following will not forsake you now."

"Too late for anything of that sort," was Catesby's decision. "There are scarce enough of us, and word will sure be sent to my Lord Harrington, quicker than we could reach the place. Remember, they will go direct, and we have come round. Nay, our only way is to gather all our friends together, and see what manner of stand we can make. In numbers is our safety."

"Every Catholic in the realm will rally to us," said Sir Everard.

"And many Protestants belike," suggested Robert Winter.

"Marry, we shall have brave following, ere we be twelve hours older," said Percy. "But which way go we now?"

"Let us first cross over to Grant's; we shall maybe increase our numbers there: then go we to Coughton, pressing such as will join us on the way."

"Done!" said Percy, always the first to agree to anything which was action, and not waiting for events.

Outside, in the meantime, Bennet Leeson was walking the horses, as he had been requested.

"Tarry a bit, Leeson: thou hast not yet handled all thou mayest gain this night," said a voice the smith knew.

"Why, whence came you, Tom Bates?"

"You've good eyes, Bennet. I've been behind you ever since we left Ashby."

"By the same token, but I never saw you."

"Well, let be seeing me or no—wilt guide me to Rugby and back here for another shilling?"

Bates and Leeson accordingly rode away to "a little town called Rugby," where at the bailiff's house they found nine more worthies, who had finished their supper, and were playing cards. One of these gentry was John Winter

—the half-brother of Robert and Thomas,—whose mother was the daughter of Queen Mary's redoubtable Secretary, Sir John Bourne.[1] He was either very simple or very clever, and at this distance of time it is not easy to say which.

Bates delivered the message with which he was charged, that "the gentlemen at Dunchurch desired their company to be merry," and the nine card-players accordingly returned with him to that place. Having paid the promised shilling to Leeson, Bates took his new convoy into the inn, whence the whole party emerged in about a quarter of an hour.

"That is for thy pains, smith, and I thank thee," said Catesby, stooping from his saddle to put two shillings in the hand of his guide.

The whole party now rode away in the direction of Coventry.

"Well, that's a queer start!" said the blacksmith to himself, looking first after the horsemen, and then down at the money in his hand. "If it hadn't a-been Muster Catesby, now, and Tom Bates, might ha' thought us 'd been out wi' the fairies this even. You're good silver, aren't you? Let we see. Ay—an Edward shovelboard,[2] and a new shilling o' King James, and three groats o' Queen Bess—that's not fairy silver, I 'count. Come along, Yethard!"[3] as he scrambled on the back of his shaggy friend. "Thee and me'll go home now. Us has done a good night's work. They shillings 'll please she, if her's not in a tantrum. Gee up wi' thee!"

[1] This is the gentleman described by the Hot Gospeller as coming to the door of the council-chamber, "looking as the wolf doth for a lamb; unto whom my two keepers delivered me," and "he took me in greedily." (Narrative of Edward Underhill, Harl. MS. 424, fol. 87, b.)

[2] The shilling of Edward VI. acquired this popular name from being so large and flat, that it was found convenient for use in the game of shovelboard.

[3] The Northamptonshire pronunciation of Edward.

CHAPTER IX.

ON THE WEARY WAY TO HOLBEACH

"And thou hast fashioned idols of thine own—
Idols of gold, of silver, and of stone :
To them hast bowed the knee, and breathed the breath,
And they must help thee in the hour of death."

—SIR EDWIN ARNOLD.

HILE the discomfited conspirators were thus speeding on their weary way, in hope of yet gathering recruits enough to raise the standard of rebellion in the interests of that Church on whose behalf they counted everything lawful, Lord Harrington, at Combe Abbey, heard the news, and hurried the little Princess off to Coventry, as a safer place than his own house, for Coventry was determinately Protestant and loyal. Elizabeth, afterwards well known as the Queen of Bohemia, was deeply impressed and horrified with the terrible discovery.

"What sort of a queen should I have been," said the true-hearted child, "when I had won to my throne through the blood of my father and my brothers? Thanked be God that it was not so!"

The metropolis was passing through a ferment of delight, amazement, and activity. Everywhere in the streets bonfires were blazing,—the first of those Gunpowder Plot bonfires which every fifth of November has seen after them.

A watch was set on Percy's house in Holborn, and his wife was guarded. A priest named Roberts was taken in the house. Mrs. Martha Percy appears to have been a fitting mate for a conspirator. She put on an affectation of the sublimest innocence. How should she know anything? she who lived so quietly, and was entirely occupied in teaching her own and other children. As to her husband, she had not seen him since Midsummer. He was attendant on my Lord of Northumberland, and lodged, as she supposed, in his house. Having thus lulled to sleep the suspicions of those set to watch her, the next morning Mrs. Percy was not to be found. Whether she slipped through a door, or climbed out of a window, or went up the chimney on a broomstick, there was no evidence to show; but three days later she made her appearance at Norbrook House in Warwickshire, the residence of her eldest brother, John Wright, and was affectionately received by her sister-in-law.

At Westminster, Lord Chief-Justice Popham and Sir Edward Coke sat in judicial ermine, and summoned before them two prisoners—Gideon Gibbons the porter, and the clever gentleman who called himself John Johnson, and whose real name was Guy Fawkes.

Gibbons was soon disposed of, for he was as innocent as he seemed to be. All that he could say was that he had been hired, in his usual way of business, with two other porters, to carry three thousand billets of wood to the Parliament House, and that Mr. Percy's servant Johnson had stacked them in the cellar. The key of the house next door had been at times left in charge of his wife. So much he knew, and no more.

The examination of "John Johnson" was another matter. The King himself had drawn up a paper containing questions to be put to him, and he answered these and all others with an appearance of perfect frankness and wish to conceal nothing. His replies were in reality a mixture of truth and falsehood, which was afterwards proved.

The catechism began as usual, " What is your name ? "

" John Johnson." To this he adhered through two more examinations.

" How old are you ? "

" Thirty-six." This was true.

" Where were you born ? "

" In Netherdale, in the county of York."

" How have you lived hitherto ? "

" By a farm of thirty pounds a year."

" How came those wounds in your breast ? "

" They are scars from the healing of a pleurisy."

The treatment of pleurisy in the seventeenth century was apparently rather severe.

Fawkes went on to reply to the articles demanded, that he had never served any man but Percy—though he had been in the service of Anthony Browne, Lord Montague, a few months before: that he obtained Percy's service "only by his own means, being a Yorkshire man"; that he had learned French in England, and increased it when abroad; that he was born a Papist, and not perverted—which was false.

Being asked why he was addressed as " Mr. Fauks " in a letter (as he alleged) from Mrs. Colonel Bostock, which was found in his pocket, Mr. ' Johnson " replied with the coolest effrontery, that it was because he had called himself so in Flanders, where Mrs. Bostock resided. This letter was subsequently discovered to come from Anne Vaux.

Thus far went King James's queries: in respect of which the King desired " if he will no other ways con-fesse, the gentle tortours to be first used unto him, *et sic per gradus ad ima tenditur;* and so God speede your good work ! "

It was not, however, necessary to urge a confession : Mr. Percy's man seemed anxious to make a clean breast of it, and promised to tell everything. He proceeded accordingly to lead his examiners astray by a little truth and a good deal of falsehood. He gave a tolerably accurate account of the hiring of the house and the cellar, the bringing in of the powder, etc., except that he refrained from implicating any one but himself. There was, at first, a certain air of nobility about Fawkes, and he sternly refused to become an informer. He declined to admit his summer journey abroad, and would not allow that the spring excursion had any other object than "to see the country and pass away the time."

"What would you have done," asked the examiners, "with the Queen and the royal issue ?"

"If they had been there, I would not have helped them."

"If all had gone, who would have been published or elected King ?"

"We never entered into that consideration."

"What form of government should have succeeded ?"

"We were too few to enter into the consideration. The people themselves would have drawn to a head."

All this was untrue, as Fawkes subsequently allowed.

A number of arrests were made, mostly of innocent persons. All in whose houses the conspirators had lodged ; Mrs. Herbert, Mrs. More, the tailor Patrick ; Mrs. Wyniard, Mrs. Bright, and their respective servants ; Lord Northumberland's gentlemen, and the Earl himself, were put under lock and key. The poor Earl bemoaned himself bitterly, and entreated that Percy might be searched for—"who alone could show him clear as the day, or dark as the night." He asserted that Percy had obtained money from him by falsehood : and seeing how exquisitely little value most of these worthy gentlemen seem to have set upon truth, it was not at all unlikely. Lady Northumberland wrote an impulsive letter to Lord Salisbury, entreating him to stand her friend by " salving " her husband's reputation, "much wounded in the opinion of the world by this wretched cousin ": but the only result of the appeal was to make the Lord Treasurer angry, and give rise to an intercession in her behalf from her lord and master, who begs Salisbury to " bear with her because she is a woman," and therefore "not able with fortitude to bear out the crosses of the world as men are : and," adds the Earl humorously, " she will sometimes have her own ways, let me do what I can, which is not unknown to you." [1]

The prisoners were remanded, and the great metropolis slept : but there was no sleep for those bemired and weary horsemen who pressed on that night journey to Norbrook. Where Grant joined them is not recorded, but Humphrey Littleton had left them at Dunchurch. His share in the plot had been insignificant, but we shall hear of him again. Catesby, John Wright, and Percy, who rode in front, beguiled their journey by a discussion as to how they could procure fresh horses. They were approaching Warwick, and it was proposed that Grant and some of the servants should be sent on in front, with instructions to make a raid on a livery-stable in the town, kept by a man named Bennock, and seize as many horses as they could get.

Robert Winter, riding behind, saw the men sent on, and pressing forward to the front, inquired the meaning of it. When told the intention, he combated it strongly, and did his best to dissuade Catesby from it. The man who had

[1] Excerpta from Burghley Papers, Addit. MS. 6178, ff. 58, 184.—Lady Northumberland was Dorothy Devereux, daughter of Walter Earl of Essex and Lettice Knolles, and sister of the famous Robert Earl of Essex, in whose rebellion so many Romanists took part. Poor Lord Northumberland, if innocent, paid dearly for his relationship to his " wretched cousin," being fined £30,000, which in 1613 was commuted to £11,000. He borrowed £12,000 from Peter Vanlore to discharge the fine, and repaid half of it within a year.

swallowed the camel of the Gunpowder Plot was scandalised at the idea of horse-stealing ![1]

"I pray you, no more of this!" said Robert Winter.
"It will but further increase the wrath of the King."

"Some of us may not look back," said Catesby.

Robert replied with some spirit, for he knew himself to
be among the less guilty of the plotters. "Yet others, I
hope, may; and therefore, I beg you, let this alone."

Catesby looked up with a faint, sad smile, and tired
sleepless eyes. "What, hast thou any hope, Robin? I
assure thee, there is none that knoweth of this action but
shall perish."

When the body of the conspirators reached Warwick,
about 3 A.M., the horses were almost ready for them to
mount. Ten were seized at the the livery-stable, and a few
more were either stolen or borrowed from the Castle.
Thus provided, and now about eighty in number, they rode
on to Grant's house at Norbrook. On arrival here, they
despatched Bates to Coughton, with a letter to Garnet from
Digby. This letter was read by Garnet to Greenway, both
of whom are represented by Bates as spotlessly ignorant
of the plot until that moment. Greenway returned with
Bates, at his earnest request, attired in "coulored satten
done with gould lace," and was met by Catesby with the
exclamation—

"Here is a gentleman who will live and die with us!"

From Norbrook Robert Winter despatched a servant in
advance, summarily ordering his wife to "go forth of the
house, and take the children with her," which the obedient
Gertrude did. About two o'clock on the afternoon of the
sixth, thirty-six worn-out men arrived at Huddington, to
be re-armed from Robert Winter's armoury; after which,

---

[1] The most comical item of this assumption of virtue is the reason, as
given by himself, for Mr. Rookwood's riding on in advance at this juncture.
"Seeing that he was so well horsed as he was—he having fifteen or sixteen good horses—he meant not to adventure himself in stealing of any!"

finding himself rather at a loss in the housekeeping depart-
ment, the master of the house recalled his Gertrude to
minister to the comfort of himself and his guests.

That submissive lady did her duty, and leaving the
children with the neighbour at whose house she had
taken refuge, returned to her own kitchen to superintend
a hastily-prepared supper for the weary travellers. Before
this was ready, Catesby and John Wright took Robert
Winter aside, and tried hard to induce him to write to his
father-in-law, attempting to draw him into the now almost
hopeless rebellion.

"There is no remedy, Robin," said John Wright, "but
thou must write a letter to thy father Talbot, to see if
thou canst therewith draw him unto us."

"Nay, that will I not," was the determined answer.

"Robin, you must," said Catesby.

"My masters, ye know not my father Talbot so well as
I," replied Robin Winter. "All the world cannot draw
him from his allegiance. Neither would I if I could, in
this case. What friends hath my poor wife and children
but he? And therefore, satisfy yourselves; I will not."

"Well, then," suggested Wright, "write as we shall say
unto thee to Master Smallpiece, that serves thy father
Talbot."

Robert Winter, who liked an easy life, suffered himself
to be persuaded on this point; and wrote the letter, of
which all that now remains is a few half-burnt lines,
written in great haste, and barely legible:

"Good Cousin, I fear it will not seem strange to you
that . . . a good number of resolved Catholics so perform
matters of such . . . will set their most strength, or hang
all those that ever . . . use your best endeavour to stir
up my father Talbot . . . which I hold much more
honourable than to be hanged after. . . . Cousin, pray for

me, I pray you, and send me all such friends . . . haste, I
commend you. From Huddington, this 6th of November."

"R. . . . ."

Having written this letter, Mr. Robert Winter proceeded, not to forward, but to pocket it, and declined to
give it up until the next morning, when he resigned it,
" to stop a peace withal."

Late in the evening of the 6th, the conspirators were
joined by Stephen Littleton and Thomas Winter, the
latter of whom had not been able to overtake them any
sooner. Before daybreak on the following morning, they
assembled in the private chapel of Huddington House,
where mass was sung by the family confessor, Mr.
Hammond, and the Sacrament was administered to all
present after due confession. Then, leaving Huddington
about sunrise, they recommenced their weary flight.

They were now " armed at all points in open rebellion,"
yet with daggers and guns only. Instead of continuing
their course, as hitherto, directly westward, they turned
towards the north, and made for Hewell Grange, the
residence of Lord Windsor, where they plundered the
armoury. The company had much decreased: one and
another every now and then dropped off stealthily, doubtful of what was coming, though Catesby and Sir Everard
rode pistol in hand, warning them that all who sought
to steal away would be shot without quarter. Percy,
Grant, John Wright, and Morgan, were placed behind
for the same purpose. As the party rode towards Hewell
Grange, they asked all whom they met to join them.
The usual response was—

" We are for King James; if you go for him, then will
we have with you."

To this the conspirators were wont to reply—" We go
for God and the country."

But the shrewd Worcestershire peasants declined to commit themselves to anything so vague as this.

At last they came to an old countryman, to whom they addressed their customary appeal. The old man planted his staff firmly in front of him, and set his back against a wall.

"I am for King James," he said, "for whom I will live and die."

Upon this the disloyalty of the company was plainly manifested by shouts of "Kill him! kill him!" But there was no time to stop for that, which probably saved the brave old loyalist's life.

Upon leaving Hewell, the conspirators rode up to the houses of all the Roman Catholic gentry in the neighbourhood, and summoned their owners to join them for God and the Church. But sore disappointments met them on every side. From door after door they were driven with horror and contumely—were openly told that "they had brought ruin on the Catholic cause." "Not one man came to take our part," is their lament, "though we had expected so many." To add to their misery, the rain began to pour down in torrents; one after another deserted them as they fled: and when at last in the darkness the heath was passed, and Holbeach House was reached, instead of the gallant company of eighty well-accoutred troops who had left Norbrook the morning before, there crept into the court-yard only eighteen wet and weary men, who had lost all, including honour.

Holbeach House was about two miles from Stourbridge, and was the home of Stephen Littleton, one of the latest to join the plot. Here the worn-out men slept—the last sleep for some of them.

So weary and worn-out were they, that they sank to sleep just as they were, in the dining-room—some pillowing their heads on the table, others casting themselves on the floor. At this very unsuitable moment, it seemed good to Mr. John Winter to inquire of Percy what he meant to do.[1]

Percy, in extremely somnolent tones, answered that he intended to go on.

"Ay, but how and whither?" responded Thomas Winter, as wide awake as he usually was in all senses.

"If you have e'er a plan in your head, out with it," replied Percy. "Just now, I've no head to put one in."

"If you will hearken to me," said Thomas, "you will now despatch Robin's letter to my cousin Smallpiece."

"What to do?"

"'What to do'!—to win his aid. He is as true a Catholic as any of us."

"Ay, he's Catholic, but he is very timorous. He has no mind to be hanged, trust me."

"Have you?"

"I should stand to it better than he. Then you'll meet old Master Talbot, who shall kick you forth ere you have time to say, 'An't please you.'"

"I'll have a care of that. Steenie, wilt have with me?"

Mr. Stephen Littleton had to be awoke before he could answer the question. As soon as he understood what was demanded of him, he professed his readiness to accompany anybody anywhere in the future, so long as he might be let alone to finish his nap at the present. Before another sentence had been uttered, he reverted to an unconscious state.

Suddenly Sir Everard sprang up.

"Mr. Catesby, methinks I shall best serve you if I go to hasten the succours. What think you?"

"If you will," said Catesby, for once a little doubtfully.

---

[1] "At Holbeach, I demanded of Mr. Percy and the rest, *being most of them asleep*, what they meant to do." (Letter of John Winter, Gunp. Plot Book, art. 110.)

Ten minutes later, one of the least wearied horses in the group carried him away.

There were troops on their way to Holbeach, but it was not for succour.   Sir Richard Walsh, the Sheriff, Sir John Folliott, a few gentlemen, and a party of the King's troops, with all the force of the county, were on the track of the wretched fugitives.   They had chased them from Northamptonshire into Warwickshire, from Warwickshire into Worcestershire, and now they were approaching their last refuge in Staffordshire.

It was still dark on the Friday morning, when Thomas Winter and Stephen Littleton rode to Pepperhill, where old Mr. Talbot was at that time.   Robert declined to accompany them, and Bates excused himself.   To obtain sight of Mr. Smallpiece, without being seen by Mr. Talbot, was the delicate business on which they were bent.   Leonard Smallpiece seems to have been an agent or bailiff of Mr. Talbot, and a relative of the Winters; he was "exceeding popishe, but very timorous."[1]   The pair of worthies settled that Stephen should remain outside in charge of the horses, while Winter tried to effect safe entrance.   They rode up to the yard door, and having dismounted, were about to investigate possibilities, when without any warning the doors were flung open, and the sturdy old loyalist owner appeared behind them.

"How dare you come hither?" was his fierce greeting to the unwelcome visitors, "considering what speech there is of your tumultuous rising."

"Sir," answered Winter, deprecatingly, "my meaning was not to speak with you, but with one in your house; and I am very sorry I have met with you."

"So am I, too!" said John Talbot.   "Your coming

---

[1] Sir Edward Coke to Lord Salisbury, Nov. 5th, "after your painful day's work" : Addit. MS. 6178, fol. 54.

may be as much as my life is worth. It is very fit you should be taken."

"I shall not easily be taken," was the reply.

"Fare you well! Get you away!" answered Talbot, as he slammed the gate in Winter's face.

They came to the conclusion that discretion would be the better part of valour, and retraced their steps to Holbeach. Here Stephen went into the house, leaving Winter outside. The former found his friends very busily engaged in making preparations for resistance, for they had now determined that at Holbeach their last stand should be made. Their gunpowder, like themselves, had been soaked in the rain, the Stour being extremely high, and the cart which they had stolen from Hewell Grange a very low one. Catesby, Rookwood, and Grant, applied themselves to the drying of the powder. They laid about sixteen pounds of it in a linen bag on the floor, and heaping about two pounds on a platter, placed it in the chimney-corner to dry by the fire. A servant entering to put fresh logs on the fire, was not sufficiently careful of the platter. A spark flew out, lighted on the powder, and it exploded. Part of the roof was blown off, the linen bag was carried through the hole thus made, and afterwards taken up uninjured in the court-yard: but the three powder-dryers, with Henry Morgan, were severely injured both in face and body. In the same pit that they had dug privily, was their own foot taken.

When the conspirators thus beheld themselves "hoist with their own petard," the first feeling among them was less fear for their safety than awe at the just judgment of God. The most guilty among them were also the most horrified. For a moment those nearest the powder were supposed to be killed. John Wright lost his head, flung himself on what he believed to be the corpse of his leader, with a wild cry—

"Woe worth the time that we have seen this day! Bring me the powder! bring me the powder, that I may set it afire, and blow up ourselves and this house together!"

Rookwood rushed to a picture of the Virgin, and throwing himself on his knees, confessed "that the act was so bloody that he desired God to forgive him;" in which prayer he was joined by some of the others. Catesby himself lost his firmness, and on recovering himself, gasped out his fear that God disapproved of their project. Robert Winter and Greenway fled in terror—so far that they never came back. Stephen Littleton went off also, but he waited long enough to send a message to Thomas Winter, who had not yet come in.

"Tell him to fly," said the valiant Stephen, "and so will I."

Whatever else Thomas Winter was, he was loyal to his oath and to his friends.

> "His honour rooted in dishonour stood,
> And faith unfaithful kept him falsely true."

He supposed the news to mean that Catesby was killed.

"Nay," said he; "I will first see the body of my friend and bury him, whatsoever befall me."

Returning to the house, Winter found his friends decidedly alive and "reasonable well."

"What resolve you to do?" he asked them.

"We mean here to die," was the answer.

"Well!" replied Winter, "I will take such part as you do."

And John Wright said, "I will live and die among you."

Not long afterwards, about noon, the Sheriff and his troops surrounded Holbeach House. After several ineffectual summonses to surrender, and the reading of a proclamation in the King's name bidding the rebels to submit themselves, which met only with blunt refusals, the Sheriff fired the house, and led an attack upon the gates. The conspirators who were left showed no lack of courage. They walked out into the court-yard, set the gate open, and took up their stand in front of it, Catesby in the middle, with Percy and Thomas Winter on either side. At the first assault, an arrow from a cross-bow had struck Winter in the shoulder, and rendered his right arm useless. The second shot struck John Wright, the third Christopher Wright, the fourth Rookwood. The two Wrights fell, and were supposed to be dead.

" Stand by me, Tom," said Catesby to Winter, " and we will die together."

" Sir," was the answer, " I have lost the use of my right arm, and I fear that will cause me to be taken."

They were the last words of Robert Catesby. The next bullet passed clean through his body,[1] and lodged in that of Percy at his side. Catesby fell, mortally wounded. He had just strength to crawl on his hands and knees into the vestibule of the house, where stood an image of the Virgin : and clasping it in his arms, he died.

Percy sank down, also wounded to death ; he expired the following day. John Wright, recovering somewhat from his wound, called to Bates, and delivered him a bag of money, entreating him to fly and take it to Mrs. Wright at Norbrook. Winter was seized ; Grant, Rookwood, and Morgan, yielded themselves to the Sheriff : but the exasperated mob, rushing in, while the Sheriff's men were lifting one of the wounded, seized upon the others, stripped and ill-used them, until wounds which might possibly have been healed were past cure. John and Christopher Wright died in two or three days.

One or two fugitives were brought into Holbeach later ;

---

[1] For this shot one of the Sheriff's men, named John Streete, received 2s. per day up to 1627.

five were arrested at Stourbridge, Sir Everard Digby at
Dudley. Bates succeeded in making good his escape with
the bag, and reached Wolverhampton in the night. His
wife Martha, who lived at Ashby, hearing a false rumour of
his capture and imprisonment in Shrewsbury Gaol, went to
see him, and both stayed for the night in the same inn at
Wolverhampton, neither of them knowing the nearness of
the other. Bates, finding himself unable to reach Lapworth,
and with no hope of escaping finally, delivered the bag of
money to a friend to convey to Martha, and departed, not
wishing to endanger his friend. He then went to Oldfield,
in Shropshire, to the house of his cousin, Richard Bates,
by whom having been betrayed, he was apprehended, and
brought to London. By his confession on his examination,
Garnet and Greenway were implicated, though Bates tried
his best to prove them innocent.

Sir Richard Walsh conveyed his prisoners to Worcester,
where he occupied himself in taking their examinations,
and sending the information obtained to the Lords of the
Council. Sir Richard Verney was sent to scour the country on the recent track of the fugitives, and to arrest the
relatives and servants of every one of them. John Winter,
Gertrude Winter at Huddington, Ludovic Grant at Dudley, Dorothy Grant at Norbrook, and at Lapworth John
Wright's wife Dorothy, and Christopher's wife Margaret;
Ambrose Rookwood's wife, and her sister; and Thomas
Rookwood of Claxton, at Bidford, were all gradually added
to the group. Mrs. Dorothy Grant, whether from fright or
loquacity, proved very candid in answering questions, and
from her they learned that the missing Martha Percy was
"not far off." Sir Richard Verney, however, found it no
easy matter to keep his prisoners when he had got them.
Twice his house was set on fire, evidently by design : but
he held stoutly to the lively ladies in his care, and delivered
them all safely in London in due time.

We must now, for a short time, follow the two conspirators who had escaped in company, and whose wanderings are not devoid of interest.   Robert Winter and Stephen
Littleton got safely away from Holbeach, thus evading the
miserable fate of their fellow-conspirators.   They succeeded
in reaching the house of a certain Christopher White, a
servant of Stephen's cousin, Humphrey Littleton, who lived
in the village of King's Rowley.   This man they bribed to
allow them to remain in his barn until the search for the
fugitives should have ceased, when they promised to give
him a substantial reward, and no longer to endanger him by
their presence.   "There they abode a great while, but with
very poor and slender fare, such as otherwise had been too
coarse and out of fashion for them."   A proclamation was
meanwhile set forth by Government for their discovery,
wherein Robert Winter was described as " of mean stature,
rather low than otherwise; brown hair and beard, not much
beard, short hair; somewhat stooping, square made, near
forty."   Stephen Littleton was "a very tall man; swarthy
complexion, no beard or little, brown coloured hair; about
thirty."   A neighbour of White's, named Smart, and apparently smart by nature as well as name, noticed the
unusual evidences of prosperity in his neighbour's dwelling,
and shrewdly surmised the reason.   Upon due consideration of the subject, Mr. Smart, like a good many people
both before and after him, came to the conclusion that
it was highly unreasonable that his neighbour should be
mounting the social ladder when he remained at the
bottom.   He therefore applied himself to the matter, discovered the refugees in the barn, and strongly recommended
his barn as far preferable to White's.   The fugitives were
persuaded to change their hiding-place.   This was no sooner
done, than another neighbour, named Hollyhead, set his wits
also to work, and dulcetly represented that Smart's barn
was a much less safe and attractive locality than his house:

each of these worthy individuals being of course moved by respect to the pecuniary reward for which he hoped. On the departure of his guests, White took fright and fled: which caused "much rumour to be blabbed abroad" concerning the vain search and the probable vicinity of the fugitives. Humphrey Littleton, who was in the secret, began to be alarmed, and removed his friends from Hollyhead's house to that of a man named John Perks, in the village of Hagley, close to Hagley Park, the residence of his widowed sister-in-law. It was before dawn on New Year's Day that they reached the cottage of Perks, a warrener or gamekeeper, who had been dismissed from Mrs. Littleton's service for dishonesty. The wearied men knocked at his door; and when Perks came forth, said they were friends, and begged him to help them to food and shelter.

"Ye be Mr. Stephen Littleton, and Mr. Winter," said Perks.

"We are so," they admitted. "Pray you, Goodman, grant us meat and lodging till we be fit for journeying; and when we can travel, then shall you bring us to London, and have a great reward from the King for taking us, we being willing to die, and not live any longer in so miserable a condition."

If Mr. Perks's eyes glistened as this distant prospect of a great reward was held out to him, they grew yet more radiant when Humphrey Littleton counted into his hand thirty golden sovereigns, twenty into that of his man, and seventeen to his sister. Perks led the way to his barn, where mounting on a barley mow, he formed a large hole in its midst, and here the unhappy gentlemen were secreted, food being brought to them by Perks as occasion served, by his sister Margaret, or at times by his man, Thomas Burford. Here they might have remained in safety for a considerable time without fear of discovery, had not Mr. Perks entertained rather too close an affection for barley in another form than heaped up in a barn—namely, in company with hops and water. Mr. Perks had a friend, named Poynter, who liked beer and rabbits quite as well as himself; and one winter night, nine days after the fugitives had been hidden in the mow, these worthies set forth on a poaching expedition. Returning home somewhat late, and "well tippled in drink," it occurred to Mr. Poynter that it would save him a walk home if his friend Perks were to lodge him for the night. The latter, however, did not see the circumstance in that light, and a tipsy altercation followed, which was ended by Perks "shaking off" Poynter, and staggering home by himself. The night was cold and wet, and Mr. Poynter's temper was scarcely so cool as the atmosphere. He was tipsily resolved that he would have a lodging at Perks's expense, whether that gentleman would or not; and bethinking himself that if Perks's house were locked against him, his barn was not, he took thither his unsteady way, and scrambling up the barley mow, to his own unfeigned astonishment dropped into the hole on the top of the sleeping conspirators.

Thus roused suddenly in the dead of night, and naturally concluding that their enemies were upon them, Winter and Littleton sprang up to defend themselves, and to sell their lives dearly. Poynter, who was quite as much amazed and terrified as they could be, as naturally fought for his own safety, and a desperate struggle ensued. It ended in the two overcoming the one, and insisting on his remaining with them, so that they could be certain of his telling no tales. For four days Poynter remained on the mow, professing resignation and contentment, and lamenting the sore pain which he suffered from a wound in the leg, received in the pursuit of his vocation as a rabbit-stealer. When Margaret Perks came with food, and afterwards Burford, Poynter pretended to be in mortal anguish, and besought them earnestly to bring him some salve, without which he was quite certain he should die. The salve was brought, and the wily Poynter then discovered that lying in the hole he had not sufficient light to apply it. He was suffered to creep up on the top of the mow, which he professed to do with the greatest difficulty. But even there the light was scarcely sufficient: might he drag himself a little nearer the door? Being now quite deceived by Mr. Poynter's excellent acting, and believing that he was much too suffering and disabled to escape, they permitted him to crawl quite to the edge of the mow nearest to the light, and of course next to the door. The moment this point was reached, the disabled cripple slipped down from the mow, and the next instant was out of the door and far away, running with a fleetness which made it hopeless to think of following him.

There was still, however, some room for that hope which springs eternal in the human breast. Poynter's friendship for Perks, and the expectation that Perks could bribe him to secrecy, weighed with the fugitives, who had not sufficiently learned that the friendship of an unprincipled man is worth nothing.

Poynter, on the other hand, considered his chances superior in the opposite direction. He made at once for Hagley Hall, intending to tell his story there; but on the way he met with Perks, who was ignorant of Poynter's recent adventure; and that gentleman suggesting a joint visit to the nearest tavern, Poynter easily suffered his steps to be diverted in that attractive direction. The precious pair of friends drank together, and departed to their respective homes.

Now, Mistress Littleton, the lady of Hagley Park, was a Protestant, and a gentlewoman of extreme discretion; and the day on which Poynter thus made his escape from the haymow had been chosen by her to commence a journey to London. Before her departure, she summoned her steward, Mr. Hazelwood, and desired him to be circumspect during her absence, "owing to the mischances happening in the county."

Mistress Littleton having ridden forth on her journey, her worthy brother, Mr. Humphrey, commonly called Red Humphrey, who certainly did not share the discretion of his sister, determined to play the mouse during the absence of his cat, and to convey his traitor-friends into his own chamber at Hagley Park. There is reason to think that Mistress Littleton was not only a sagacious but also a somewhat managing dame, who rode Red Humphrey with a tighter curb than that reckless individual approved. Accordingly, having heard of Poynter's escape, and taking one person only into his confidence, he repaired to the barn about eleven o'clock that night, and smuggled his cousin and friend away from the barley mow into the pleasanter shelter of his own room in Hagley Park. The one person thus selected as Humphrey's confidant, was John Fynwood or Fynes, alias "Jobber," also known as John Cook, from the office which he bore in the household. Humphrey had brought him up, and when come to suitable age, had induced his sister-in-law to engage him as cook: he therefore expected this man, being thus beholden to him, to remain faithful to his interests. But there was another person whose interests were considerably dearer to John Cook, and that was himself.

The trio reached Master Humphrey's chamber in safety, aided by John Cook. Robert Winter turned round as he entered, and grasped the cook's hand.

"Ah, Jack!" said he, "little wots thy mistress what guests are now in her house, that in so long a space did never so much as look upon a fire!"

"Welcome, heartily!" answered Humphrey, motioning to his guests to approach nearer to the cheerful hearth. "Jack, lad, the time being thus late, canst kill some hen or chickens about the house, to serve and fit the present occasion withal? I will recompense it to thee afterward."

Jack readily undertook the commission, and brought up

a very appetising dish with great diligence and promptness.

"Master," said he, " you shall need drink, and the butler is in bed ; to call on him for the key might rouse suspicion. Pray you, shall I run in the town to my mother, and fetch you drink from thence ? "

"So do, honest Jack, and hie thee back quickly. See, here is a tester for thee."

Honest Jack picked up the tester, and disappeared.

It does seem strange, considering the danger which was thus run, that the fugitives should not have been satisfied to drink water with their supper, since even thus they would have fared much better than they had done for some time past. But in truth, the very idea of drinking water was foreign to men's minds in those days, except in the light of a very cruel hardship, and about the last strait to which a starving man could be reduced.

The mother of Jack kept a small tavern in the village. Thither he ran to fill his jug, and to pour into the ears of the hostess the interesting fact that the traitors then sought for by the King's proclamation were at that moment entertained in Master Humphrey's chamber at Hagley Park.

"Pray you, Mother," he added, " when morning breaketh, raise the town to take them, for I fear lest I may not, unsuspected, get forth again to do it."

Having made which little arrangement, honest Jack and his jug returned to the Park, where the trio of traitors finished their supper, and proceeded to sleep three in a bed.

To make assurance doubly sure, Jack rapped at Mr. Hazelwood's door, and bestowed upon him the same interesting information already given to Mrs. Fynwood.

The morning being come, the cook paid another visit to his prisoners, whom he found nearly dressed, and looking out of the window to see the meaning of the noise they heard, which was in fact the arrival of the Sheriff's officer and his men.   Even then, so complete was their confidence in Jack, that they never imagined themselves betrayed, and Humphrey, having stowed his friends for more complete security in a closet-room opening out of his chamber, went down into the hall—and met the officer of the law.

"Sir, I understand there be in this house certain traitors, so charged by proclamation of his sacred Majesty, whom you have in keeping."

"Never an one, my master, I do ensure you," answered Humphrey, as lightly as if he spoke the truth : and he cut a large slice from the loaf standing on the table.   "Pray you, sit down and break your fast ; you are full welcome, as I am sure my good sister should tell you were she at home.   After that ye have eaten, ye shall search the house an' ye will.— See here, Jack Cook! make a good toast for these worthy masters; and thou, David Butler, go up to my chamber for my cup—thou shalt find it on the window-ledge, I think."

Outside, Mr. Hazelwood was giving directions for the search, hints being constantly supplied to him by the cook as to what transpired within.   The butler, David Bate, went to fetch his master's cup, and of course found the room empty.   As he came to the foot of the back-stair, Master Humphrey met him.

"Good David, help me to the key of the back-door into the cellar," he said in a hurried whisper.   "As ever thou wilt do anything for me, stick now to me, and help save my life."

"Sir, I have not the key," answered the astonished butler. "The brewer hath it."

The brewer was hastily summoned, delivered the key, and was as hurriedly dismissed.   Then Humphrey ran up to his closet, brought down his concealed guests, and conducted them through the buttery towards the cellar.   The butler slipped away from them, and told the officers.   The situation was now desperate.   Inside the house the officers were pursuing them; outside, a crowd, in league with the authorities, was shouting itself hoarse in execration of them. The wretched men made one last frantic dash around the house, and Robert Winter and Stephen Littleton were arrested in the stable-yard, and prevented from reaching the neighbouring wood.

But what had become of Red Humphrey? The instant he saw the game was up, he hurriedly mounted his horse, and eluded his pursuers. But he was not to escape much longer. The searching party which Poynter had led to the barn, disappointed there, scoured the neighbourhood; and at Prestwood the fugitive was taken, and committed to safe custody in Stafford Gaol. Even after they were secured, it was no easy matter to carry the other prisoners to Worcester. While they were "refreshing themselves" in an alehouse at Hagley—probably the tavern kept by Mrs. Fynwood—a tumult arose among the people outside which almost led to their rescue; and a few miles from Hagley, Sir Thomas Undirhood and his company overtook the Sheriff, and vainly attempted to gain possession of them to take them back to Staffordshire. The Worcestershire men, however, held on grimly to their prize, and at last triumphantly lodged their prisoners in the gaol at Worcester.

The examinations of the culprits in London went on. They were mainly characterised by Mr. Fawkes's contradictions on every occasion of something which he had previously said; by the addition of a little information each time; and by the very small amount of light that could be obtained from any outsiders. On his third examination, Mr. "John Johnson" owned that his name was Guy Fawkes; that he was born at York, the son of Edward Fawkes, a younger brother, who had left him "but small living," which he ran through with equally small delay. He denied on his conscience that he was in orders, "major or minor, regular or secular": on which occasion he told the truth.   Fawkes added that he did not now desire to destroy the King.

"It is past," he said, "and I am now sorry for it, for that I now perceive that God did not concur with it."

He admitted also the design on the Lady Elizabeth, but he still declined to name his accomplices, and proved obdurate to all attempts—and the attempts were basely made—to persuade him to accuse the prisoners in the Tower, of whom the chief was Sir Walter Raleigh.   The utmost he could be induced to admit concerning this point was that it had been "under consultation that the prisoners in the Tower should have intelligence" of the intended plot, and that Raleigh and several others had been named in this connection.

"We should have been glad to have drawn any, of what religion soever, unto us," he said : "we meant to have made use of all the discontented people of England."

But he would not allow, even to the last, that any communication had actually been made.

In his fourth examination Fawkes gave the names of those who had been "made privy afterwards," but he still refused to reveal those of the original traitors.   He was accordingly put to the torture.   Gentle or ungentle, this worked its office : and on the ninth of November, after half-an-hour on the rack, Fawkes recounted the names of all his accomplices.   He made also an admission which proved of considerable importance—he mentioned a house in Enfield Chase, "where Walley [Garnet] doth lie."

Every examination is signed by the prisoner.   To the first he signs "Guido Faukes" in a free, elegant Italian hand, the hand of an educated man.   But it is pitiful to see the few faint strokes which sign the fifth, even the "Guido" being left unfinished.   He is supposed to have fainted before the word could be written.   The subsequent reports are fully signed, and in a firmer hand ; but the old free elegant signature never comes again.

That night an unheard-of event occurred at the White Bear. Hans Floriszoon was two hours late in coming home.

"My lad!" said Edith, meeting him in the hall, "we feared some ill had befallen thee."

"It hath not befallen *me*, Mrs. Edith," was the answer; "and may God avert it from us all! But these men that Aubrey was wont to visit—Mr. Catesby, Mr. Winter, and the rest—are now confessed by the caitiff in the Tower to have an hand in the plot."

"Aubrey?" The word was only just breathed from Edith's lips.

"I went thither at once, and spake with Aubrey, whom I found to have heard nought, and to be very sore troubled touching Mr. Winter, whose friendship I can see hath been right dear unto him. I besought him to lie very close,— not to come forth at all, and if he would communicate with us these next few days, to send a messenger to me at Mr. Leigh's, and not here, for it seemed to me there was need of caution. After a time, if all blow over, there may be less need. Will you tell my Lady Lettice, or no?"

"Dear Hans, thou art ever thoughtful and good. Thou hast done very well. But I think my mother must be told. Better softly now, than roughly after—as it may be if it be let alone."

Lady Louvaine sat silent for a few minutes after that gentle communication had been made. Then she said,—

"'The floods lift up themselves, and rage mightily: but yet the Lord, who dwelleth on high, is mightier.' 'Tis strange that it should be so much harder to trust Him with the body than with the soul! O Father, keep my boy from evil!—what is evil, Thou knowest: 'undertake for us!'"

On the 23rd of November, one of the prisoners in the Tower escaped the sentence of the law, by an inevitable summons to the higher tribunal of God Almighty. Francis Tresham died in his prison cell, retracting with his last breath, and "upon his salvation," the previous confession by which he had implicated Garnet in the Spanish negotiations. It has been suggested that he was poisoned by Government because he knew too much; but there is no foundation for the charge except the possibility that his death might have been convenient to the Government, and the fact that they allowed his wife and servant to be with him in his last illness goes far to disprove this improbable accusation.

The authorities were now engaged in lively pursuit of the new track which Fawkes had indicated to them. A house in Enfield Chase where Garnet was or might be found, was too appetising a dainty to be lightly resigned. On the 23rd, they obtained a full confession from Thomas Winter, and the actual name of White Webbs. From this moment White Webbs became their Ultima Thule of hope and expectation.

A poor and mean revenge was taken on the dead Catesby and Percy. Their bodies were exhumed, and beheaded, and their heads set on the pinnacles of the Houses of Parliament. The spectators noticed with superstitious terror that blood flowed from Percy's wound. The authorities seem to have regarded Percy as the head and front of the conspiracy; they term him "the arch-traitor." But by the testimony of both Fawkes and Winter, Catesby was the original deviser of the Gunpowder Plot.

CHAPTER X.

THE CHAIN OF OUR SINS.

" When on the problems of the past
  A flood of light has come ;
  When we see the evil that we did,
  And the good we might have done."
                        —CYRUS THORNTON.

N the 27th of January, Robert and Thomas Winter, Guy Fawkes, John Grant, Ambrose Rookwood, Robert Keyes, and Thomas Bates were placed upon their trial at Westminster. Grant and Bates were really guilty of very little beyond knowing of the plot and keeping silence. But they all received the same sentence—to be hung, drawn, and quartered. Sir Everard Digby was tried separately, but to the same end. He alone pleaded guilty ; his principal anxiety seemed to be to save the priests—a wish wherein all the conspirators agreed. On leaving the dock, Sir Everard, " bowing himself towards the Lords, said, ' If I may but hear any of your Lordships say, you forgive me, I shall go more cheerfully to the gallows.' Whereupon the Lords said, ' God forgive you, and we do.' "

Of all the conspirators, Sir Everard won the greatest sympathy, from his rank, his youth, his accomplishments, and especially his fine person—which last drew expressions of pity from the Queen, who was afflicted with that fatal worship of beauty which was the bane of the Stuart race.

Three days later, the scaffold was set up at the west end of St. Paul's Cathedral, and four of the traitors were brought forth to die. They were the four least guilty of the group —Sir Everard Digby, Robert Winter, John Grant, and Thomas Bates.

As the prisoners were being drawn to the scaffold upon hurdles, a pathetic incident took place. Martha Bates had followed her husband to London, and as the procession passed by, she rushed from the crowd of spectators, and flung herself upon the hurdle in an agony. Bates then told her of the money entrusted to him by Wright, which he wished her to keep for her own relief, and it was afterwards granted to her by the Crown.

Arrived at the place of execution, Sir Everard was the first to ascend the ladder. Very pale, yet very self-controlled, he spoke to the people, saying that his conscience had led him into this offence, which in respect of religion he held to be no sin at all, but in respect of the law he confessed that he had done wrong; and he asked forgiveness of God, the King, and the kingdom. He declined the ministrations of the clergy, and after a few Latin prayers, crossed himself, and so "made an end of his wicked days in this world"—an example for all time how little education and accomplishments can do to keep man from sin, a martyr to a priest-ridden conscience unenlightened by the Word of God.

Robert Winter followed next. He scarcely spoke, asked no forgiveness, but after a few silent prayers, passed calmly into the Silent Land.

The next was John Grant. This grave, melancholy man went smiling to his death. When he was entreated to seek for pardon for his crimes, his reply was, in a triumphant tone, "I am satisfied that our project was so far from being

sinful, that I rely entirely upon my merits in bearing a part
of that noble action, as an abundant satisfaction and expia-
tion for all sins committed by me during the rest of my
life!" He died thus with a lie in his right hand, and went
to present the filthy rags of his own righteousness before
His eyes in whose sight the heavens are not pure, and
whose command is "Thou shalt do no murder."

Last came poor Bates, who "seemed sorry for his
offence," and said that only his love for his dead master
had drawn him to forget his duty to God, his King and
country. And "thus ended that day's business."

In Old Palace Yard, "over against the Parliament House"
—namely, where now stands the statue of Godfrey de
Bouillon—the second scaffold was erected on the following
day. The four prisoners who were now to suffer were, the
priests excepted, the most guilty of those left alive. They
were drawn from the Tower on hurdles, as was usual. As
they passed along the Strand, from an open window the
beautiful Elizabeth Rookwood called to her husband—

"Ambrose, be of good courage! Thou art to suffer for a
great and noble cause."

Raising himself from the hurdle as well as he could,
Rookwood answered, "My dear, pray for me."

"I will, I will!" she cried. "And do you offer yourself
with a good heart to God and your Creator. I yield you to
Him, with as full an assurance that you will be accepted of
Him as when He gave you to me."

And so the procession passed on.

The first to suffer of these was Thomas Winter. He
was extremely pale, and seemed sorry for his offence "after
a sort;" but he spoke little, merely protesting that he died
"a true Catholic."

Rookwood, who came next, made a long speech. He
said that he asked forgiveness of God, whom he had offended
in seeking to shed blood, of the King, and of the people.

He prayed for the King and Royal Family, entreating that the King might become a "Catholic:"[1] and he besought the King's goodness to his Elizabeth and her children. He was spared the worst, for he drew his last breath ere it began.

The next to follow was Keyes. He had said on the trial that his fortunes being desperate, his fate was "as good now as another time, and for this cause rather than another." In this hardened, reckless spirit, he flung himself from the ladder, with such force as to break the halter.

Last came "the great devil of all," Guy Fawkes, who, "being weak with torture and sickness, was scarce able to go up the ladder." He made no long speech, but "after a sort, seemed to be sorry" and asked forgiveness: and "with his crosses and his idle ceremonies" was cast off, dying instantaneously.

So ended the awful scenes which were the reward of the Gunpowder Plot.

But not yet had justice overtaken all the perpetrators of this villainy. Three important traitors were yet at large, and they were all Jesuit priests. Greenway, who had fled from Holbeach with Robert Winter, had not continued in his company. For ten days he hid in barns and cottages in Worcestershire; but when the proclamation was made for his arrest, thinking it safest to be lost in a crowd in the metropolis, he came to London. Here he was one day seized by a man, as they stood among others reading the proclamation for his arrest. Greenway, with artful composure, denied the identity, but went quietly with his captor till they reached an unfrequented street, when the priest, who was a very powerful man, suddenly set upon his companion, and escaping from him, after a few days' concealment fled to the coast, whence he safely crossed to the Continent. He

[1] To which the reporter adds, "otherwise a Papist, which God for His mercy ever forbid!"

afterwards wrote for his superiors a narrative of the plot, wherein all the conspirators are impeccable heroes of the romantic novel type, and the plot—which during its existence he upheld and fervently encouraged—is condemned as a "rash, desperate, and wicked" piece of business. He succeeded so well in deceiving his superiors (or else they were equally hypocritical with himself), that he was appointed Penitentiary to the Pope, and ended his life in the full favour of that potentate.

Gerard, also, who had originally assisted the plotters in taking their oath of secrecy, had now disappeared. So excellent an opinion had the Roman Catholics of him, that many refused to believe "that holy, good man" could have had any share in the conspiracy. The description of this worthy, as given in the proclamation for his arrest, is curious in its detail, and the better worth quoting since it has apparently not been printed :—

"John Gerrarde the Jesuit is about xxx[tie] years old, of a good stature, something higher than Sir Thomas Leighton [this name is crossed out, and replaced by the word] ordinary, and upright in his pace and countenance ; somewhat staring in his looke and Eyes, curled headed by Nature, and blackish, and not apt to have much hair on his beard. His Nose somewhat wide, and turning up ; blebberd lipped,[1] turning outward, especially the upper lip, upward toward the Nose. Curious in speech, if he do continue his custom, and in his speech he flewreth[2] and smiles much, and a faltering, lisping, or doubling of his tongue in his speech."[3]

What a picture of a Jesuit! This is the type of man

---

[1] Thick-lipped.

[2] To flewer or fleer is to smile in that grinning manner which shows all the teeth. Our forefathers considered it a mark of a sneering, envious man.

[3] Dom. State Papers, James I., vol. xviii. art. 20.

who practises an art which I never saw to such perfection as
once in the Principal of a Jesuit College—that of

> " Washing the hands with invisible soap
>   In imperceptible water."

Lastly, what had become of Garnet?   He had not escaped
nor left England, yet he seemed in some inscrutable manner
to have vanished from the face of the earth, as completely as
a morning mist.

The next step was to secure White Webbs.   Commis-
sioners were sent down to Enfield Chase, with directions to
search for that undiscoverable house, to make thorough investigation of it, and to take into custody every individual
therein.   They found the place—an old rambling house in
the heart of the Chase, full of trap-doors, passages, unexpected steps up or down, holes, corners, and cupboards at
every turn.   But it had no inhabitants save servants, and
they could tell little.   Their mistress was Mrs. Perkins, the
widowed sister of Mr. Mease, a Berkshire farmer.   It was
quite true they were Catholics, all allowed; and Elizabeth
Shepherd admitted that mass had been performed in the
house.   But what connection could there be between the
Gunpowder Plot and worthy Mr. Mease the farmer, or
innocent Mrs. Perkins the widow?

Many persons would have resigned the search: but not
so Sir William Wade.   Sir William Wade, the Keeper of
the Tower, had an uncommonly keen scent for a heretic
which term was in his eyes the equivalent of a Jesuit.   He
could see much further than any one else through a mill-
stone, and detected a Jesuit where no less acute person
suspected anything but a farmer or a horse-dealer.   Not
only was a Jesuit capable of every crime that man could
commit, but every criminal was pretty nearly certain to
turn out a Jesuit.   Moreover, Sir William loved a joke only
less than he hated a Jesuit; and apathy in any pursuit was

not one of his failings who wrote that "he thanked God on the knees of his soul" for the discovery of the Gunpowder Plot.

Mr. Mease was not to escape Sir William's penetration. He was anxious to see a little more of Mr. Mease, and of Mrs. Perkins also.

For the moment, however, he was doomed to disappointment. Sturdy James Johnson, Mrs. Perkins' servant, would not betray his employers, even when put to the rack, until he had suffered appallingly. Half-an-hour had been sufficient to exhaust Guy Fawkes' endurance, but James Johnson bore three hours. Even then he could tell little. For his mistress's brother he knew no name but Mease, except that he had heard him addressed as "Farmer:" but he did know, and had known for two years, that the real name of his mistress was Anne Vaux. He could also say that she had been visited by a Mr. and Mrs. Skinner, a Mr. and Mrs. Thomas Jennings, a Mr. Catesby, and a little gentleman whom the latter called Tom, and whose name he said was Winter. As to himself, Johnson asserted that he was "a Romishe Catholic," and "never was at church nor yet at mass in his life." Frightened little Jane Robinson, aged fourteen, admitted that mass had been said in the house, but when asked what vestments the priest wore, could only answer that "he was apparelled like a gentleman."

Sir William Wade went down once more upon the knees of his soul, when his ears were refreshed by these delightful names. At Harrowden, the seat of Lord Vaux, the family had already been questioned to no purpose. Mrs. Vaux, the mother of the young Lord, and the sister-in-law of Anne, was astonished that anybody should suspect her of a guilty knowledge of the plot. Having previously denied that she knew any such person as Gerard, she subsequently confessed that Gerard and Garnet had been frequently at her house, and that she had a vague suspicion that "something was going to happen." Harrowden must be further investigated; and admissions were wrung from the servants at White Webbs which satisfied the commission that the relations between Anne Vaux and Garnet had been of an intimate character. Sir William Wade was now on the track of a Jesuit, and might be trusted to pursue that enticing path with eager and untiring accuracy.

The watch set at Harrowden was removed just too soon. Had it lasted two days longer, Gerard would have been starved out, for he lay concealed in the priest's hiding-place. As soon as the watching party took their leave, he emerged from his refuge, and succeeded through multifarious difficulties in safely escaping over seas.

About this time—from what source is uncertain—a hint reached the Government to the effect that Gerard might possibly, and Hall would probably, be found in one of the priest's hiding-places at Hendlip Hall in Worcestershire, the residence of Mr. Thomas Abington. Edward Hall, alias Oldcorne,[1] was Mr. Abington's private chaplain; and though there is little evidence extant to connect him with the plot, the Government appear to have been extremely suspicious of him. When, therefore, the suggestion reached them that they might as well inspect the curiosities of Hendlip Hall, the authorities lost no time in sending down Sir Henry Bromley, of Holt Castle, at the head of a searching party, for that purpose.

Until 1825 or thereabouts, Hendlip Hall remained standing, on the highest ground in the neighbourhood between Droitwich and Worcester, and rather nearer to the latter. A most curious, cunningly-planned, perplexing house it was —a house of houses wherein to secrete a political refugee or a Jesuit priest—full of surprises, unexpected turnings,

---

[1] This most untruthful gentleman asserted that " his true name was Oldcorne ;" but Garnet and Anne Vaux both call him Hall in writing to each other.

sliding panels, and inconceivable closets without apparent entrances. "There is scarcely an apartment," wrote a spectator shortly before its destruction, "that has not secret ways of going in or going out; some have back staircases concealed in the walls; others have places of retreat in their chimneys; some have trap-doors, and all present a picture of gloom, insecurity, and suspicion." On one side was a high tower, from which the approach of any enemy could be easily observed. The house had been built in 1572, by John Abington, cofferer to Queen Elizabeth; but his son Thomas, the owner in 1605, had added the hiding-places. Such concealed chambers were very common in houses belonging to Roman Catholic families; and in the safest of all those at Hendlip Hall, two priests were at that moment in close confinement. The Government had been so far truly informed. Hall, too, was one of them: but Gerard was not the other. Sir William Wade would have danced in delight, could he have known that his colleagues were on the track of the great Provincial of the Jesuit Mission to this heathen country of England, the chief of all the conspirators yet left at large.

About two months before this, Garnet had come to the conclusion that he was no longer safe at Coughton, which, as the property of Mr. Throckmorton, and lately in the occupation of Sir Everard Digby, would be likely to obtain a thorough overhauling. From Mr. Hall he had received a pressing invitation to Hendlip for himself and his confidential servant, Nicholas Owen, who went by the name of "Little John." The latter was an old acquaintance at Hendlip, for it was his ingenuity that had devised the numerous hiding-places which had been added to the Hall by its present owner. To Hendlip accordingly Garnet removed from Coughton,— accompanied by Anne Vaux and the Brooksbys,—about the 16th of December, and for some weeks resided with the family without concealment. But on Monday, the 20th of January, as the day broke, Sir Henry Bromley and his troops marched up to and invested Hendlip Hall.

The Hon. Mrs. Abington was a sister of Lord Monteagle, and was quite as good an actress as her brother was an actor. She possessed the power of assuming the most complete outward composure, as if nothing whatever were the matter, however adversely things might be going to her wishes. She had also a very quiet, very firm, very unmanageable will. Mr. Abington was not at home; but that signified little, for the grey mare was unquestionably the superior creature of the pair.

. If the information imparted to her so early on that morning had been that the cat had mewed, or that a hen had dropped a feather, the lady of Hendlip could scarcely have received it with more repose of manner.

"That is what we might look for," said she. "If it please you, holy Fathers, it might be as well that you should repair to one of your chambers for a while.—Bid Edward come to me."

Edward, a white-headed confidential servant with an aspect of appalling respectability, presented himself at once in response to his mistress's summons.

"Edward," said Mrs. Abington, "I would have you, quickly, take up these holy Fathers to the hole in your chamber, and set Little John and Chambers in the next safest. There are enemies approaching."

Edward bowed his dignified head, and obeyed.

He led Garnet and Hall up the chief staircase, and into the bedroom occupied by Edward himself, which stood behind that of his master.

Garnet cast his eyes round the chamber.

"Truly, good Edward," said he, "I scarce see means to hide so much as a mouse in this chamber, other than in yonder closet, which is as plain as the door or the window."

Edward replied by an amused smile.

"You've a deal of book-learning, Father Garnet," said he, "but under your leave, there's a few things you don't know in this world."

He walked into the chimney-corner.

Chimneys, be it remembered, were much wider in the seventeenth century than they have been since the invention of grates. There was room in every chimney-corner, not only for the fire, but for one or two chairs and settles, where people could sit when they wished to warm themselves; and as there was no fire on Edward's hearth, moving about on it was as easy as in a closet.

"Are we to fly up the chimney on a pair of broomsticks?" laughed Hall.

Edward only smiled again, and after a moment's feeling with his hand among the bricks at the side of the chimney, they heard a sound as of the pushing back of bolts. Slowly, as if it moved with some difficulty, a square door opened in the chimney, so cleverly concealed that it required a skilful detective indeed to guess its existence. The door was of wood, "curiously covered over with brick, mortared and made fast" to it, "and coloured black like the other parts of the chimney, that very diligent inquiry might well have past by." Behind it was a very small square recess, large enough to hold the two, though not sufficiently high for them to stand upright. A narrow tunnel, in outward appearance like a chimney, led up to the top of the house, designed for the admission of light and air to the hiding-place, but capable of conveying no great quantity of either. Having fetched a short ladder, Edward placed it in position, so that the priests could climb up into the chamber.

"It had been more to your comfort, Fathers, could we have cast forth some of this furniture," he said, looking round it: "but it were scarce wise to defer the matter, the house being already invested."

"Let be, we will serve ourselves of it as it is, and well."

The priests mounted into the tiny hiding-place.

"See you, holy Fathers," Edward asked, "a vessel of tin, standing below a little hole in the wall? Have a care that you move it not without you first stop the hole, for it runneth through into my mistress's chamber, and by a quill or reed therein laid can she minister warm drinks unto you, as broths and caudle. She can likewise speak to you through the hole, and be heard: but if you hear the noise of feet or strange voices in that chamber, have a care to lie as squat[1] and close as ever you can. So may you safely hover;[2] for the cleverest soldier of them all shall be hard put to it to find you here, if it please God."

Would it please God? Did no memory come to either of those well-read priestly refugees of a familiar question—"Shall the throne of iniquity have fellowship with Thee?"

"A tight fit this, for two!" said Hall.

"Ay, it is. There hath not been above one here aforetime. But it is the safest hilling[3] in the house. Good-day, holy Fathers, and God keep you safe!"

While these scenes were enacting in one part of the house, in another Sir Henry Bromley was introducing himself to the lady of Hendlip Hall, and, with plumed hat in hand, apologising for his intrusion, and civilly requesting her permission to examine the house. A kindly, tender-hearted man was the commander of this searching party, but at the same time a conscientious one, and a determined Protestant.

If anything could be more considerate and cordial than Sir Henry's appeal, it was to all appearances the spirit wherein it was received. Mrs. Abington begged her visitor not to speak of intrusion. His Majesty the King had no

---

[1] Quiet.   [2] Lie concealed.   [3] Hiding-place.

subjects more loyal than every man and woman in that
house. It was really a source of pleasure to her that her
abode should be scrutinised in the most critical manner,
and her perfect innocence and submission to law thus made
manifest. The lady at once delivered her keys—she did
not say that a few of them were on a separate bunch—and
requested that no quarter might be given. Appearances
were so charming, and innocence apparently so clear, that
they might have deluded a more astute man than Sir
Henry Bromley.

Sir Henry, however, had come to do his duty, and he
did it in spite of appearances. Lord Salisbury had furnished him with minute instructions, which pointed decidedly to probable need of caution in this respect. He
was to search for a suspected vault at the east end of the
dining-room; for a similar erection beneath the cellars;
for ingenious closets squeezed in between the walls of upper
rooms; for possible holes in corners and chimneys, wainscots which could be pierced by gimlets, double lofts, and
concealed chambers in the rafters. Sir Henry set to work.

"Madam," said he to Mrs. Abington, "were it not more
to the conveniency of yourself and these gentlewomen your
friends, that you should take occasion to pay some visit
forth of the house? I fear the noise made by my men, not
to speak of the turning about of your chambers by taking
up of boards and trying of wainscots, shall greatly incommode you if you tarry."

Sir Henry wanted sadly to get the ladies away. But
Mrs. Abington was quite as sagacious as himself, and more
determined. She assured him that the noise was nothing,
and the little novelties of holes in her dining-room floor
and broken wainscots in her drawing-room would be rather
amusing than otherwise. Poor Sir Henry, baffled by this
clever woman, laments to Lord Salisbury,—"I did never
hear so impudent liars as I find here—all recusants, and all

resolved to confess nothing, what danger soever they incur. . . . I could by no means persuade the gentlewoman of the house to depart the house, without I should have carried her, which I held uncivil, as being so nobly born ; as I have and do undergo the greater difficulties thereby."

The Monday night brought home the master of the house. He answered the queries of the gentlemen in possession with as much apparent frankness as his wife, but assured Sir Henry that the persons for whom he was searching were absolute strangers to him ; he had never seen any of them save Gerard, and him only some five and twenty years before. For suspecting him of harbouring priests, not to speak of traitors, there was not a shadow of reason !

Sir Henry went on searching, though he was out of hope. In the first place, he discovered some parcels of " books and writing," which showed at that time that "some scholars " must have used them ; an ordinary country gentleman was not expected to have any books, except Bible and prayer-books, one or two on law, needed in his capacity as a magistrate, a book on etiquette, and a few dog's-eared plays. On the Wednesday a discovery of more importance was made, for in three or four places where boards were uplifted, a quantity of "Popish trash " was brought to light. Thus encouraged, the searchers resolved to continue their work, which they were on the point of giving up. Mr. Abington continued to protest his supreme innocence of all knowledge or connivance. The books were none of his ; the " Popish stuff " astonished him as much as it did the searchers. This assumption of exquisite stainlessness lasted until one day a hiding-place was discovered, which contained his family muniments and the title-deeds of his estate. After that, Mr. Abington protested no more ; and it was needless, for he would not have been believed had he done so. Sir Henry at once despatched him to Worcester to be taken care of by a magistrate; and "being much wearied," on Wednesday night returned to his own house to take rest, leaving his brother Sir Edward in charge.

On the Thursday morning, when he returned to Hendlip, he was met by two wan, gaunt men, whose countenances showed privation and suffering. They gave their names as William Andrews and George Chambers.

By some unexplained want of care or foresight, these two unfortunate men had been suffered to secrete themselves without provisions, and had nothing but one apple between them from Monday to Thursday.

Sir Henry was delighted, for at first he thought he had secured Greenway and Hall. A little further examination, however, showed him that his captives were only the priests' servants; yet he shrewdly surmised that the servants being there, the masters in all probability were not far away.

For four days more the search was pursued in vain: but on the 27th news came that not only was Hall certainly concealed in the house, but that the most important of all the implicated Jesuits, Garnet, would probably be found by a diligent continuance of the search. It came from an unexpected quarter—no other than Red Humphrey Littleton.

Justice had not been slow in overtaking the harbourers of Robert Winter and Stephen Littleton. White and his brothers had got clear away; but Smart, Hollyhead, Perks, and Burford, suffered the last penalty of the law. Margaret Perks was pardoned, though condemned to death. Humphrey Littleton received the torture; and when apparently at the point of death, entreated permission to confess important facts, which he promised to do if his life might be spared. His appeal was granted, and he then told the authorities that the most important criminal still at large would be found in the priest's hiding-place at Hendlip Hall.

Fortified by this encouraging news, though the prisoners already taken denied all knowledge of any others being hidden in the house, Sir Henry pushed on his search; and at last, on the 28th, eight days after his arrival, one of his men broke into the cunningly contrived hiding-place in the chimney of Edward's room. This brave discoverer was so terrified by his own success that he ran away lest the priests should shoot him; but others coming rapidly to his assistance, the priests offered to come out if they might do so with quietude. "So they helped us out," says Garnet, "very charitably."

Garnet's account of their experiences in "the hoale," as he terms it, is not suggestive of an inviting place. "We were in the hoale seven days and seven nights and some hours, and were well wearied;" the place was so encumbered with books and furniture that they "could not find place for their legs" even when seated; and the cramped positions which they were compelled to assume caused their legs to swell greatly. Garnet seems to have suffered more of the two. Yet he adds that they were "very merry and content," and could have stayed three months, though when they came out at last, "we appeared like two ghosts."

Sir Henry Bromley at once recognised the Provincial of the Jesuit Mission; but which of his various aliases really belonged to him puzzled his captor not a little, and Garnet declined to enlighten him.

"Call me as you will," said he; "I refer all to my meeting with my Lord of Salisbury, and he will know me. In truth, I say not thus for any discourtesy, but that I will not, in the places we are, be made an obloquy: but when I come to London, I will not be ashamed of my name."

Sir Henry now marshalled his prisoners for transport to Worcester. He described them to the authorities as "Humphrey Phillips alias Henry Garnet; John Vincent

alias Hall; Thomas Abington, Esq.; William Androwes
alias Nicholas Owen, either a priest or servant to Garnet;
George Chambers, servant of Hall; Edward Jarrett, servant
of Mrs. Dorathie Abington; William Glandishe, servant of
Mr. Abington."[1] Mr. Abington and the priests were taken
to Worcester in Sir Henry's coach. The mind of that
gentleman was somewhat exercised as to what he was to
do with them when he got them there. Before leaving
Hendlip he had promised to place them in the house of some
bailiff or citizen; but as they were driving into Worcester,
he said uneasily—

"My masters, I cannot do for you as I would; I must
needs send you to the gaol."

"In God's name!"[2] responded Garnet. "But I hope you
will provide we have not irons, for we are lame already, and
shall not be able to ride after, to London."

Sir Henry's tender heart was touched at once.

"Well," said he, "I will think of it."

He thought of it to such purpose, that when they reached
the inn, he placed Garnet in a private room, with a guard
—his Reverence says, "to avoid the people's gazing;" Sir
Henry would probably have added that it was also in order
to prevent the prisoner's disappearance. After despatching
his business he ordered his coach, and took his prisoners
home with him to Holt Castle. Here, on their own testimony, they were "exceeding well used, and dined and
supped with him and his every day,"—not without some
apprehension on the part of their kindly gaoler that they
might reward him by perverting his young daughters from
the Protestant faith.

[1] Dom. State Papers, Jac. I., vol. xviii., art. 64. Mrs. Dorathie Abington
was Mr. Abington's maiden sister, who lived at Hendlip Hall, and had a
priest of her own, a Jesuit, named Butler or Lyster. He does not appear
in this narrative, and was very likely absent.

[2] This was not meant profanely, but was simply equivalent to saying,
"God's will be done!"

When Candlemas Day came, Sir Henry "made a great dinner to end Christmas," and sent for wine to drink the King's health. It was then customary for gentlemen always to dine with their hats on, and to uncover when a royal toast was proposed. The hats were doffed accordingly. The wine came in, and with it a wax candle, lighted—a blessed candle taken at Hendlip, among the "Popish trash," and destined. for use on the services of that very day, having "Jesus" painted on one side of it, and "Maria" on the other. Garnet's heart leaped at the familiar sight, and he begged leave to take the candle in his hand. Passing it to Mr. Hall, he said, half joyfully, half sadly,—

"I am glad yet, that I have carried a holy candle on Candlemas Day."

Restoring the holy wax to the unholy candlestick, the priests drank the King's health in what Mr. Garnet is kind enough to tell us was "a reasonable glass"—a piece of information the more valuable, since this adjective was not always applicable to his Reverence's glasses.

When they came to leave Worcester, the parting between Garnet and the ladies was almost affectionate. The priest was evidently possessed of that strong personal magnetism which some men and women have, and which is oftener exercised for the purposes of Satan than in the service of God.

"Madam," he said to Lady Bromley, "I desire you all to think well of me till you see whether I can justify myself in this cause."

The journey to London took longer than would otherwise have been needed, on account of the condition of the prisoners. Garnet, whose sufferings had been the more severe, was also the one in whom their results lasted longest ; and on the 5th of February, Sir Henry wrote that he was "but a weak and wearisome traveller." He was, however, " passing well used at the King's charge, and that by express orders from my Lord Salisbury," and "had always the best horse in the company." Garnet adds, "I had some bickering with ministers by the way. Two very good scholars, and courteous, Mr. Abbott and Mr. Barlow, met us at an inn; but two other rude fellows met us on the way, whose discourtesy I rewarded with plain words, and so adieu." The Jesuit Superior apparently rather enjoyed a little brisk brushing of wits with well-educated gentlemanly clerics, but felt some disgust of abuse which passed for argument with others. On the evening of the 6th of February they reached London, where they were lodged in the Gate-house, and Garnet was "very sick the first two nights with ill lodging." It was not until the 13th that the first examination took place before the Privy Council at Whitehall.

CHAPTER XI.

ACCORDING TO THAT BEGINNING.

"Carry him forth and bury him.   Death's peace
Rest on his memory !   Mercy by his bier
Sits silent, or says only these few words—
Let him who is without sin 'mongst ye all
Cast the first stone."

—DINAH MULOCK.

GREAT crowd had assembled near Whitehall, and was lining Charing Cross and the Tilt-yard below, on the morning of that 13th of February, when Sir Henry Bromley and his guard, with the prisoners in their midst, marched down the street to the Palace.   Among them were Temperance Murthwaite and Rachel, and near them was Mrs. Abbott.   The crowd was deeply interested in the prisoners, especially the two priests.

"There is a Provincial!" said a respectable-looking man who stood next to Rachel.

"Ay, and there goeth a young Pope!" returned Temperance, grimly, in allusion to Hall.

"They bear a good brag, most of 'em," said the man.

"Would we were rid of 'em all, neck and crop!" said another.

"Pack 'em off to the American plantations!" suggested a third.

"If I dwelt there, I shouldn't give you thanks," replied the first.

"Find some land where nought dwelleth save baboons and snakes, and send 'em all there in a lump," was the response.

"What think you, Rachel?" demanded Mrs. Abbott, who was not often silent for so long at once.

"Why, they're men, just like other folks!" was Rachel's contribution.

"Did you think they'd have horns and tails?" said Temperance.

"Well, nay, not justly that," answered Rachel: "but I reckoned they'd ha' looked a bit more like wastrels.[1] Yon lad's none so bad-looking as many a man you may meet i' th' street. And th' owd un's meterly,[2] too. Happen[3] they aren't any o' the worst."

"Why, maid," said the man who had first spoken, "that's Father Garnet, the head of all the Jesuits in this country; there isn't a craftier fox in all England than he."

"Well, I shouldn't ha' thought it," saith Rachel.

"Faces tell not alway truth," said Temperance.

"He's good eyes, though," remarked Mrs. Abbott, "though they be a bit heavy, as though he'd had a poor night's rest."

"He's one o' them long, narrow faces," said the man; "I never trust such. And a long nose, too—just like a fox."

"Ay, I'll be bound he's a fause[4] un," commented Rachel.

"His mouth's the worst thing about him," said Temperance.

"It's a little un," observed Rachel.

"Little or big, it's a false one," answered Temperance. "There's a prim, fixed, sanctimonious look about it that I wouldn't trust with anything I cared to see safe."

---

[1] Scoundrels.　　[2] Middling.　　[3] Perhaps.　　[4] Cunning.

"Eh, I'd none trust one o' them—not *to* sell a pound o' butter," said Rachel. "And by th' same token, Mrs. Temperance, I mun be home to skim th' cream, or Charity'll take it off like a gaumless [1] lass as hoo [2] is. Hoo can do some things, well enough, but hoo cannot skim cream!"

"Go, good maid, if thou canst win out of this crowd, but methinks thou shalt have thy work cut out to do so."

"Eh, she will," said Mrs. Abbott. "And mind you, Rachel! if you pull yourself forth, you'll find your gown in rags by the time you're at home. I do hope, neighbour, you deal not with Simpkinson, in the Strand; that rogue sold me ten ells of green stamyn, and charged me thirty shillings the ell, and I vow it was scarce made up ere it began a-coming to bits. I'll give it him when I can catch him! and if I serve not our Seth out for dinting in the black jack last night, I'm a Dutch woman, and no mistake! Black jacks are half-a-crown a-piece, and so I told him; but I'll give him a bit more afore I've done with him; trust me. There is no keeping lads in order. The mischievousness of 'em's past count. My husband, he says, 'Lads will be lads,'—he's that easy, if a mouse ran away with his supper from under his nose, he'd only call after it, 'Much good may it do thee.' Do you ever hear mice in your house, Mrs. Murthwaite? I'm for ever and the day after plagued wi' them, and I do wish those lads 'ud make theirselves a bit useful and catch 'em, instead o' dinting in black jacks. But, dear heart, you'll as soon catch the mice as catch them at aught that's useful. They'll——"

"My mistress," said Mrs. Abbott's next neighbour, "may I ask if your husband be a very silent man?"

"I'm sure o' that," said the man who followed him.

"Eh, bless you, they all talk and chatter at our house while I can't slip a word in," was the lady's answer.

[1] Stupid.   [2] She.

"That's why she has so many to let go out o' door," remarked the last speaker.

"I thought so," observed the neighbour, "because I have marked that men and women do mostly wed with their contraries."

"Why, what mean you?" inquired Mrs. Abbott, turning round to look him in the face.

"That my way lieth down this by-street," said he, working himself out of the crush into Channon Row, "and so I bid you all good-morrow."

Temperance Murthwaite laughed to herself, as she let herself in at the door of the White Bear, while Mrs. Abbott hurried into the Angel with a box on the ear to Dorcas and Hester, who leaned upon the gate watching the crowd.

"Get you in to your business!" said she. "Chatter, chatter, chatter! One might as well live in a cage o' magpies at once, and ha' done with it. Be off with the pair of ye!"

Garnet's admissions in answer to the questions put to him were few and cautious. He allowed that for twenty years he had been the Superior of the English Jesuits, but denied any knowledge of the negotiations with Spain, carried on before the death of Queen Elizabeth. As to Fawkes, he had never seen him but once in his life, at the previous Easter. Questioned about White Webbs, he flatly denied that he ever was there, or anywhere near Enfield Chase "since Bartholomewtide." He was not in London or the suburbs in November. The Attorney-General was very kind to the prisoner, and promised "to make the best construction that he could" of his answers to the King; but Sir William Wade was not the man to accept the word of a Jesuit, unless it should be the word "Guilty." He accused Garnet of wholesale violation of the Decalogue in the plainest English, and coolly told him that he could not believe him on his oath, since the Pope could absolve him for any extent of lying or equivocation. It was plainly no easy matter to beguile Sir William Wade.

The next day, February 14th, Garnet and Hall were removed to the Tower of London, where the former found himself, to his satisfaction, lodged in " a very fine chamber," next to that of his brother priest. Here, as he records in a letter to his friends, he received the best treatment, being *"allowed every meal a good draught of excellent claret wine,"* as well as permitted to send for additional sack out of his own purse for himself and the keeper: and he was suffered to vegetate as he thought proper, with only one sorrow to vex his soul—Sir William Wade.

Sir William Wade, the Lieutenant of the Tower, constituted himself the torment of poor Garnet's life. He was perpetually passing through his room, or at the furthest, loitering in the gallery beyond. Sometimes he treated the prisoner as beneath contempt, and would not utter a word to him; at other times he sat down and regaled him with conversation of a free and easy character. The scornful silence was bad enough, but the conversation was considerably worse. Whatever else Garnet was, he was an English gentleman, as his letters testify; and Sir William Wade was not. He was, on the contrary, one of those distressing people who pride themselves on being outspoken, and calling a spade a spade, which they do in the most vulgar and disagreeable manner. He favoured the prisoner with his unvarnished opinion of the Society to which he belonged, and with unsavoury anecdotes of its members, mingled with the bitterest abuse: and the worthy knight was not the man to spare his adjectives when a sufficient seasoning of them would add zest to a dish of nouns. At other times Sir William dipped his tongue in honey, and used the sweetest language imaginable. It is manifest from the manner in which Garnet mentions him, that the smallest of his trials was not Sir William Wade.

Mr. Garnet's first act, on being inducted into these comfortable quarters in his Majesty's Tower, was to bribe his keeper to wink at his peccadilloes. A few cups of that supernumerary sack, and an occasional piece of silver, were worth expending on the safe carriage of his letters and other necessities which might in time arise. He made affectionate inquiries as to the keeper's domestic relations, and discovered that he was blessed with a wife and a mother. To the wife he despatched a little of that excellent sack, and secured permission for his letters to be placed in the custody of the mother, who dwelt just outside the walls. But he was especially rejoiced when, a few days after his incarceration, the keeper sidled up to him, with a finger on his lips and a wink in his eye, and beckoned him to a particular part of the room, where with great parade of care and silence he showed him a concealed door between his own cell and that of Hall, intimating by signs that secret communications might be held after this fashion, and he, the keeper, would take care to be conveniently blind and deaf.

This was a comfort indeed, for the imprisoned priests could now mutually forgive each others' sins. There was a little cranny in the top of the door, which might be utilised for a mere occasional whisper; but when a regular confession was to be made, the door of communication could be opened for an inch or two. The one drawback was that the vexatious door insisted on creaking, as if it were a Protestant door desirous of giving warning of Popish practices. But the Jesuits were equal to the difficulty. When the door was to be shut, the unemployed one either fell to shovelling coals upon the fire, or was suddenly seized with a severe bronchial cough, so that the ominous creak should not be heard outside. The comfort, therefore, remained; and heartily glad were the imprisoned Jesuits to have found this means of communication by the kind help of their tender-hearted keeper.

Alas, poor Jesuits! They little knew that they were caught in their own trap. The treacherous keeper drank their sack, and pocketed their angels, but their letters rarely went further than my Lord of Salisbury's desk; and in a convenient closet unseen by them, close to the creaking door, Mr. Forset, a Justice of the Peace, and Mr. Locherson, Lord Salisbury's secretary, were listening with all their ears to their confidential whispers, and taking thereby bad " coulds " which they subsequently had to go home and nurse. It was fox *versus* fox. As soon as the door was closed under cover of cough or coals, the hidden spies came quickly forth, and in another chamber wrote down the conversation just passed for the benefit of his Majesty's Judges.

Benighted Protestants were evidently Messrs. Forset and Locherson, for the " Catholic practice " of auricular confession was to them a strange and perplexing matter. They innocently record that " the confession was short, with a prayer in Latin before they did confess to each other, and beating their hands on their breasts." The Confiteor was succeeded by the whispered confession, in such low tones that scarcely anything reached the disappointed spies. Hall made his confession first, and Garnet followed. The subsequent conversation was in louder tones, though still whispered. Garnet informed his fellow-conspirator that he was suspicious of the good faith of some one whose name the spies failed to hear—to which frailty he allowed that he was very subject; that he had received a note from Thomas Rookwood, who told him of Greenway's escape, and from Gerard, who therefore was evidently in safety, though "he had been put to great plunges ; " that he believed Mrs. Anne was in the Town, and would let them hear from their friends ; that the keeper had accepted an angel, and sundry cups of sack for himself and his wife, and taken them very kindly,—recommending similar treatment on Hall's part ;

that Garnet was very much afraid he should be driven to confess White Webbs, but if so, he would say that he " was there, but knew nothing of the matter." Then Hall made a remark lost by the spies, to which Garnet answered, with a profane invocation—too common in all ranks at that day— "How did they know that!" If he were pressed as to his treasonable practices before the Queen's death, he would admit them, seeing that he held a general pardon up to that time. Garnet bemoaned himself concerning Sir William Wade, and expressed his annoyance at the persistent questioning of the Court touching White Webbs.

"I think it not convenient," said he, "to deny that we were at White Webbs, they do so much insist upon that place. Since I came out of Essex I was there two times, and so I may say I was there; but they press me to be there in October last, which I will by no means confess, but I shall tell them I was not there since Bartholomew-tide."

He expressed his apprehension lest the servants at White Webbs should be examined and tortured, which might "make them yield to some confession;" a fear which made him more resolute to admit nothing concerning the place. He was also very much afraid of being asked about certain letters which Lord Monteagle had written.

"But in truth I am well persuaded," he concluded, "that I shall wind myself out of that matter; and for any former business, I care not."

Just as Garnet whispered these words, footsteps were heard approaching the chamber.

"Hark you, hark you, Mr. Hall!" cried Garnet in haste; "whilst I shut the door, make a hawking and a spitting."

Mr. Hall obediently and energetically cleared his throat, under cover of which Garnet closed the door, and presented himself the next moment to the edified eyes of Sir William Wade in the pious aspect of a priest telling his beads.

Another conference through the door was held on the 25th of February, wherein Garnet was heard to lament to Hall that he "held not better concurrence"—namely, that he did not use diligence to tell exactly the arranged falsehoods on which the two had previously agreed. The poor spies found themselves in difficulties on this occasion through "a cock crowing under the window of the room, and the cackling of a hen at the very same instant." Hall, however, was heard to undertake a better adherence to his lesson. It is more than once noted by the spies that in these conferences the prisoners "used not one word of godliness or religion, or recommending themselves or their cause to God; but all hath been how to contrive safe answers."

During Garnet's imprisonment in the Tower, if his gaolers may be trusted, his consumption of that extra sack was not regulated by the rules of the Blue Ribbon Army. They averred that he was "indulgent to himself" in this particular, and "daily drank sack so liberally as if he meant to drown sorrow."

On the 26th, Garnet knew that one of his apprehensions was verified, when he was confronted with poor James Johnson, who had borne the torture so bravely, and who now admitted that the prisoner thus shown to him was the man whom he had known at White Webbs as Mr. Mease, the supposed brother of his mistress, Mrs. Perkins. He confessed that he had seen him many times. After this, it was useless to deny White Webbs any longer. Hall was examined on the same day; but being ignorant of the evidence given by Johnson, he audaciously affirmed that he had not visited White Webbs, and knew of no such place.

That evening, Garnet gave a shilling to his keeper, with a request to have some oranges brought to him. This fruit, first introduced into England about 1568, was at that time very cheap and plentiful, about eighteen-pence the hundred

being the usual price. Sir William Wade, lounging about
the gallery as usual, met the keeper as he came out of the
cell with the money in his hand.

"What would the old fox now?" demanded he.

"An 't please you, Sir, Mr. Garnet asked for oranges."

"Oh, come! he may have an orange or two—he can't do
any harm with them without he choke himself, and that
should spare the King the cost of a rope to hang him," said
shrewd Sir William.

But he was not quite shrewd enough, for it never occurred
to his non-Jesuitical mind that one of those innocent oranges
was destined to play the part of a traitorous inkstand by the
Rev. Henry Garnet.

A large sheet of paper, folded letter-wise, came out of the
prison in the keeper's hand an hour later. It was addressed
to the Rev. Thomas Rookwood, and contained only—in appearance—the following very unobjectionable words. They
were written in ink, at the top of the first page:—

"Let these spectacles be set in leather, and with a leather
case, or let the fould be fitter for the nose.—Yours for ever,
"HENRY GARNETT."

Who could think of detaining so innocent a missive, or
prevent the poor prisoner from obtaining a pair of comfortable spectacles? But when the sheet of paper was held to
the fire, a very different letter started out, in faint tracings
of orange juice:—

"This bearer knoweth that I write thus, but thinks it
must be read with water. The papers sent with bisket-
bread I was forced to burn, and did not read. I am sorry
they have, without advise of freinds, adventured in so wicked
an action. . . . I must needs acknowledge my being with

---

[1] Gunpowder Plot Book, art. 241.

the two sisters, and that at White Webbs, as is trew, for they are so jealous of White Webbs that I can no way else satisfy. My names I all confesse but that last. . . . I have acknowledged that I went from Sir Everard's to Coughton. . . . Where is Mrs. Anne?"

A few days later, on the 2nd of March, after a careful reconnoitre to avoid the ubiquitous Sir William, Garnet applied his lips to the cranny in the door.

"Hark you! is all well? Let us go to confession first, if you will."

The spies, ensconced in secret, confess that they heard nothing of Hall's confession, but that Garnet several times interrupted it with "Well, well!"

Garnet then made his own confession, "very much more softlier than he used to whisper in their interloqucions." It was short, but unless the spy was mistaken, "he confessed that he had drunk so extraordinarily that he was forced to go two nights to bed betimes." Then something was said concerning Jesuits, to which Garnet added,—

"That cannot be; I am Chancellor. It might proceed of the malice of the priests."

The conversation on this occasion was brought to a hasty close by Garnet's departure to read or write a letter; Mr. Hall being requested to "make a noise with the shovel" while he was shutting the door.

The second letter to Mr. Thomas Rookwood followed this interview. It was equally short in its ostensible length, and piously acknowledged the receipt of two bands, two hand-kerchiefs, one pair of socks, and a Bible. Beneath came the important postscript.

"Your last letter I could not read; the pen did not cast incke. Mr. Catesby did me much wrong, and hath con-fessed that he asked me the question in Queen Elizabeth's time of the powder action, and I said it was lawfull: all

which is most untrew. He did it to draw in others. I
see no advantage they have against me for the powder
action." [1]

Garnet added that his friend might communicate with him
through letters left in charge of the keeper's mother; but
he begged him not to pay a personal visit unless he could
first make sure that the redoubtable Wade was absent.

An answer from the Rev. Thomas consisted, to all appearance, of a simple sheet of writing-paper, enclosing a pair of
spectacles in their case, and bearing the few words written
outside—" I pray you prove whether the spectacles do fit
your sight." Inside, in orange juice, was the real communication, from Anne Vaux, wherein she promised to
come to the garden, and begged Garnet to appoint a time
when she might hope to see him.[2] This seems to show
that Garnet was sometimes allowed the liberty of the Tower
garden.

On the 5th of March, Hall and Garnet were re-examined,
when Hall confessed the truth of the conversations through
the door, and Garnet denied them. The same day, the
latter wrote a long letter, addressed to Mrs. Anne Vaux or
any of his friends, giving a full account of his sufferings
while in "the hoale" at Hendlip Hall, and of his present
condition in the Tower. Remarking that he was permitted
to purchase sherry out of his own purse, Garnet adds,—

"This is the greatest charge I shall be at, for fire will
soon be unnecessary, if I live so long, whereof I am very
uncertain, and as careless. . . . They say I was at White
Webbs with the conspirators; I said, if I was ever there
after the 1st of September, I was guilty of the powder
action. The time of my going to Coughton is a great pre-
sumption, but all Catholics know it was necessary. I thank
God, I am and have been *intrepidus*, wherein I marvail at

myself, having had such apprehension before; but it is
God's grace."

On the third examination, which was on the 6th of
March, both Garnet and Hall confessed White Webbs at
last,—the former, that he had hired the house for the meetings of the conspirators, the latter that they had met there
twice in the year. Garnet also allowed that Perkins was
the alias of the Hon. Anne Vaux, to avoid whose indictment he afterwards said his confession had been made. It
is evident, from several allusions in his letters, that Garnet
was terribly afraid of torture, and almost equally averse to
confronting witnesses. The first was merely human nature;
the second speaks ill for his consciousness of that innocence
which he repeatedly asserts.

But not yet had the Gunpowder Plot secured its latest or
its saddest victim. Soon after Sir Henry Bromley's departure from Hendlip, Mrs. Abington came to London, bringing Anne Vaux with her, and they took lodgings in Fetter
Lane, then a more aristocratic locality than now. Here
they remained for a few weeks, doing all that could be done
to help Garnet, and poor Anne continually haunting the
neighbourhood of his prison, and trying to catch glimpses
of him, if not to obtain stolen interviews, at the garden
gate. But on the 10th of March the authorities interfered,
and Anne Vaux was a prisoner of the Tower. Examined
on the following day, she deposed that she "kept the house
at White Webbs at her own charge;" that she was visited
there by Catesby, Thomas Winter, Tresham, and others,
but said that she could not remember dates nor further
names. She refused to admit that Garnet had been there,
but she allowed that she had been among the party of
pilgrims to St. Winifred's Well, in company with Lady
Digby and others whom she declined to name. Lastly, she
persisted in saying that she had known nothing of the plot.

She was told—not improbably by Sir William Wade, and if so, we may be sure, not very tenderly—that Garnet had been one of the chief criminals. A few sorrowful lines remain showing the spirit in which she heard it. They were written on the 12th of March.

"I am most sore to here that Father Garnet shoulde be ane wease pryue to this most wicked actione, as himselfe euer cauled it, for that hee made to mee maney greate prostertations to the contrari diuerstimes sence.

"ANNE VAUX."[1]

After this, Garnet gave up the fiction of his total ignorance of the conspirators' object. In his fourth examination, on the 13th of March, he said that on the demise of Queen Elizabeth, he had received a letter from the General of the Jesuits, stating that the new Pope Clement had confirmed the order of his predecessor that no such plot should be set on foot, and that Garnet had accordingly done what in him lay to turn Catesby from the idea. Catesby, however, thought himself authorised by two briefs received by Garnet about twelve months earlier, commanding the Roman Catholics of England not to consent to any successor of Elizabeth who should refuse to submit to Rome. These Garnet had shown to Catesby before destroying them. It is evident from these admissions, not only that Garnet had been privy to the plot from the first, but also that it was known at Rome, and controlled from the Vatican—forbidden when success appeared unlikely, and smiled on as soon as it seemed probable.

Shortly after this, a letter came from Anne Vaux—a letter which sadly reveals the character of its writer, and shows how different life might have been for this poor passionate-hearted woman, had she not been crushed under the iron heel of Rome.

---

[1] Gunpowder Plot Book, art. 201.

"To live without you," she writes to Garnet, "it is not life, but death! Now I see my los. I am and euer will be yours, and so I humbly beseche you to account me. O that I might see you!"

Her second examination took place a few days later, on the 24th of March. She now acknowledged that Tresham Catesby, and Garnet, used to meet at her house at Wandsworth: and that Garnet was wont to say to them, when they were engaged in discussion,—"Good gentlemen, be quiet; God will do all for the best; and we must get it by prayer at God's hands, in whose hands are the hearts of princes." The confession was carried to Garnet. Poor frail, loving heart! she meant to save him, and he knew it. He wrote calmly underneath,—

"I do acknowledge these meetings.—H. GARNETT."[1]

Even her very gaolers dealt pitifully with Anne Vaux. "This gentlewoman," said Lord Salisbury to Garnet, "hath harboured you these twelve years last past, and seems to speak for you in her confessions; I think she would sacrifice herself for you to do you good, and you likewise for her."

Garnet made no answer.

Letters continued to pass between the cells. A remarkable one was sent to Anne on the 2nd of April, written principally in orange-juice, on the question which she had submitted to Garnet as to her living abroad after her release.

"Concerning the disposal of yourself, I give you leave to go over to them. The vow of obedience ceaseth, being made to the Superior of this Mission: you may, upon deliberation, make it to some there. If you like to stay here, then I exempt you, till a Superior be appointed,

[1] Gunpowder Plot Book, art 212.

whom you may acquaint: but tell him that you made your vow yourself, and then told me; and that I limited certain conditions, as that *you are not bound to sin* [1] *except you be commanded in virtute obedientiæ.* We may accept no vows, but men may make them as they list, and we after give directions accordingly. Mr. Hall dreamed that the General . . . provided two fair tabernacles or seats for us: and this he dreamed twice." [2]

The sentence in italics is terrible. No Protestant ever penned a darker indictment against Popery.

Anne Vaux received this letter, for she answered it at once. She speaks of her " vow of poverty," and adds,—

" Mr. Haule his dreame had been a great cumfert, if at the fute of the throne there had bin a place for me. God and you know my unworthenes.—Yours and not my own,

" ANNE VAUX." [3]

On the following day, Garnet wrote again—eight closely covered pages, in his own hand throughout. I append a few extracts from this pathetic letter.

" MY VERY LOVING AND MOST DEAR SISTER,—I will say what I think it best for you to do, when it please God to set you at liberty. If you can stay in England, and enjoy the use of the Sacraments as heretofore, it would be best: and then I wish that you and your sister live as before in a house of common repair of the Society, or where the Superior of the Mission shall ordinarily remain : or if this cannot be, then make choice of some one of the Society, as you shall like, which I am sure will be granted you. If you like to go over, stay at St. Omer, and send for

---

[1] This word is plainly *sin*, though Mr. Lemon in his copy tried to read it *him*—an interpretation which he was obliged to abandon.

[2] Gunpowder Plot Book, art. 245.

[3] Ibid., art. 246.

Friar Baldwin, with whom consult where to live : but I think St. Omer less healthy than Brussels. In respect of your weakness, I think it better for you to live abroad, and not in a monastery. Your vow of obedience, being made to the Superior of the Mission here, when you are over, ceaseth : and then may you consult how to make it again. None of the Society can accept a vow of obedience of any; but any one may vow as he will, and then one of the Society may direct accordingly."

Garnet proceeds to say that the vow of poverty was to cease in like manner, and might be similarly renewed. " All that which is for annuities " he had always meant to be hers, in the hope that she would afterwards leave it to the Jesuit Mission : but she is at liberty, if she wish it, to alienate a third of this, or if she should desire at any time to " retire into religion "—*i.e.*, to become a nun—and require a portion, she is to help herself freely. He " thanks God most humbly that in all his speeches and practices he has had a desire to do nothing against the glory of God." He was so much annoyed by having been misunderstood by the two spies that he " thought it would make our actions much more excusable to tell the truth, than to stand to the torture, or trial by witnesses." As to his acquaintance with the plot, he sought to hinder it more than men can imagine, as the Pope can tell : how could he have dissuaded the conspirators if he had absolutely known nothing? But he thought it not allowable to tell what he knew. None of them ever told him anything, though they used his name freely—he implies, more freely than truth justified them in doing : " yet have I hurt nobody." He ordered the removal of certain books which he does not further describe ; if they be found, " you can challenge them as your own, as in truth they are." He will " die not as a victorious martyr, but as a penitent thief :" but " let God

work His will." The most touching words are the last.
Up to this point, the spiritual director has been addressing
his subject. Now the priest disappears, and the man's
heart breaks out.

"Howsoever I shall die a thief, yet you may assure yourself your innocence is such, that but if you die by reason
of your imprisonment, you shall die a martyr.[1] 'The
time is come that judgment must begin at the house of
God.' Farewell, my ever beloved in Christ, and pray for
me." [2]

Yet a few words were to be written before the end. The
execution of Hall, which took place at Worcester on the
7th of April, unnerved Garnet as nothing else had done.
He wrote, a fortnight later, to her who was his last and
had always been his truest friend—a few hurried, incoherent words, which betray the troubled state of his
mind.

"It pleaseth God daily to multiply my crosses. I beseech Him give me patience and perseverance to the end.
I was, after a week's hiding, taken in a friend's house, where
our confessions and secret conferences were heard, and my
letters taken by some indiscretion abroad;—then the taking
of yourself;—after, my arraignment;—then the taking of
Mr. Greenwell;—then the slander of us both abroad;—then
the ransacking anew of Erith and the other house;—then
the execution of Mr. Hall;—and now, last of all, the apprehension of Richard and Robert: with a cipher, I know not
of whose, laid to my charge, and that which was a singular
oversight, a letter in cipher, together with the ciphers—
which letter may bring many into question.
"'The patience of Job ye have heard, and have seen the

---

[1] From this point the letter is in Latin.
[2] Dom. State Pap., Jac. I., vol. xx., art. 11.

end of the Lord,—that the Lord is very pitiful, and of tender mercy.' Blessed be the name of the Lord![1]—Yours, eternally, as I hope,　　　　　　　　　　　H. G."

"21*st Apr.*—I thought verily my chamber in Thames Street had been given over, and therefore I used it to save Erith; but I might have done otherwise."

At the end of the letter is a symbolic sketch. The mystic letters I. H. S., within a circle, are surmounted by a cross, and beneath them is a heart pierced by three nails. Underneath is written, in Latin—"God is [the strength] of my heart, and God is my portion for ever."[1]

So end the last words which passed between the unhappy pair.

In his sixth examination, four days later, Garnet admitted that as often as he and Greenway had met, he had asked concerning the plot, "being careful of the matter;" and that "in general" he had inquired who was to be chosen protector after the explosion; Greenway having answered that this "was to be deferred until the blow was passed, and then the protector to be chosen out of the noblemen that should be saved." This completely settles the question as to Garnet's guilty knowledge of the plot before he received Digby's letter. Greenway is here shown to be Garnet's informant; whereas the letter was addressed to Garnet himself, and the occasion on which he received it was the last time that he ever saw Greenway!

A few days before his execution, the prisoner received a visit from three Deans, who essayed to converse with him upon various points of doctrine. Garnet, however, declined any discussion, on the ground that "it was unlawful for him." He was asked whether he thought that he should die a martyr.

[1] These quotations are in Latin.

"I a martyr!" exclaimed Garnet, with a deep sigh.
"Oh, what a martyr should I be! God forbid! If, indeed,
I were really about to suffer death for the sake of the
Catholic religion, and if I had never known of this project
except by the means of sacramental confession, I might perhaps be accounted worthy of the honour of martyrdom, and
might deservedly be glorified in the opinion of the Church.
As it is, I acknowledge myself to have sinned in this respect,
and deny not the justice of the sentence passed upon me."
Then, after a moment's pause, he added with apparent
earnestness, "Would to God that I could recall that which
has been done! Would to God that anything had happened
rather than that this stain of treason should hang upon my
name! I know that my offence is most grievous, though
I have confidence in Christ to pardon me on my hearty
penitence: but I would give the whole world, if I possessed
it, to be able to die without the weight of this sin upon my
soul."

The 1st of May had been originally fixed for the execution, but it was delayed until the 3rd. To the last moment
when he received notice of it, which was on the 29th of
April, Garnet fully expected a reprieve. He "could hardly
be persuaded to believe" in approaching death. Yet even
then, on the very night before his execution—if we may
believe the testimony of his keepers—he drank so copiously
that the gaoler thought it necessary to inform the Lieutenant, who came to see for himself, and was invited, in
thick and incoherent accents, to join Garnet in his potations.
Sir William Wade was not the man to allow such a fact
to rest in silence; and Garnet is neither the first nor the
last whose words have been better than his actions.

On the 3rd of May, he was drawn on a hurdle to the
west end of St. Paul's Churchyard, where the first conspirators had suffered, and where the scaffold was again set up.
His conduct on the scaffold was certainly not that of a

martyr, nor that of a penitent thief : the impenitent thief appeared rather to be his model. Advised by the attendant Deans of St. Paul's and Winchester to " prepare and settle himself for another world, and to commence his reconciliation with God by a sincere and saving repentance," Garnet answered that he had already done so. He showed himself very unwilling to address the people ; but being strongly urged by the Recorder, he uttered a few sentences, the purport of which was that he considered all treason detestable ; that he prayed the King's pardon for not revealing that of which he had a general knowledge from Catesby, but not otherwise ; that he never knew anything of the design of blowing up the Parliament House. The Dean of Winchester reminded him that he had confessed that Greenway told him all the circumstances in Essex. " That was in secret confession," said Garnet, " which I could by no means reveal." The Dean having reminded him that he had already allowed the contrary, the Recorder was about to read his written confessions to the people—a course commanded by the King if Garnet should deny his guilt upon the scaffold : but Garnet stopped this conviction from his own mouth, by telling the Recorder that he might spare himself that trouble ; he would stand to the confessions he had signed, and acknowledge himself justly condemned for not having declared his general knowledge of the plot. He then spoke of Anne Vaux, and denounced as slander all the injurious reports concerning his relations with her : then he asked what time would be permitted him for prayer. He was told that he should choose his own time, and should not be interrupted. Kneeling down at the foot of the ladder, Garnet proceeded to his devotions in such a manner as to show that they were to him the purest formalities : as the words fell from his lips, he was gazing at the crowd, listening to the attendants, sometimes even replying to remarks they made. When he rose from his knees, he was urged once more to confess his guilt in plain terms. He answered that he had no more to confess; his guilt had been exaggerated. As he undressed for execution, he said in a low voice to those nearest to him, " There is no salvation for you, unless you hold the Catholic faith." Their reply was that they were under the impression they did hold it. " But the only Catholic faith," responded Garnet, " is that professed by the Church of Rome." Having ascended the ladder, he addressed the people. He expressed in these closing words his grief that he had offended the King, and that he had not used more diligence in preventing the execution of the plot ; he was sorry that he had dissembled with the Lords of the Council, and that he did not declare the truth until it was proved against him : " but," he said, " I did not think they had such sure proofs against me " ! He besought all men " not to allow the Catholics to fare worse for his sake," and bade the latter keep out of sedition. Then he crossed himself, and added—" *Jesus Maria !* Mary, mother of grace, mother of mercy ! Save me from mine enemies, and receive me in the hour of death. In Thine hands I commend my spirit : Thou hast redeemed me, O Lord God of truth ! " Crossing himself once more, he added—always in Latin—" By this sign of the cross, may all evil things be dispersed. Plant Thy cross, Lord, in mine heart ! " But his last words were, " Jesus Maria ! Mary, mother of grace ! " Then the ladder was drawn away, and Henry Garnet, the conspirator and liar, stood before that Lord God of truth who will by no means clear the guilty. By express command of the King, the after-horrors of a traitor's death were omitted.

Three months after that sad close of life, the Tower gates opened again—this time to release a prisoner. The Hon. Anne Vaux was bidden to go whither she would. Whither she would !—what a mockery to her to whom all the earth and the heavens had been made one vaulted grave—who had no home left anywhere in the world, for her home had been in the heart of that dead man. To what part of that great wilderness of earth she carried her bitter grief and her name of scorn, no record has been left to tell us, except one.

Thirty years later, in 1635, a Jesuit school for "Catholic youths of the nobility and gentry" was dispersed by authority. It was at Stanley, a small hamlet about six miles to the north-east of Derby, a short distance from the Nottingham road. The house was known as Stanley Grange, and it was the residence of the Hon. Anne Vaux.

So she passes out of our sight, old and full of days, true to the end to the faith for which she had so sorely suffered, and to the memory of the friend whom she had loved too well.

"O solitary love that was so strong!"

Let us leave her to the mercy of Him who died for men, and who only can presume to sit in judgment on that faithful, passionate, broken heart.

CHAPTER XII.

THE FRUIT OF HIS OWN WAY.

"Say not, This brackish well I will not taste;
 Ere long thou may'st give thanks that even this
 Is left for thee in such a burning waste."
                          —Rev. HORATIUS BONAR.

ELL Mr. Louvaine that I desire speech of him."
The page who received this order looked up in apprehension. So exceedingly stern were Lady Oxford's tones, and so frowning her aspect, that he trembled for himself, apart from Aubrey. Escaping from that awful presence at the earliest moment possible, he carried the message to Aubrey, who when he received it was lounging on a day-bed, or sofa, with his arms crossed behind his head.

"And you'd best go soon, Sir," said the page, "for her Ladyship looks as though she could swallow me in two bites."

"Then I rather count I'd best not," said Aubrey, looking very much indisposed to stir. "What on earth would she have of me? There's no end to the whims and conceits of women."

He unwreathed his arms and stood up, yawned, and very slowly went up-stairs to the gallery where he had learned that the Countess was awaiting him.

Aubrey Louvaine was at that moment a most unhappy

young man. The first sensation of amazement and horror at the discovery of the treachery and wickedness of his chosen friends was past, but the apprehensions for his own safety were not; and as the time went on, the sense of loss, weariness, and disgust of life, rather grew than lessened. Worst of all, and beyond all, were two better feelings—the honest affection which Aubrey had scarcely realised before that he entertained for Thomas Winter, and the shock and pain of his miserable fate: and even beyond this, a sense of humiliation, very wholesome yet very distiessing, at the folly of his course, and the wreck which he had made of his life. How complete a wreck it was he had not discovered even now: but that he had been very foolish, he knew in his inmost heart. And when a man is just making that valuable discovery is not the best time for other men to tell him of it.

That Fate was preparing for him not a sedative but a stimulant, he had little doubt as he went slowly on his way to the gallery: but of the astringent nature of that mixture he had equally small idea, until he turned the last corner, and came in sight of the Countess's face. There was an aspect of the avenging angel about Lady Oxford, as she stood up, tall and stately, in that corner of the gallery, and held out to Aubrey what that indiscreet young gentleman recognised as a lost solitaire that was wont to fasten the lace ruffles on his wrist.

" Is this yours, Mr. Louvaine?" Her voice said, "Guilty or not guilty?" so plainly that he was almost ready to respond, "Of what?"

Aubrey gave the garnet solitaire a more prolonged examination than it needed. He felt no doubt of its identity.

" Yes, Madam, I think it is," he answered slowly. " At the least, I have lost one that resembles it."

" I think it is, too," said the Countess no less sternly. " Do you know where this was found, Mr. Louvaine?"

Aubrey began to feel thoroughly alarmed.

" No, Madam," he faltered.

" In the chamber of Thomas Winter, the traitor and Papist, at the sign of the Duck, in the Strand. Perhaps you can tell me how it came thither ? "

Aubrey was silent, from sheer terror. A gulf seemed to yawn before his feet, and the Countess appeared to him in the light of the minister of wrath waiting to push him into it. With the rapidity of lightning, his whole life seemed to pass in sudden review before him—his happy childhood and guarded youth at Selwick Hall, the changed circumstances of his London experiences, his foolish ways and extravagant expenditure, his friendship with Winter, the quiet home at the White Bear into which his fall would bring such disgrace and sorrow, the possible prison and scaffold as the close of all. Was it to end thus ? He had meant so little ill, had done so little wrong. Yet how was he to convince any one that he had not meant the one, or even that he had not done the other?

In that moment, one circumstance of his early life stood out bright and vivid as if touched with a sunbeam :—an act of childish folly, done fifteen years before, for which his grandfather had made him learn the text, " Thou God seest me." It came flashing back upon him now. Had God seen him all this while? Then He knew all his foolishness —ay, and his innocence as well. Could He—would He— help him in this emergency? Aubrey Louvaine had never left off the outward habit of saying prayers; but it was years since he had really prayed before that unheard cry went up in the gallery of Oxford House—" Lord, save me, for my grandmother's sake ! " He felt as if he dared not ask it for his own.

All these thoughts followed each other in so short a time that Lady Oxford was conscious of little more than a momentary hesitation, before Aubrey said—

"I suppose I can, Madam."

He had made up his mind to speak the plain, full truth. Even that slight touch of the hem of Christ's garment had given him strength.

"Then do so.   Have you visited this man?"

"I have, Madam."

"How many times?"

"Several times, Madam.   I could not say with certainty how many."

"How long knew you this Thomas Winter?"

"Almost as long as I have dwelt in your Ladyship's house—not fully that time."

"Who made you acquaint with him?"

"Mr. Percy."

"What, the arch-traitor?"   Percy was then supposed to be what Catesby really was—the head and front of the offending.

"He, Madam.   I will not deceive your Ladyship."

"And pray who made you acquaint with him?" demanded the Countess, grimly.   In her heart, as she looked into the eyes honestly raised to hers, she was saying, "The lad is innocent of all ill meaning—a foolish daw that these kites have plucked:" but she showed no sign of the relenting she really felt.

"Madam, that was Mr. Thomas Rookwood."

"He that dwells beside the Lady Lettice?"

"His son, Madam."

"Were you acquaint with any of their wicked designs?"

"Not one of them, Madam, nor I never imagined no such a thing of any of those gentlemen."

"Who of them all have you seen?"

"Madam, I have seen divers of whom I knew no more than to see them, whose names—but no more—I can specify if your Ladyship desire it.   But those that I did really know and at all consort with were three only beside

Mr. Tom Rookwood—to wit, Mr. Percy, Mr. Catesby, and Mr. Thomas Winter: and I saw but little save of the last."

" The boy's telling truth," said Lady Oxford to herself. " He has been exceedingly foolish, but no worse." Then aloud she asked,—" Saw you ever any priests there ? "

" Not to know them for such, Madam."

" Tampered they with you in any wise as to religion ? "

" Never, Madam."

" And you are yet at heart a true Protestant, and loyal to King James ? "

" As much so as I ever was, Madam."

But as Aubrey spoke, the question arose in his con-science,—What had he ever cared about either ? Not half as much as he had cared for Tom Winter,—nay, not so much as he had cared for Tom Winter's tobacco.

" Mr. Louvaine," said the Countess, suddenly, " have you discovered that you are a very foolish young man ? "

Aubrey flushed red, and remained silent.

" It seems to me," she continued, " that you speak truth, and that you have been no worser than foolish. Yet, so being, you must surely guess that for your own sake, no less than for the Earl's, you must leave this house, and that quickly."

He had not guessed it, and it came upon him like a bomb-shell. Leave Oxford House ! What was to become of him ?

" And if you will take my advice, you will not essay to win into any other service. Tarry as still as you can some whither, till matters be blown over, and men begin to for-get the inwards of this affair : not in Town. Have you no friend in the country that would take you in for a while ? 'Tis for your own good, and for my Lady Lettice' sake, that I give you this counsel."

" Lie hidden in the country ! " Aubrey's tones were

perfectly aghast. Such an expectation had never visited
his least coherent dreams.

"Mr. Louvaine," said Lady Oxford in a kinder voice, "I
can see that you have never reckoned till this moment
whither your course should lead you, nor what lay at the
end of the road you traversed. I am sorry for you, rather
than angered; for I believe you thought no ill: you simply
failed to think at all, as so many have done before you.
Yet is it the truest kindness not to cover your path by a
deluding mist, but to point out to you plainly the end of
the way you are going. Trust me, if this witness in mine
hand were traced to you by them in power, they should not
take your testimony for truth so easily as I may. I know
you, and the stock whence you come; to them, you were
but one of a thousand, without favour or distinction.
Maybe you think me hard; yet I ensure you, you have no
better friend, nor one that shall give you truer counsel than
this which I have given. Go you into the country, the
further from London the better, and lie as quiet as you
may, till the whole matter be blown over, and maybe some
time hence, it shall be possible to sue you a pardon from
his Majesty to cover all."

"Some time!" broke from Aubrey's lips.

"Ay, and be thankful it is no worse. He that leaps into
a volcano, counting it but a puddle, shall not find it a
puddle, but a volcano. You have played with firebrands,
Mr. Louvaine, and must not marvel nor grumble to feel the
scorching of your fingers."

Aubrey's silence was the issue of sheer despair.

"You must leave this house to-day," said the Countess
firmly, "and not as though you went on a journey. Go
forth this afternoon, as for a walk of pleasure, and carrying
nothing save what you can put in your pockets. When you
have set a few miles betwixt yourself and the town, you
may then hire an horse, and ride quickly. I would counsel

you not to journey too direct—if you go north or south, tack about somewhat to east and west; one may ride with far more safety than many. I am not, as you know, over rich, yet I will, for my Lady Lettice' sake, lend you a sufficiency to carry you an hundred miles—and if it fall out that you are not able to return the loan, trouble yourself not thereabout. I am doing my best for you, Mr. Louvaine, not my worst."

"I thank your Ladyship," faltered the unhappy youth. "But—must I not so much as visit my grandmother?"

It was no very long time since the White Bear had been to Aubrey a troublesome nuisance. Now it presented itself to his eyes in the enticing form of a haven of peace. He was loved there: and he began to perceive that love, even when it crossed his wishes, was better worth having than the due reward of his deeds.

"Too great a risk to run," said the Countess, gravely. "If any inquiration be made for you, and you not found here, the officers of justice should go straight thither. No: I will visit my Lady Lettice myself, and soften the thing as best I may to her and to Mrs. Louvaine. The only thing ——" she paused a moment in thought. "What other friends have you in London?"

"Truly, none, Madam, save my cousin David——"

"Not a relative. Is there no clergyman that knows you, who is of good account, and a staunch Protestant?"

"There is truly Mr. Marshall, a friend of my grandmother, and an ejected Puritan."

"Where dwelleth he?"

"In Shoe Lane, Madam."

"Is he a wise and discreet man?"

"I think, Madam, my grandmother holds him for such."

"It is possible," said Lady Oxford, meditatively, "that you might be safe in his house for a day or two, and your

T

friends from the White Bear could go as if to see him and
his wife—hath he a wife?"

"He buried his wife this last summer, Madam: he
bath a daughter that keeps his house, of about mine own
years."

"If you think it worth to run the risk, you might ask
this good gentleman to give you a day's shelter, so as to
speak with your friends ere you depart. It were a risk:
yet not, perchance, too great. You must judge for yourself. If you choose this way, I will take it on myself to let
your friends know how it is with you."

It was a bitter pill to swallow. Mr. Marshall was about
the last man in his world to whom Aubrey felt any inclina-
tion to lay himself under an obligation. Both as a clergyman, a Puritan, and an ejected minister, this undiscerning
youth had looked down exceedingly upon his superior.
The popular estimate of the clergy was just then at the
lowest ebb, and it required some moral courage for any man
to take holy orders, who was neither very high up in rank,
nor very low down. This was the result partly of the evil
lives, and partly of the gross ignorance, of the pre-Refor-
mation priests; the lives were now greatly amended, but too
much of the ignorance remained, and the time had not
been sufficient to remove the stigma. A clergyman was
expected to apprentice his children to a trade, or at best
to place them in domestic service; and he would have been
thought forward and impertinent if, when dining with lay-
men in a good position, he had not spontaneously taken
his departure before dessert made its appearance. To be
indebted, therefore, for an essential service to one of this
lowly class, Aubrey was sufficiently foolish to account a
small degradation.

Happily for him, he had just enough sense left, and had
been sufficiently humiliated, to perceive that he could not
escape the necessity of devouring this unpalatable piece of

humble pie, and that the only choice left him was a choice of bitters. The false manliness which he had been diligently cultivating had vanished into thin air, and something of the child's spirit, so long despised, was coming back to him,—the longing for the sound of a familiar voice, and the touch of a tender hand. Even Aunt Temperance would have received, just then, a welcome which might have astonished her. But it showed the character of the women of his family that in this emergency Aubrey's thoughts scarcely touched his mother, and dwelt longingly on his grandmother and his Aunt Edith.

The wise Countess waited quietly till Aubrey's meditations had taken time to settle themselves into resolution.

"Madam, I thank your Ladyship," he said at last, as he looked up, with an expression which had not dwelt for many a month in his eyes. "I think I perceive now how matters stand. Suffer me to say that I never knew, until now, how foolish I have been. Under your Ladyship's leave, I will take your kindly counsel, and seek aid of Mr. Marshall. I would like to see them again."

His voice faltered as the last words were spoken.

"So will you do well," said the Countess, more kindly than before. "All is not yet lost, Mr. Louvaine. You have been foolish, but there is time before you wherein you may be wise."

Aubrey bowed, took his leave, and went to his own room, where he filled his pockets with a few immediate necessaries and what little money he had. It was hard to bear, this going forth into the wilderness, not at God's call, but as the consequence of his own folly—Egypt left behind, and no Canaan in prospect. He must take leave of none save Lady Oxford—must appear to none to be what he was— a homeless fugitive with his life in his hand. As he came down-stairs, he was met in the hall by the same page who had previously summoned him.

"My Lady would speak a word with you in her cabinet ere you walk forth."

Aubrey found Lady Oxford at her desk, busied with household accounts, and a little pile of gold beside her. When she had reminded him that she was not rich, she had spoken very truly. That deceased husband of hers, as wanting in reason in his age as in his youth, having reduced the great Vere estates to almost nothing, his second wife, the Countess Elizabeth, and her young son Earl Henry, had to sustain the dignity of the House upon a very insufficient number of gold pieces. Twenty months had elapsed since the death of Earl Edward, and the excellent management and strict economy of the widowed Countess had done something to retrieve the ruined fortunes of the family, but much still remained to do.

Lady Oxford glanced up at Aubrey as he entered.

"Mr. Louvaine, I owe you your quarter's wages," she said; "at least, so little time remains that it need not tarry, and 'tis to my conveniency to reckon with you this afternoon." This was said in a voice that the page could hear. Then, as Aubrey came up to her, with a significant look, she laid another ten pounds in his hand, with a few words for his private ear. "Let me hear of you in time to come as a good man. God go with you! Farewell."

Ten minutes later, Aubrey closed the door of Oxford House for the last time, and went out, truly not knowing whither he went. His primary destination of course was Shoe Lane; but after that—whither?

Through back streets he made his way to Aldersgate, and passed through it out of the City; over Snow Hill and Holborn Bridge, and down Shoe Lane to the small house where Mr. Marshall "had his lodging"—to use the phrase of the time—in other words, where he and Agnes made their home in three rooms, the kitchen being open to all

the lodgers to cook for themselves. Two of the rooms
were moderately large; these formed the sitting-room, and
the clergyman's bedroom and study, the bedroom end being
parted from the study end by a curtain between the two.
The remaining room, a mere closet, was his daughter's bedchamber. Pleasantest of the three was the sitting-room,
the front half of which was the general and public portion,
while the back was reserved as Agnes's boudoir, where her
little work-table and stool were set by a small window,
looking out over the little garden towards Fetter Lane,
bounded on the right hand by the wall of St. Andrew's
Church. The door was opened by a rather slipshod girl,
the landlady's daughter.

"Pray you, is Mr. Marshall at home?"

"He's not, Sir; he's gone for a country walk."

"What time look you for him?"

"Well, about dark, I dare say. Mrs. Agnes, she's in."

"Thank you; I will come again about dusk."

Aubrey walked up the lane, turned aimlessly to the left,
and sauntered on towards Bloomsbury. It was no matter
where he went—no matter to any one, himself least of all.
Passing St. Giles's Church, he turned to the right, up a
broad country road lined by flowery banks, wherein the
first primroses of spring were just beginning to appear.
There are primroses there yet—in flower-girls' baskets: they
bloom now no otherwise in Tottenham Court Road.

When he had gone some little distance, Aubrey grew
tired. It was a warm day for the season; he sat down
to rest on the flowery bank, and lost himself in unhappy
thought.

A mile further on, Mr Marshall was coming home down
the same road, in a more despondent mood than was usual
with him. Things were going badly for the Puritans
abroad, and for the Marshalls at home. An ejected
minister was at all times an unfashionable person, and

usually a very poor man. His income was small, was growing smaller, and was not at all likely to take a turn and increase. His wife was gone, and he felt her loss rather more than less as time passed on ; and Agnes had her private trouble, for her affianced husband, a young tradesman to whom she had been engaged for two years, had jilted her when he heard of her father's ejectment. Altogether, the prospect before the Marshalls was not pleasant. Rent was due, and clothes were needed, and money was exceedingly scanty.

In the outside world, too, the sky was dull and gloomy. The Puritans were in no greater favour than they had been, though the Papists were at the lowest ebb. That there was any inconsistency in their conduct did not apparently occur to the authorities, nor that the true way to repress Popery was by cultivating Puritanism. Believing the true principles of the Church of England to be the golden mean between the two, they acted under the pleasing illusion that when both halves were cut off, the middle would be left intact, and all the better for the operation.

As Mr. Marshall walked on in the Tottenham road, he saw a figure seated on the grassy bank at some distance before him. When he came nearer, he perceived that it was a young man, who sat with his head cast down, in an attitude of meditation, and a light cane in his hand, with which now and then he switched off the head of an unoffending dandelion. Drawing nearer still, the minister began to suspect that the youth's face was not unfamiliar ; and when he came close, instead of passing the sitter on the bank, he stepped down, and took a seat beside him.

The youth had paid no apparent attention to his companion until that moment. His face was turned away northward, and only when Mr. Marshall sat down close to him did he seem to perceive that he was not alone.

"How goes the world with you this afternoon, Mr. Louvaine?"

"Mr. Marshall! I ask your pardon. I had not seen you."

"I thought not. You have taken a long walk."

Aubrey made no reply.

"Now, how am I to get at this shut-up heart?" said Mr. Marshall to himself. "To say the wrong thing just now may do considerable harm. Yet what is the right one?" Aloud he said only,—"I hope my Lady Lettice is well? I know not whether you or I saw her last."

"I have not seen her for months," said Aubrey, curtly.

"Then I am happier than you, for I saw her three weeks since. I thought her looking somewhat frail and feeble, even more so than her wont; yet very ripe for Heaven, when as it shall please God to take her."

There was no answer again. Aubrey's cane applied itself diligently to making a plantain leaf lie to the right of its neighbour instead of the left.

"Mr. Louvaine, did you ever hear that my mother and your grandfather were friends of old time?"

For the first time Aubrey turned his head fully, and looked at his companion. The face which Mr. Marshall saw was not, as he had imagined it might be, sullen and reluctant to converse. It was only very, very weary and sad, with heavy eyes as though they had slept little, or were holding back unshed tears.

"No, never," was all he said.

"My mother," said Mr. Marshall, "was an Oxfordshire woman, of Minster Lovel by her birth, but she wedded a bookseller in Oxford town, where she was in service to a lady. I think you were not present when I told this to my Lady Lettice. But do you remember your old friend Mrs. Elizabeth Wolvercot, that she told me you were wont to call Cousin Bess?"

"Remember Cousin Bess! Of course I do," said Aubrey, a tone of interest coming into his voice. "What of her?"

"My mother was her sister Ellen."

"Why, Mr. Marshall! are you my cousin?"

"If it please you to acknowledge me, Cousin Aubrey."

"That I will, indeed!" said Aubrey, clasping the hand of the ejected minister. Then, with a sudden and complete change of tone,—"But, maybe, if you knew all I know, you were not over ready to acknowledge me."

"You are in trouble, my friend," answered Mr. Marshall sympathisingly. "Can I help you thereout? At least I can feel for you in it, if I may do no more."

There was another minute of dead silence. The next question came suddenly and bluntly.

"Mr. Marshall, did you ever in your life feel that you had been a grand fool?"

"Yes," was the short, quiet answer.

"I am glad to hear it, though I should not have thought so. I thought you had always been a precisely proper person, and I did not suppose you could feel for me a whit. But I must tell my trouble to somebody, or I shall grow desperate. Look you, I have lost my place, and I can get none other, and I have not twenty pounds in the world, and I owe an hundred pounds, and I can't go home."

"Thank God!" was the strange answer.

"Well, to be sure,—Mr. Marshall, what on earth are you thanking God for?"

"That your husks have lost their flavour, my son. So long as the prodigal finds the husks sweet, there is little hope of him. But let him once discover that they are dry husks, and not sweet fruits, and that his companions are swine, and not princes—then he is coming to himself, and there is hope of making a man of him again. I say therefore, Thank God!"

"I shall never make anything better than a fool."

"A man commonly ceases to be a fool when he begins to reckon himself one."

"You know not the worst yet. But—Mr. Marshall, if I tell it you, you will not betray me, for my poor old grandmother's sake? I never gave her much cause to love me, but I know she doth, and it would grieve her if I came to public hurt and shame."

"It would grieve me, my cousin, more than you know. Fear not, but speak freely."

"Well,—I know not if my grandmother told you that I was intimate with some of these poor gentlemen that have paid the penalty of their treason of late?"

"I know that you knew Percy and Winter—and, I dare say, Rookwood."

"I knew them all, and Catesby too. And though I was not privy to the plot—not quite so bad as that!—yet I would have followed Mr. Tom Winter almost anywhere,—ay, even into worse than I did."

"Surely, Aubrey Louvaine, you never dreamed of perversion!"

"Mr. Marshall, I was ready to do anything Tom Winter bade me; but he never meddled with my religion. And—come, I may as well make a clean breast, as I have begun—I loved Dorothy Rookwood, and if she had held up a finger, I should have gone after. You think the Rookwoods Protestants, don't you? They are not."

Mr. Marshall sat in dismayed silence, for a moment.

"I doubted them somewhat," he said : "but I never knew so much as you have told me. Then Mrs. Dorothy——"

"Oh, she would have none of me. She told me I was a beggar and a fool both, and she spake but the bitter truth. Yet it was bitter when she said it."

"My poor boy!" said Mr. Marshall, compassionately.

"I thought Hans but a fool when he went and bound himself to yon mercer—he, the son of a Dutch Baron!

But I see now—I was the fool, not he. Had I spent my days in selling silk stockings instead of wearing them, and taken my wages home to my mother like a good little boy, it had been better for me. I see, now,—now that the doors are all shut against me, and I dare not go home."

"Yet tell me, Aubrey, for I scarce understand it—why dare you not go home?"

As Aubrey laid the matter before him from the point of view presented by Lady Oxford, Mr. Marshall's face grew graver every moment. He began to see that the circumstances were much more serious than he had apprehended. There was silence for a few minutes when Aubrey finished his account. Then the clergyman said,—

"'Tis a tangle, and a tight one, my boy. Yet, by God's blessing, we may see our way out. Let us take one point at a time. These debts of yours—will you tell me, are they 'debts of honour,' falsely so-called?"

"Only twenty pounds. The rest is due partly to Patrick the tailor and others for goods, and partly to Tom Rookwood for money I borrowed of him."

"How much to Tom Rookwood?"

"Twenty pounds."

"I will see what I can do with him," said Mr. Marshall, thoughtfully. "If these Rookwoods are in no wise dragged into the plot, so that they have no land escheated, nor fines to pay, then I think he can afford to wait for his money—better, very like, than the tradesfolk. But, Aubrey, you must get another place. Bear with me if I ask you,—Could you bring your pride down to serve in a shop?"

The young shapely head went up suddenly, as if in proud protest against this most unacceptable proposal. Then it dropped again, and the cane toyed with the plantain.

"I thought my pride was down," he said in a low voice, "but I see it might be lowered yet further. Mr. Marshall, I will try to humble myself even to that, if it be needful."

Aubrey did not suspect that Mr. Marshall had never come so near respecting him as at that moment.

"Well," he said, quietly, "I will do what I can to help you. I will see Tom Rookwood; and I know a bookseller in Oxford town to whom I could speak for you if you wish it. The question for you at this moment is not, What is easy and pleasant?—but, What is right? '*Facilis descensus Averni*'—you know—'*sed revocare gradum!*' It is always hard work turning back. There is a bitter cup to be drunk; and if you would win back your lost self-respect—if you would bring help and comfort to your grandmother in her old age—if you would light up the lamp of joy where hitherto you have wrought darkness —nay, if you would win a smile from the blessed lips which said 'Father, forgive them' *for you*—then, Aubrey Louvaine, be a man, and drink off that bitter draught. You will find it sweeter afterwards than all the dainties you have been searching after for so long."

Aubrey sat still and silent for some time, and his companion let him alone to consider his ways. Mr. Marshall was a wise man; and never gave more strokes to a nail than were needful to drive it in. At last the question came, in low, unsteady tones,—

"Mr. Marshall, did God send you up this road this afternoon?"

"I have no doubt He did, my friend, if anything I say or do can help you to the right way. You see, I knew not of your being here, and He did."

"When you came up," said the low voice, "I thought all was over, and my mind was very near made up to enlist as a common soldier, and leave no trace behind. I see now, it should have been an ill deed to do."

"An ill deed in truth for your poor friends, if the only news they had ever heard of you were your name in a list of the dead."

"Yes, I wished to be killed as soon as might be—get to the end as fast as possible."

"Would that have been the end, Aubrey?"

The reply was barely audible. "No, I suppose not."

"Take up your burden instead, my son, and bear it by God's grace. He does not refuse that, even when the burden is heaped and bound by our own hands. Unlike men, His compassion faileth never. He has maybe emptied thine heart, Aubrey, that He may fill it with Himself."

Aubrey made no reply, but Mr. Marshall did not think that a bad sign.

"Well, come now," said he, rising from the bank, and in a more cheerful tone. "Let us go to Shoe Lane, and see if Agnes hath any supper for us. The prodigal son was not more welcome to his old father than you shall be to my poor lodging, for so long a time as may stand with your safety and conveniency. My Lady Oxford, you say, was to give my Lady Lettice to know how things went with you? but methinks it shall do none ill if I likewise visit her this evening. 'Two heads are better than one,' and though 'tis said 'o'er many cooks spoil the broth,' yet three may be better than two."

The feeling of humiliation which grew and deepened in Aubrey's mind, was one of the best things which could have come to him. Vanity and self-sufficiency had always been his chief failings; and he was now finding, to his surprise, that while his chosen friends surrounded him with difficulties, the people whom he had slighted and despised came forward to help him out of them. He had looked down on no one more than on Mr. Marshall, and Agnes had received a share of his contempt, partly because

of her father's calling and comparative poverty, partly
because she was not pretty, and partly because she showed
no power of repartee or spirit in conversation. In
Aubrey's eyes she had been "a dull, humdrum thing,"
only fit to cook and sew, and utterly beneath the notice of
any one so elevated and *spirituel* as himself.

During the last few hours, Aubrey's estimate of things
in general had sustained some rude shocks, and his
hitherto unfaltering faith in his own infallibility was
considerably shaken. It suffered an additional blow when
Mr. Marshall led him into his quiet parlour, and he saw
Agnes seated at her work, the supper-table spread, and
a cheerful fire blazing upon a clean hearth. An expression of slight surprise came into her eyes as she rose to
greet Aubrey.

"You see, daughter, I have brought home a guest," said
her father. "He will tarry with us a little season."

Then, stepping across the room, he opened a closed
door, and showed Aubrey another chamber, the size of the
first, across which a red curtain was drawn.

"This is my chamber, and shall be also yours," said he:
"I pray you use it freely. At this end is my study, and
beyond the curtain my bedchamber. I somewhat fear
my library may scarce be to your liking," he added, an
amused smile playing round his lips; "but if you can
find therein anything to please you, I shall be glad.—Now,
daughter, what have we here? We so rarely have guests
to supper, I fear Mr. Louvaine may find our fare somewhat meagre: though 'better is a dinner of herbs where
love is, than a stalled ox and hatred therewith.'"

"It is a dinner of herbs, Father," said Agnes, echoing
the smile; "for 'tis a bit of gammon of bacon and spinach,
with eggs in poach."

"How say you, my friend?" asked Mr. Marshall of
Aubrey. "Can you make your supper of so simple a dish?"

"Indeed I can, Sir, and thankfully," was the answer.

Agnes Marshall, though very quiet, was observant, and she perceived in a moment that something was wrong with the magnificent youth who had scarcely deigned to look at her when they had met on previous occasions. She saw also that his manner had greatly changed, and very much for the better. He spoke to her now on terms of equality, and actually addressed her father in a tone of respect. Something must have happened.

Aubrey, naturally the less observant of the two, was looking on just now with quickened senses; and discovered, also to his surprise, that the simple supper was served with as much dainty neatness as at Lord Oxford's table; that Mr. Marshall could talk intelligently and interestingly on other than religious subjects; that Agnes really was not dull, but quite able to respond to her father's remarks; that her eyes were clear and bright, her complexion not at all bad, and her smile decidedly pleasant: and lastly, that both his hosts, though taken thus unawares, were exceedingly kind to him, and ready to put themselves to any trouble or inconvenience in order to accommodate him. He had learned more, when he lay down to sleep that night, in twelve hours than in any previous twelve months of his life, since his infancy. The lessons were of higher value, and they were not likely to be lost.

When supper was over, Mr. Marshall repaired to the White Bear, and Aubrey was left to Agnes as entertainer. She was sewing a long seam, and her needle went in and out with unfailing regularity. For a few minutes he watched her in silence, discovering a sunny gleam on her hair that he had never before noticed. Then he suddenly spoke out one of his thoughts.

"Don't you find that exceeding wearisome?"

Agnes looked up with amused surprise.

"Truly," she said, "I never thought about it."

"I am sure I could not work at it ten minutes," replied Aubrey.

Agnes laughed—a low, soft, musical laugh, which struck pleasantly on the ear.

"My father would be ill off for shirts if I could not," she answered. "You see, Mr. Louvaine, things have to be done. 'Tis to no good purpose to be impatient with them. It doth but weary more the worker, and furthers not the work a whit."

"Would you not like to lead a different life?—such a life as other young maids do—amid flowers, and sunshine, and jewels, and dancing, and laughter, and all manner of jollity?"

He was curious to hear what she would say to the question.

Agnes answered by a rather wondering smile. Then her eyes went out of the window, to the steeple of St. Andrew's, and the blue sky beyond it.

"I might well enjoy some of them," she said slowly, as if the different ideas were passing in review before her. "I love sunshine, and flowers. But there is one thing I love far better."

"And that is——?"

A light "that never was from sun nor moon" flooded the grave grey eyes of Agnes Marshall. Her voice was very low and subdued as she answered.

"That is, to do the will of God. There is nothing upon earth that I desire in comparison of Him."

"Is not that a gloomsome, dismal sort of thing?"

There was Divine compassion, mingled with human amusement, in the smile which was on Agnes's lips as she looked up at him.

"Have you tried it, Mr. Louvaine?"

Aubrey shook his head. "I have tried a good many

things, but not Puritan piety. It ever seemed to me a most weary and dreary matter,—an eternal 'Thou shalt not' carved o'er the gate of every garden of delight that I would fain enter. They may be angels that stand there, but they bear flaming swords."

He spoke lightly, yet there was an accent in his voice which revealed to Agnes a deep unfilled void in his heart.

"Don't try piety," she said quietly. "Try Jesus Christ instead. There are no flaming swords in the way to Him, and the truest and deepest satisfaction cannot be reached without Him."

"Have you found it thus, Mrs. Agnes?"

"I have, Mr. Louvaine."

"But, then,—you see,—you have not tried other fashions of pleasure, maybe," said Aubrey, slowly.

"Have you?" said Agnes.

"Ay—a good many."

"And did you find them satisfying? I say not, pleasant at the moment, but satisfying?"

"Well, that is a large word," said Aubrey.

"It is a large word," was the reply, "yet Christ can fill it: and none can do it but He. Know you any thing or creature else that can?"

"I cannot say, for I have not needed it."

"That is, you have not been down yet into deep places, methinks, where the floods have overflowed you. I have not visited many, in truth; yet have I been in one or two where I should have lost my footing, had not my Lord held me up."

A very sorrowful look came into the gentle eyes. Agnes was thinking of the faithless Jonas Derwent, who had cast her off in the day of her calamity. Aubrey made no answer. He was beginning to find out that life was not, as he had always imagined it, a field of flowers, but a very

sore and real battlefield, wherein to lose the victory meant
to lose his very self, and to win it meant to reign for ever
and ever.

And then Mr. Marshall's voice said on the other side
of the door,—"This is the way"—and another voice,
dearly welcome to Aubrey, responded as Aunt Edith came
into the room,—

"Mine own dear boy! God be thanked that we see
thee safe from harm!"

And again, for the twentieth time, Aubrey felt as he
kissed her that he had not deserved it.

CHAPTER XIII.

WHICH IS FULL OF SURPRISES.

"Ah, who am I, that God hath saved
Me from the doom I did desire,
And crossed the lot myself had craved,
To set me higher?"

—JEAN INGELOW.

S Mr. Marshall approached the White Bear that evening, he was unexpectedly pounced upon by Silence Abbott.

"Eh, Parson, I declare it's you! How fares Mrs. Agnes this cold even? Marry, I do believe we shall have snow ere the day break again. The White Bear'll be a bit whiter, I reckon, if he be well snowed o'er. Are you going in there? You'll have some work to peace Mrs. Louvaine; she's lamenting and weeping, you never heard!—and all for her son as cometh not home, and she is fair sure he'll be hung, because she saith he was in with those rogues yonder."

"He was nothing of the sort," said Mr. Marshall, breaking in sternly on the flow of Silence's tide of words: "and let me tell you, Mrs. Abbott, if you spread such a lie, you may have a death at your door, as like as not. Mr. Louvaine, I have no doubt, is safe and well, and had no more ado with the Gunpowder Plot than you had: and I saw you with mine own eyes

talking with Fawkes, that rascal that called himself
Johnson."

"Eh deary, Parson, but you'd never go to tell on a
poor woman, and as honest as any in Westminster, if
I did pass the time o' day to a fellow, that I never
guessed to be a villain? I do assure you, on my truth
as——"

"I hope you are an honest woman, Mrs. Abbott; and so
is Mr. Louvaine an honest man; and if you would have
me keep my tongue off your doings, see that you keep
yours off his. Now I have given you warning: that is a
bargain."

"Eh deary, deary! but I never heard Parson i' such a
way afore!" lamented Mrs. Abbott to her daughter Mary,
the only listener she had left, for Mr. Marshall had walked
straight into the White Bear. "I'll say the lad's a Prince
of the Blood, or an angel, or anything he's a mind, if he'll
but let me be. Me talk to Guy Fawkes, indeed! I never
said no worser to him than 'Fine morning,' or 'Wet, isn't
it?' as it might be: and to think o' me being had up afore
the Lords of the Council for just passing a word like that—
and the parson, too! Eh, deary me! whatever must I say
to content him, now?"

"I fancy, Mother," said Mary, who took after her quiet
father, "he'll be content if you'll hold your peace."

Mr. Marshall found the ladies at the White Bear all
assembled in the parlour. Mrs. Louvaine had the ear of
the House as he entered.

"So unfeeling as you are, Temperance, to a poor widow!
and my only child as good as lost, and never found
again. And officers and thirdboroughs and constables all
going about, making all manner of inquirations, trying
to bring folks to justice, and Aubrey in with those wicked
people, and going to sup with them, and all—and nobody
ever trying to prevent him, and not a soul to care but

me whether he went right or wrong—I do believe you
thought more of the price of herrings than you ever did of
the dear boy—and now, he's completely lost and nobody
knows what has become of him——"

Mr. Marshall's quiet voice effected a diversion.

"Mrs. Louvaine, pardon me. Aubrey is at my house,
safe and sound. There is no need for your trouble."

"Of course!" responded Temperance. "I told her so.
Might as well talk to the fire-bricks, when she takes a
fancy of this sort. If the lad had come to any harm,
we should have heard it. Faith never will think that 'no
news is good news.'"

"I am glad Aubrey is with you, Mr. Marshall," said
the gentle voice of Lady Louvaine.

"I met with him, Madam, in a walk this afternoon,
and brought him so far with me."

"And why not a bit further, trow?" asked Temperance.

"That am I come to say.. Madam,"—and he addressed
himself to Lady Louvaine,—"having told you that your
grandson is well in body, and safe at my lodging, I trust
it shall not greatly touch you to learn that he is in some
trouble of mind."

"Didn't I tell you?" demanded Mrs. Louvaine, in
tones suited to Cassandra amid the ruins of Troy. "I
said I was sure some harm had come to the boy, and
you laughed me to scorn, and not one of you went to
see——"

"Nobody laughed at you but me, my dear," said her
sister: "and as to going to see, when his mother did
not reckon it worth while to budge, I don't see why his
aunts should not sit quiet."

"Why, you never looked for *me* to go?" responded
Mrs. Louvaine, with a faint scream of horror. "Me,
a poor widow, and with my feeble health! When I

haven't been out of the door except to church for nigh
a month!"

"More's the pity! If you knocked about a bit more,
and went to market of a morrow, and such like, maybe
your health would not be so feeble."

"Temperance, you barbarous creature, how *can* you?"

"Well, I know there are folks that can, Faith, and
there are folks that can't. You never heard me ask my
Lady Lettice why she didn't stir up and go a-market-
ing. She can't; she'd be only too glad if she could,
and would want no asking. But you could if you would
—it's true, my dear, and you don't need to stare, as if
you'd never seen me before this evening. As for looking
for you to go, I didn't indeed; I never look for aught but
cumber, and so I'm not disappointed.—Mr. Marshall, I ask
your pardon; I'm staying you from speaking."

Mr. Marshall accepted the apology with a smile.

"Well, the upshot of the matter is this. Mr. Louvaine,
though in truth, as I do verily believe, innocent of all
ill, is in danger to fall in some suspicion through a
certain jewel of his being found in the lodging of one
of the caitiffs lately execute. He saith that he knew not
where he had lost it: no doubt it dropped out of his
apparel when he was there, as he allows he hath been
divers times. He never heard, saith he, a word of any
traitorous designs, nor did they tamper at all with his
religion. But this jewel being carried to my Lady Oxford
—truly, whether by some suspicion that it should be Mr.
Louvaine's, or how, I know not, nor am sure that he
doth himself—she charged him withal, yet kindly, and
made haste to have him forth of the house, warning
him that he must in no wise tarry in the town, but
must with all haste hie him down into the country,
and there lie squat until all suspicion had passed. She
would not even have him come hither, where she said

he should be sought if any inquiry were made. The
utmost she would suffer was that he should lie hid for
a day or twain in my lodging, whither you might come
as if to speak with Agnes, and so might agree whither he
should go, and so forth. My Lady paid him his wage,
well-nigh nine pound, and further counted ten pounds
into his hand to help him on his journey. Truly, she
gave him good counsel, and dealt well with him. But
the poor lad is very downcast, and knows not what to
do; and he tells me he hath debts that he cannot pay.
So I carried him to my lodging, where he now lieth:
and I wait your further wishes."

"I thank you right truly for that your goodness," said
Lady Louvaine.

"There, now! didn't I say the boy was sure to run
into debt?" moaned Mrs. Louvaine.

"How much be these debts, Mr. Marshall?" asked the
old lady.

"Twenty pounds borrowed from Mr. Thomas Rookwood;
twenty lost at play; and about sixty owing to tailors,
mercers, and the like."

"Ay, I reckoned that velvet would be over a penny
the yard."

"I see, the lad hath disburdened himself to you," said
Lady Louvaine, with a sad smile. "Truly, I am sorry to
hear this, though little astonied. Mr. Marshall, I have
been much troubled at times, thinking whether, in suffering Aubrey to enter my Lord Oxford's service, I had
done ill: and yet in very deed, at the time I could see
nothing else to do. It seemed to be the way wherein
God meant us to go—and yet——"

"Madam, the Lord's mercies are great enough to cover
our mistakes along with our sins. And it may be you
made none. I have never seen Mr. Louvaine so softened
and humbled as he now looks to be."

"May the Lord lead him forth by the right way! What do you advise, true friend?"

"I see two courses, Madam, which under your good leave I will lay before you. Mr. Louvaine can either lie hid in the country with some friend of yours,—or, what were maybe better, some friend of your friend: or, if he would be doing at once towards the discharging of his debts, he can take the part Mr. Floriszoon hath chosen, and serve some tradesman in his shop."

"Trade! Aubrey!" shrieked Mrs. Louvaine in horror. "He never will! My boy hath so delicate a soul——"

"He said he would," answered Mr. Marshall quietly, "and thereby won my high respect."

"Nay, you never mean it!" exclaimed Temperance. "Bless the lad! I ne'er gave him credit for half the sense."

"If Aubrey be brought down to that, he must have learned a good lesson," said his grandmother. "Not that I could behold it myself entirely without a pang."

Edith, who had hitherto been silent, now put in a suggestion.

"Our Charity is true as steel," she said. "Why not let Aubrey lie close with her kindred, where none should think to look for him?"

"In Pendle?—what, amid all the witches!" said Temperance.

"Edith, I'm amazed at you! I could never lie quiet in my bed!" wailed Mrs. Louvaine. "Only to think of the poor boy being bewitched by those wicked creatures! Why, they spend Sunday nights dancing round the church-yard with the devil."

"And the place is chokefull of em', Charity says," added Temperance. "She once met Mother Demdike her own self, muttering under her breath, and she gave her the evillest look as she passed her that the maid ever saw."

"Ay, saying the Lord's Prayer backwards, of course."

"Well, I can't say," said Temperance, dubiously: "it did not seem to do Charity any ill. I shouldn't wonder, truly——"

"For mercy's sake, stop her!" cried Mrs. Louvaine. "She's going to say something wicked—I know she is! She'll say there are no witches, or no devil, or something horrible."

"Nay, I'll say nought o' the sort," responded Temperance. "Whether there be witches or no, the Lord knows, and there I leave it; but that there is a devil I'm very sure, for he has tempted me over and over again. All I say is, if Charity could meet a witch, and get no ill, why should not Aubrey too?"

"I won't have it!" cried Mrs. Louvaine in an agony. "My poor darling boy! I won't have it! My fatherless child shall not go among snakes and witches and demons——"

"Now, Faith, do be quiet, or you'll have a fit of the mother.[1] Nobody wants to send the lad amongst snakes —I don't know that there's so much as an adder there. As to devils, he'll find them where'er he goeth, and some of them in men's and women's bodies, or I mistake."

"If your Ladyship liked better," suggested Mr. Marshall, quietly, "to take the other road I named, I am acquaint with a bookseller in Oxford town, that is a cousin of my sister's husband, a good honest man, and a God-fearing, with whom, if you so pleased, he might be put. 'Tis a clean trade, and a seemly, that need not disgrace any to handle: and methinks there were no need to mention wherefore it were, save that the place were sought for a young gentleman that had lost money through disputes touching lands. That is true, and it

_____
[1] Hysteria.

should be sufficient to account for all that the master might otherwise note as strange in a servant."

" My poor fatherless boy ! " sobbed Mrs. Louvaine, with her handkerchief at her eyes. " Servant to a trades-fellow ! "

" We are all servants," answered Mr. Marshall : " and we need think no scorn thereof, since our Lord Himself took on Him the form of a servant. Howbeit, for this even, the chief question is, Doth any of you gentlewomen desire to return with me ?—Mrs. Louvaine ? "

" I could not bear it ! " came in a stifled voice from behind the handkerchief. " To see my poor child in his misery—it would break mine heart outright. 'Tis enough to think of, and too-too[1] great to brook, even so."

" Let her pass ; she'll be ne'er a bit of good," said Temperance in a contemptuous whisper. Then raising her voice, she added,—" Now, Lady Lettice, don't you think thereof. There's no need, for Edith and I can settle everything, and you'd just go and lay yourself by, that you should have no good of your life for a month or more. Be ruled by me, and let Edith go back and talk matters o'er with Aubrey, and see whether in her judgment it were better he lay hid or went to the bookseller. She's as good a wit as any of us, yourself except. Said I well ? "

" If your Ladyship would suffer me to add a word," said the clergyman, " I think Mrs. Temperance has well spoken."

There was a moment's hesitation, as if Lady Louvaine were balancing duties. Mr. Marshall noticed how her thin hand trembled, and how the pink flush came and went on her delicate cheek.

" Well, children, have it as you will," said the old lady at last. " It costs me much to give it up ; but

[1] Exceedingly.

were I to persist, maybe it should cost more to you
than I have a right to ask at your hands. Let be: I
will tarry."

"Dearest Mother, you have a right to all that our hands
can give you," answered Edith, tenderly: "but, I pray you,
tarry until the morrow, and then if need be, and your
strength sufficient, you can ride to Shoe Lane."

So Edith went with Mr. Marshall alone. Even after
all she had heard, Aubrey's condition was a delightful surprise. Never before had she seen him in so
softened, humbled, grateful a mood as now. They talked
the matter over, and in the end decided that, subject to
Lady Louvaine's approval, Aubrey should go to the bookseller.

When the White Bear was reached on her return,
Edith found Lady Oxford in the parlour. The sternness
with which the Countess had treated Aubrey was quite
laid aside. To Lady Louvaine she showed a graceful and
grateful mixture of sympathy and respect, endeavoured to
reassure her, hoped there would be no search nor inquiry,
thought it was almost too late, highly approved of Edith's
decision, promised to send over all Aubrey's possessions
to the White Bear, and bade them let her know if she
could do them any service.

"Will you suffer me to ask you one thing?" she
said. "If Mr. Louvaine go to Oxford, shall you tarry
here, or no?"

"Would it be safe for us to follow him?"

"Follow him—no! I did but think you might better
love to be forth of this smoky town."

"Amen, with all my heart!" said Temperance. "But,
Madam, and saving your Ladyship's presence, crowns
bloom not on our raspberry bushes, nor may horses be
bought for a groat a-piece down this way."

Mrs. Louvaine, behind the cambric, was heard to

murmur something about a sordid spirit, people whose minds never soared, and old maids who knew nothing of the strength of maternal love.

"Strength o' fiddlesticks!" said Temperance, turning on her. "Madam, I ask your Ladyship's pardon."

"My dear lady, I cannot answer you as now," was Lady Louvaine's reply. "The pillar of cloud hath not moved as yet; and so long as it tarrieth, so long must I also. It may be, as seemeth but like, that my next home will be the churchyard vault. that let my Father judge. If it had been His will, that I might have laid my bones in mine own country, and by the side of my beloved, it had been pleasant to flesh and blood: but I know well that *I* go to meet him, wherever my dust may lie. I am well-nigh fourscore years old this day; and if the Lord say, 'Go not over this Jordan,' let Him do as seemeth Him good. Methinks the glory of the blessed City burst no less effulgent on the vision of Moses, because he had seen the earthly Canaan but far off. And what I love the best is not here, but there."

Temperance and Edith accompanied Lady Oxford to her coach. She paused a moment before stepping in.

"Mrs. Edith," she said, "methinks your good mother would fain see Mr. Louvaine ere he depart. If so, she shall not be balked thereof. I have made inquiry touching Mr. Marshall's house, and I find there is a little gate from the garden thereof into St. Andrew's churchyard. I will call for her as to-morrow in my coach, and carry her to take the air. An ancient servant of mine, that is wedded to the clerk of St. Andrew's, dwelleth by the churchyard, and I will stay me there as though to speak with her, sending away the coach upon another errand that I can devise. Then from her house my Lady may safely win to Mr. Marshall's lodging, and be back again ere the coach return."

"Your Ladyship is most good unto us," responded Edith, thankfully. "I am assured it should greatly comfort my dear mother."

Lady Oxford turned with a smile to Temperance.

"It seems to me, Mrs. Temperance, that your words be something sharp."

"Well, Madam, to tell truth, folks do put me out now and again more than a little. Many's the time I long to give Faith a good shaking; and I could have laid a stick on Aubrey's back middling often,—I'll not say I couldn't: but if the lad sees his blunders and is sorry for 'em, I'll put my stick in the corner."

"I think I would leave it tarry there for the present," said Lady Oxford, with a soft little laugh. "God grant you a good even!"

The coach had only just rolled away, and four youthful Abbotts, whom it had glued to the window, were still flattening their noses against the diamond panes, when a clear, strong, sweet voice rang out on the evening air in the back road which led by the palings of St. James's Park. Both Edith and Temperance knew well whose voice it was. They heard it every night, lifted up in one of the Psalms of David, as Hans Floriszoon came home from his work with the mercer. Hans was no longer an apprentice. Mr. Leigh had taken such a fancy to him, and entertained so complete a trust both in his skill and honesty, that six months before he had voluntarily cancelled his indentures, and made him his partner in the business. Nothing changed Hans Floriszoon. He had sung as cheerily in his humble apprenticeship, and would have done so had he been Lord Mayor of London, as now when he came down the back road, lantern in hand, every evening as regularly as the clock struck four. Mrs. Abbott declared that she set her clock by Hans whenever it stopped, which it did frequently, for it was an ancient piece of goods, and suffered from an asthmatic affection.

"There's Mestur 'Ans!" said Charity. "See thee, Rachel, I'll teem them eggs into th' pan; thou doesn't need to come."

Rachel sat by the window, trying to finish making a new apron before supper.

"That's a good lass," she said. "Eh, but it's a dark day; they'll none see a white horse a mile off to-night." [1]

"They'd have better e'en nor me to see it any night," said Charity, breaking the eggs into the pan.

"Hearken to th' lad!" said Rachel. "Eh, it's gradely [2] music, is that!"

"He sings well, does Mestur 'Ans."

The words were audible now, as the singer unlatched the gate, and turned into the garden.

> "And in the presence of my foes
>   My table Thou shalt spread':
> Thou shalt, O Lord, fill full my cup,
>   And eke anoint mine head.
>
> "Through all my life Thy favour is
>   So frankly showed to me,
> That in Thy house for evermore
>   My dwelling-place shall be.'

Hans lifted the latch and came into the kitchen.

"Here's a clean floor, Rachel! Tarry a minute, while I pluck off my shoes, and I will run across in my stocking-feet. It shall be 'February Fill-dyke,' methinks, ere the day break."

---

[1] "On Candlemas Day, you should see a white horse a mile off," is a proverb in the North, and perhaps elsewhere.

[2] Excellent, exactly right.

"He's as good as my Lady and Mrs. Edith, for not making work," said Charity as Hans disappeared.

"I would we could set him i' th' garden, and have a crop on him," responded Rachel. "He's th' only man I ever knew that 'd think for a woman."

"Eh, lass, yo' never knew Sir Aubrey!" was Charity's grave comment.

There was a good deal for Hans to hear that evening, and he listened silently while Edith told the tale, and Temperance now and then interspersed sarcastic observations. When at last the story was told, Hans said quietly,—

"Say you that you look to see Aubrey again to-morrow?"

"Lady Lettice doth, and Edith. Not I," said Temperance. " 'Tis a case wherein too many cooks might spoil the broth, and the lad shall be all the easier in his mind for his old crusty Aunt Temperance to tarry at home. But I say, Edith, I would you had asked him for a schedule of his debts. 'Tailors and silkmen' is scarce enough to go to market withal, if we had the means to pay them."

"So did I, Temperance, and he told me—twenty pounds to Mr. Tom Rookwood, and forty to Patrick at the Irish Boy; fifteen to Cohen, of the Three Tuns in Knight-riders' Street; and about ten more to Bennett, at the Bible in Paternoster Row."

"Lancaster and Derby! Why, however many suits can the lad have in his wardrobe? It should fit me out for life, such a sum as that."

"Well! I would we could discharge them," said Lady Louvaine with a sigh. "Twenty to Tom Rookwood, and forty to Patrick!"

"Make your mind easy, Madam," came in the quietest tones from Hans: "not a penny is owing to either."

"What can you mean, Hans?"

"I am sure of it."

"Who told you so much?"

"Nay, ask Mr. Rookwood, and see what he saith."

"I'll go this minute," said Temperance, rising. "I wis not what bee thou hast in thy bonnet, but I don't believe thee, lad."

"Maybe you will when you come back," was the calm response.

Away flashed Temperance, and demanded an interview with Mr. Thomas Rookwood, if he were at home. Mr. Thomas was at home, and did not express the surprise he felt at the demand. But when the subject of Aubrey's debt was introduced, Mr. Thomas's eyebrows went up.

"Mr. Louvaine owes me nothing, I do ensure you."

"I heard you had lent him twenty pounds?"

"I did; but it was repaid a month ago."

"By Aubrey?"

"So I suppose. I understood so much," was the answer, in a slightly puzzled tone.

"He repaid it not himself, then?"

"Himself, nay—he sent it to me; but I gave the quittance as to Mr. Louvaine."

"I thank you, Mr. Rookwood. Then that ends the matter."

Out of the Golden Fish, and into the White Bear, ran Temperance, with drops of rain lying on her gown and hood.

"Madam," she announced in a stern voice, "I am that flabbergasted as never was! Here's Mr. Tom Rookwood saith that Aubrey paid him his money a month gone."

"Why, Aubrey told me this afternoon that he owed him twenty pounds," replied Edith in a tone of astonished perplexity.

" Hans, what meaneth this ? "

" Methinks, Madam, it means merely that I told you the truth.   Mr. Rookwood, you see, bears me out."

" He saith Aubrey sent the money by a messenger, unto whom he gave the quittance.   Dear heart, but if he lost it ! "

" Yet Aubrey must have known, if he sent the money," said Edith in the same tone as before.

"The messenger lost not the quittance," said Hans.   " It is quite safe."

He had been out of the room for a minute while Temperance was away, and now, passing his hand into his pocket, he took out a slip of paper, which he laid in the hand of Lady Louvaine.

She drew forth her gold spectacles, and was fitting them on, when Edith impulsively sprang up, and read the paper over her mother's shoulder.

" Received of Mr. Aubrey Louvaine, gent., the sum of twenty pounds, for moneys heretofore lent by me, this fifteenth of January, the year of our Lord God MDCV., according to the computation of the Church of England.

" THO. ROOKWOOD."

" Northumberland, Cumberland, Westmoreland, and Durham ! " was the comment from Temperance.

"Hans ! " said Edith, a light flashing on her, " wert thou the messenger ? "

" I was not sent," was the placid answer.

" Hans, thou admirable rascal ! " cried Temperance, laying her hands on his shoulders, " I do believe thou didst pay this money.   If thou own not the truth, I'll shake thee in twenty bits."

Hans looked up laughingly into her face.

"Methinks, Mrs. Temperance, you should shake yourself in forty ere you did it."

"Answer me this minute, thou wicked knave! didst thou pay this money, or no?"

"I was there when it was paid."

"I'll wager my best boots thou wert! Was any else there?"

"Certainly."

"Who beside?"

"The cat, I believe."

Temperance gave him a shake, which he stood with complete calm, only looking a little amused, more about his eyes than his lips.

"Hans, tell me!" said Lady Louvaine. "Is it possible these debts were paid with thy money? How shall I repay thee, my true and dear friend?"

Hans freed himself from Temperance's grasp, and knelt down beside Lady Louvaine.

"Nay, Madam! do you forget that you paid me first —that I owe unto you mine own self and my very life? From the time we came hither I have seen pretty clearly which way Aubrey was going; and having failed to stay him, methought my next duty was to save all I could, that you should not at some after-time be cumbered with his debts. Mr. Rookwood's and Patrick's, whereof I knew, have I discharged; and the other, for which I have a sufficiency, will I deal withal to-morrow, so that you can tell Aubrey he is not a penny in debt——"

"Save to thee, my darling boy."

"There are no debts between brothers, Madam, or should not be."

"Hans, thou downright angel, do forgive me!" burst from Temperance.

"Dear Mrs. Temperance, I should make a very poor angel; but I will forgive you with all mine heart when I know wherefore I should do it."

"Why, lad, here have I been, like an old curmudgeon

x

as I am, well-nigh setting thee down as a pennyfather, because I knew not what thou didst with thy money. It was plain as a pikestaff what Aubrey did with his, for he set it all out on his back; but thy habit is alway plain and decent, and whither thy crowns went could I never tell. Eh, but I am sorry I misjudged thee thus! 'Tis a lesson for me, and shall be my life long. I do believe thou art the best lad ever trod shoe-leather."

"Well, 'tis a very proper deed, Hans, and I am glad to see in you so right a feeling," said Mrs. Louvaine.

"The Lord bless thee, my boy!" added Lady Louvaine, with emotion. "But how may I suffer thee to pay Aubrey's debts?"

"I scarce see how you shall set about to help it, Madam," said Hans with a little laugh of pleasure. "I thank God I have just enough to pay all."

"And leave thyself bare, my boy?" said Edith.

"Of what, Mrs. Edith?" asked Hans with a smile. "'A man's life consisteth not in the abundance of the things which he possesseth.' I am one of the richest men in England, I take it, and my wealth is not of a sort that shall make it hard to enter into the Kingdom of God. The corn and wine and oil may be good things, and are such, being God's gifts: yet the gladness which He giveth is a better, and will abide when they are spent."

Lady Oxford kept her word, and his grandmother and Aunt Edith had a farewell interview with Aubrey. His face was a study for a painter when the receipts were shown him. Tom Rookwood had refused him a second loan only a few weeks earlier, and had pressed him to repay the former: Hans Floriszoon had paid his debts without even letting him know it. Yet he had lent many a gold piece to Tom Rookwood, while the memory of that base, cruel blow given to Hans made his cheek burn with shame. Had he not been treasuring the pebble, and flinging away the pearl?

"Hans has paid my debts!" he said, in an exceedingly troubled voice. "Hans! out of his own pocket? May God forgive me! Tell him—" and Aubrey's voice was almost choked—"tell him he hath heaped coals of fire on mine head."

Edith asked no questions, but she gave a shrewd guess which was not far off the truth, and she was confirmed in it by the fact that Hans received the message with a smile, and expressed no doubt what it meant.

That night there were twenty-two miles between Aubrey and London: and the next day he rode into Oxford, and delivered Mr. Marshall's letter of recommendation to the bookseller, Mr. Whitstable, whose shop was situated just inside the West Gate—namely, in close contiguity to that aristocratic part of the city now known as Paradise Square.

Mr. Whitstable was a white-haired man who seemed the essence of respectability. He stooped slightly in the shoulders, and looked Aubrey through and over, with a pair of dark, brilliant, penetrating eyes, in a way not exactly calculated to add to that young gentleman's comfort, nor to restore that excellent opinion of his own virtues which had been somewhat shaken of late.

"You are of kin to the writer of this letter, Mr. Marshall?"

Aubrey admitted it.

"And you desire to learn my trade?"

"I am afeared I scarce do desire it, Master: but I am content, and needs must."

"What have you hitherto done?"

"Master," said Aubrey, looking frankly at his questioner, "I fear I have hitherto done nothing save to spend money and make a fool of myself. That is no recommendation, I know."

"You have done one other thing, young man," said the old bookseller: "you have told the truth. That is a recommendation. Mr. Marshall tells me not that, yet can I read betwixt the lines. I shall ask you no questions, and as you deal with me, so shall I with you. Have you eaten and drunk since you entered the city? Good: take this cloth, and dust that row of books. I shall give you your diet, three pound by the year, and a suit of livery."

And Mr. Whitstable walked away into the back part of his shop, leaving Aubrey to digest what he had just heard.

The idea of wearing livery was not in his eyes, what it would be in ours, a part of his humiliation, for it was then customary for gentlemen, as well as servants, to wear the livery of their employers. Even ladies did it, when in the service of royal or noble mistresses. This, therefore, was merely what he might expect in the circumstances: and as his own meanest suit was not in keeping with his new position, it was rather a relief than otherwise. But he was slightly disconcerted to find how accurately his master had read him in the first minute. A little wholesome reflection brought Aubrey to the conclusion that his best plan—nay, his only plan in present circumstances—was to accommodate himself to them, and to do his very best in his new calling. Almost unconsciously, he set Hans before him as a suitable example, and dusted the row of books under this influence in a creditable manner.

His experiences for the evening were new and strange.

Now an undergraduate entered for the Epistles of Casau-
bon or the Paraphrases of Erasmus ; now a portly citizen
demanded the Mirrour of Magistrates ; a labouring man
asked for the Shepherd's Calendar ; a schoolmaster required a dozen horn-books, and a lady wanted a hand-
somely-bound Communion Book. Psalters, at two shillings
each ; grammars, from sixpence to a shilling ; Speed's
Chronicle at fifty shillings, a map of England at thirty,
the Life of Sir Philip Sidney at fourpence, a "paper
book" at sixteenpence, an Italian Dictionary at fifteen
shillings—classics, song-books, prayer-books, chronicles,
law-books—Aubrey learned to handle them all, and to
repeat their prices glibly, in a style which astonished
himself. At the end of a week, Mr. Whitstable told
him, in his usual grave and rather curt manner, that if
he would go on as he had begun, he should be satisfied
with him.

The going on as he had begun was precisely the
difficulty with Aubrey. To do some magnificent deed
by a sudden spurt of heroism, or behave angelically for
a day, might be possible to him ; but that quiet daily
fulfilment of uninteresting duties—that patient continuance in well-doing, which seemed as if it came naturally
to Hans, was to Aubrey Louvaine the hardest thing on
earth. Had the lesson been a little less sharp, humanly
speaking, he would have failed. But Aubrey's conscience
had been startled into life, and he was beginning to see
that it would be too little profit to gain the whole world,
if in so doing he lost his own soul, which was himself.
Men are apt to look on their souls not as themselves, but
as a sort of sacred possession, a rich jewel to be worn
on Sundays, and carefully put up in cotton-wool for the
rest of the week—of immense value, theoretically, of
course, yet not at all the same thing as the "*me*" which
is the centre of sensation to each one, and for which

every man will give all that he hath. The mountain was
terribly steep, but Aubrey climbed it—only God knew with
how much inward suffering, and with how many fervent
prayers. The Aubrey who sold Mr. Whitstable's books that
spring in the shop at the West Gate of Oxford, was a
wholly different youth from my Lord Oxford's gentleman
only a few weeks before.

Three months had passed by, and no further apprehensions were entertained at the White Bear of any Government inquiries. If Lady Oxford still felt any, she kept
them to herself.

It was a summer evening; Hans had come home, and
the little family party were seated in the parlour, when a
summons of Charity to the front door was followed by her
appearance before the ladies.

"Madam," said she, "here's one would have speech of
your Ladyship, and he'll not take a civil nay, neither. I
told him he might ha' come i' daylight, and he said
you'd be just as fain of him i' th' dark. He's none aila,[1]
for sure."

"Well, let him come in, Charity," said Lady Louvaine
smiling.

Charity drew back, and admitted a man of about five-
and-twenty years, clad in respectable but not fashionable
garments, and with an amused look in his eyes.

"I do believe your maid thinks I've come to steal the
spoons," said he. "I could scarce win her to let me
in. Well, does nobody know me? Don't you, Grandmother?"

"Why, sure! 'tis never David Lewthwaite?" responded
Lady Louvaine in some excitement.

"'Tis David Lewthwaite, the son of your daughter Milisent," said he, laughing.

---

[1] Bashful.

"Why, who was to know you, my boy?" asked his Aunt Edith. "We have not seen you but once since we came, and you have changed mightily since then."

"When last we saw you," said Temperance, "your chin was as smooth as the hearthstone, and now you've got beard enough to fit out a flock of goats."

"Ah! I'd forgot my beard was new. Well, I have been remiss, I own: but I will expound another time the reasons why you saw me not oftener. To-night, methinks, you'll have enough to do to hearken to the cause which has brought me at last."

"No ill news, David, I trust?" asked his grandmother, growing a shade paler.

"None, Madam. And yet I come to bring news of death."

"Of whose death?"

"Of the death of Oswald Louvaine, of Selwick Hall."

There was a cry from Edith—"O David, can you possibly mean—is Selwick come back to us?"

"Oswald Louvaine died unwedded, and hath left no will. His heir-at-law is my cousin Aubrey here."

"May the Lord help him to use it wisely!" said his grandmother, with emotion.

"Amen!" said David, heartily. "And now, Madam, as I have not stolen the spoons, may I let somebody else in, that I left round the corner?—whom, perchance, you may care rather to see than me."

"Prithee bring whom thou wilt, David; there shall be an hearty welcome for him."

"Well, I rather guess there will be," said David, as he walked out of the parlour. "Dear heart, but who] is talking fast enough to shame a race-horse?"

"Well, now, you don't say so!" was what met David's ear as he unlatched the gate of the White Bear. "And you've come from Camberwell, you say? Well, that's a good bit o' walking, and I dare be bound you're weary. I'd——"

"I cry you mercy,—Cumberland," said a silvery voice in amused tones.

"Dear heart! why, that's a hundred mile off or more, isn't it? And how many days did it take you?—and how did you come—o' horseback?—and be the roads very miry?—and how many of you be there?—and what kin are you to my Lady Lettice, now? and how long look you to tarry with her?"

"My mistress," said David, doffing his hat, "an't like you, I am a lawyer; and to-morrow morning, at nine o'clock, if you desire it, will I be at your service in the witness-box, for two shillings the week and my diet. For to-night, I wish you good even."

"Lack-a-daisy!" was all that Mrs. Abbott could utter, as David rescued the owner of the silvery voice, and bore her off, laughing, to the White Bear.

"Madam, and my mistresses," he said, as he threw open the door, "I have the honour to announce the most excellent Mistress Milisent Lewthwaite."

Tears and laughter were mixed for more than one present, as Milisent flew into her mother's arms, and then gave a fervent hug to her sister Edith.

"I would come with Robin!" she cried. "It feels like a whole age since I saw one of you!"

"My dear heart, such a journey!" said her mother. "And where is the dear Robin, then?"

"Oh, he shall be here anon. He tarried but to see to the horses, and such like; and I set off with Davie—I felt as though I could not bear another minute."

"Madam, I give you to wit," said David, with fun in his eyes, "this mother of mine, that had not seen me for an whole year, spake but three words to me—'How fare you, my boy?' 'Help me to 'light,' and 'Now let us be off to Westminster.'"

" Well, I had seen thee in a year," answered Milisent, echoing his laugh, "and them not for three years, less a month."

A little soft echoing laugh came from Lady Louvaine.

" Shall I tell thee, my dear heart, what I think Aunt Joyce should say to thee? ' Well done, Lettice Eden's daughter!'"

"Ah, Mother dear!" said Milisent, kissing her mother's hand, "I may be like what you were as a young maid, but never shall I make by one-half so blessed a saint in mine old age."

"That must you ask your grandchildren," said Temperance.

"Nay, I will ask somebody that can judge better," replied Milisent, laughing. "What sayest thou, Robin?"

Mr. Lewthwaite had entered so quietly that only his wife's quick eyes had detected his presence. He came forward now, kissed Lady Louvaine's hand, and then laying his hand on Milisent's bright head, he said softly—

"'The heart of her husband doth safely trust in her; she will do him good and not evil all the days of her life. She openeth her mouth with wisdom, and in her tongue is the law of kindness. Her children arise up and call her blessed; her husband also, and he praiseth her.'"

Whether he would have gone further was never to be known, for a sudden rap at the door preceded Charity.

"Madam, here's Mistress Abbott, and hoo will come in. I cannot keep her out. I've done my best."

And they were all feeling so happy, and yet, for various reasons, so humble,—the two are very apt to go together, —that, as Edith observed afterwards, there was charity enough and to spare even for Silence Abbott.

CHAPTER XIV.

ENDS WITH JOYCE MORRELL.

> " Vanished is each bright illusion ;
>   They have faded one by one :
> Yet they gaze with happy faces,
>   Westwards to the setting sun :—
>
> " Talking softly of the future,
>   Looking o'er the golden sands,
> Towards a never-fading city,
>   Builded not with earthly hands."
>
> —Cyrus Thornton.

WELL, to be sure ! My man wouldn't let me come no sooner—'tis his fault, not mine. But I did want to know which of them lads o' ours told his tale the rightest. Here's Seth will have it you've had a thousand left you by the year, and Ben he saith young Master Floriszoon's to be a lord."

"Dear ! I hope not," said Hans.

"Well ! but they're a-saying so much all up and down the King's Street, I can tell you."

"How could it have crept forth ? " said Edith.

"Then 'tis true ? Eh, but I'm as glad as if I'd had forty shillings left me,—I am, so ! " cried Mrs. Abbott; and she was sincere, for a fresh subject for conversation was worth quite that to her. "And is it true, as our Seth said, that you've a fine house and a park in

Northamptonshire come to you, and fifteen hundred head o' red deer and a lake to fish in ?"

" Quite true," said Robert Lewthwaite, with a grave bow, "allowing, my mistress, of four corrections : there is not a park, it is not in Northamptonshire, there be no red deer, and the lake 'longeth not to the house."

" And jewels worth ever so many thousands, as our Ben saith, for Mistress Lettice, and ten Barbary horses o' th' best, and a caroche fine enough for the King's Majesty ?"

" Ah, I would that last were true," said Edith.

" My mistress, the Barbary horses be all there saving ten, and the caroche is a-building in the air: as to the jewels, seeing they be Mistress Lettice's, I leave her to reply."

Lettice was in no condition to do it, for she was suffering torments from suppressed laughter. Her Uncle Robert's preternatural gravity, and Mrs. Abbott's total incapacity to see the fun, were barely endurable.

" Eh, but you will be mortal fine !" said Mrs. Abbott, turning her artillery on the afflicted Lettice. " I only wish our Mall had such a chance. If she——"

" Mrs. Abbott, I cry you mercy, but here comes your Caleb," said Hans calmly. " I reckon he shall be after you."

" I reckon he shall, the caitiff ! That man o' mine, he's for ever and the day after a-sending the childer after me."

" I rejoice to hear you have so loving an husband," Mr. Lewthwaite was sufficiently inconsiderate to respond.

" Eh, bless you, there's no love about it. Just like them men ! they'd shut a woman's mouth up as tight as a fish, and never give her no leave to speak a word, if they had their way. But I'm not one of your meek bag-puddings, that'll take any shape you pinch 'em,—

not I, forsooth; and he knows it.   I'll have my say,
soon or late, and Prissy, she's a downright chatter-box.
Not that I'm that, you know—not a bit of it: but
Prissy, she is; and I can tell you, when Prissy and
Dorcas and Ben they're all at it, the house isn't over
quiet, for none on 'em hearkens what t'others are saying,
and their father whacks 'em by times—ay, he doth! Now,
Caleb, what's to do?"

"Nothing particular, Mother," said slow, deliberate
Caleb through the open window: "only there's yon
pedlar with the mercery, and he willn't tarry only ten
minutes more——"

"Thou lack-halter rascal, and ne'er told me while I
asked thee!"

The parlour of the White Bear was free in another
moment.

"There's a deliverance!" said Mr. Lewthwaite.   "Blessed
be the pedlar!—Have you been much pestered by that
gadfly?"

"There's been a bit of buzzing by times," replied Temperance.

"Now, Mother, darling," said Milisent, "how are we to
carry you down home?"

"My dear child!" was the response.   "Methinks, if
you would do that, it should be only in my coffin.   I have
one journey to go soon, and it is like to be the next."

"Mother, sweet heart, I won't have it! You shall yet
win to Selwick, if I carry you every foot of the way."

"Nay, nay, my dear heart, I cannot hope that at fourscore."

"Fourscore! ay, or forty score!" cried Milisent.   "Why,
old Mistress Outhwaite journeyed right to the Border but
just ere we came, and she's four years over the fourscore—
and on horseback belike.   Sure, you might go in a waggon
or a caroche!"

" Where is the caroche, Milly ? "

" Well ! but at any rate we might find a waggon."

"There is a travelling waggon," said Hans, "leaves the Chequers in Holborn for York, once in the month—methinks 'tis the first Thursday in every month."

"That is three weeks hence. Why not ? Sure, your landlord would suffer you to let this house, and you might leave some behind till it were off your hands. What saith Temperance ?—or Hans ? "

" That where my Lady goeth, I go," was the answer from Hans.

" Is it needful, Milly, to settle all our futures ere the clock strike ? " humorously inquired Mr. Lewthwaite. " Methinks we might leave that for the morrow."

Milisent laughed, and let the subject drop.

Mr. Lewthwaite and Temperance happened to be the last up that night. When all the rest had departed, and Charity came with the turf to bank up the parlour fire for the night, Temperance was saying,—

" One thing can I promise you,—which is, if Aubrey return to Selwick as lord and master, you may trust Faith to go withal. As for me, I live but in other lives, and where I am most needed, there will I be, if God be served : but truly, I see not how we shall move my Lady Lettice. I would fain with all my heart have her back yonder, and so she would herself,—of that am I right sure. But to ride so far on an horse, at her years, and with her often pains—how could she ? And though the waggon were safer, it were too long and weary a journey. Think you not so ? "

Charity, having now settled her peat-sod to her satisfaction, left the room, with a hearty—" Good-night, Mrs. Temperance ! Good-night, Mestur Robin ! "

" Truly, I think with you," said Mr. Lewthwaite, when she was gone : " but there is time to consider the matter. Let us decide nothing in haste."

The next morning, for the first time for many weeks, Charity asked for a holiday. It was granted her, and she was out till twelve o'clock, when she came home with a very satisfied face.

Ways and means were discussed that day, but to little practical purpose. Of course Aubrey must be informed of the good fortune which had fallen to him: and after some consideration, it was settled that if Hans could make arrangements with Mr. Leigh, he should be the messenger in this direction, setting forth when Sunday was over. People did not rush off by the next train in those days, and scald their tongues with hot coffee in order to be in time.

The Saturday evening came, and with it the calm quiet which most Puritan families loved to have on the eve of the Lord's Day. While it was not necessary, it was nevertheless deemed becoming to lay aside secular occupations, and to let worldly cares rest. There was therefore some astonishment in the parlour when a sudden rap came on the door, and Charity's face and cap made their appearance.

"If you please, Madam, when'll you be wanting your coach, think you?"

"My coach, Charity!" said Lady Louvaine in amazement.

Everybody was staring at Charity.

"It's ready, Madam," said that damsel with much placidity. "He's only got to put the horses to, hasn't 'Zekiel, and they're at Tomkins' stable yon, by th' Tilt Yard—Spring Gardens, I reckon they call it."

"Charity, lass, are you in your right senses, think you?" demanded Temperance.

"Well, Mrs. Temperance, I reckon you'll be best judge o' that," said Charity coolly. "Seems to me I am: but that scarce makes sure, I count."

"But, Charity!—what Ezekiel?"

"''Zekiel Cavell, Mrs. Edith. He's i' th' kitchen: you can see him if you've a mind."

"Ezekiel Cavell! Aunt Joyce's coachman! Where on earth has he come from?"

"Well, I rather think it was somewhere on earth," answered the calm Charity, "and I expect it was somewhere i' Oxfordshire. Howbeit, here he is, and so's th' coach, and so's th' horses: and he says to me, 'Charity,' says he, 'will you ask my Lady when she'll be wanting th' coach?' So I come."

Everybody looked at everybody else.

"Is it possible?" cried Edith. "Has dear Aunt Joyce sent her coach to carry down Mother home?"

"Nay, it's none hers, it's my Lady's," said Charity, "and nobry else's; and if she's a mind to bid me chop it up for firewood, I can, if Mestur 'Ans 'll help me. We can eat th' horses too, if she likes; but they mun be put in salt, for we's ne'er get through 'em else. There's six on 'em. Shall I tell Rachel to get th' brine ready?"

"Charity, what have you been doing?" said Hans, laughing.

"I've done nought, Mestur 'Ans, nobut carry a letter where it belonged, and serve 'Zekiel his four-hours."

They began to see light dawning on the mystery.

"A letter to whom, Charity? and who writ it?"

"To Mestur Marshall: and Mrs. Joyce Morrell writ it—leastwise her man did, at her bidding."

"What said it?"

"I didn't read it, Sir," responded Charity, demurely.

"Come, I reckon you know what was in it," said Mr. Lewthwaite. "Out with it, Charity."

"Come forward into the room, Charity, and tell your tale like a man," said Temperance.

"I amn't a man, Mrs. Temperance," answered Charity,

doing as she was bid: "but I'll tell it like a woman. Well, when I were with Mrs. Joyce, afore we came hither, hoo gave me a letter,—let's see! nay, it were two letters, one lapped of a green paper, and one of a white. And hoo said, as soon as yo' geet[1] here, I were to ask my way to Shoe Lane, just outside o' th' City gate, and gi'e th' letter i' th' white paper to Mestur Marshall. And th' green un I were to keep safe by me, till it came —if it did come—that my Lady lacked a coach either to journey home or to Minster Lovel, and when I heard that, I were to carry it to Mestur Marshall too. So I did as I were bid. What were i' th' letters I cannot tell you, but Mestur Marshall come to see you as soon as he geet th' white un, and when he geet th' green un come 'Zekiel wi' th' coach and th' tits. Mrs. Joyce, hoo said hoo were feared nobry'd tell her if a coach were wanted, and that were why she gave me th' letter. So now you know as much as I know: and I hope you're weel pleased wi' it: and if you please, what am I to say to 'Zekiel?"

"Dear Aunt Joyce!" said Edith under her breath.

"Make Ezekiel comfortable, Charity," said Lady Louvaine, as she drew off her glasses and wiped them: "and on Monday we will talk over the matter and come to some decision thereupon."

The decision unanimously come to on the Monday was that Hans should ride down to Oxford and see Aubrey before anything else was settled. Lady Louvaine would have liked dearly to return home to Selwick, but Aubrey was its master, and was of age, and he might be contemplating matrimony when he could afford it. If so, she would make a long visit—possibly a life-long one— to her beloved Joyce at Minster Lovel, accompanied by Edith. Temperance and Lettice were to return to Kes-

[1] Got.

wick: Faith must please herself. That Faith would please herself, and would not much trouble herself about the pleasing of any one else, they were tolerably convinced : and of course Aubrey's own mother had a greater claim on him than more distant relatives. She would probably queen it at Selwick, unless Aubrey provided the Hall with a younger queen in her place.

It was on a lovely summer afternoon that Hans rode into Oxford by the Water Gate or Little Gate, from which a short street led up northwards to Christ Church and St. Aldate's. Just beyond these, he passed through the city portal of South Gate, and turning to the left down Brewers' Street, he soon came to Mr. Whitstable's shop under the shadow of West Gate. Just on the eastern side was a livery stable, where Hans put up his horse : and then, wishing to see Aubrey before he should be recognised, he walked straight into the shop. At the further end, Aubrey was showing some solid-looking tomes to two solid-looking dons, while Mr. Whitstable himself was just delivering a purchase to a gentleman in canonicals. Hans stepped up to the bookseller, and in a low tone asked him for a Book of Articles. This meant the famous Thirty-Nine, then sold separate from the Prayer-Book at a cost of about sixpence.

Mr. Whitstable laid three copies on the counter, of which Hans selected one, and then said, still speaking low,—

" May I, with your good leave, tarry till my brother yonder is at liberty, and have speech of him ? I have ridden from London to see him."

The keen eyes examined Hans critically.

" You—brothers ? " was all the reply of the old bookseller.

" Not by blood," said Hans with a smile, " nor truly by nation : but we were bred up as brothers from our cradles."

"You may tarry. Pray you, sit."

Hans complied, and sat for a few minutes watching Aubrey. He perceived with satisfaction that his costume was simple and suitable, entirely devoid of frippery and foppery; that his mind seemed to be taken up with his employment; that he was looking well, and appeared to understand his business. At last the grave and reverend signors had made their choice; Bullinger's Decades, at nine shillings, was selected, and Beza's New Testament, at sixteen: Aubrey received the money, gave the change, and delivered the books. He was following his customers down the shop when his eyes fell on Hans. Whether on this occasion he was welcome or not, Hans was not left to doubt. Every feature of Aubrey's face, every accent of his voice, spoke gratification in no measured tones.

"Hans, my dear brother!" he said as they clasped hands. "When came you? and have you had to eat since? How left you all at home?"

Mr. Whitstable was looking on, with eyes that saw.

"I came but now, and have left all well, God be thanked," said Hans. "I have not yet eaten, for I wished to see you first. I will now go and break bread, and we can meet in the evening, when you are at large."

There was a momentary look of extreme disappointment, and then Aubrey said,—

"That is right, as you alway are. Where meet we? under West Gate?"

Mr. Whitstable spoke. "Methinks, Mr. Louvaine, it were pity to snatch the crust from an hungry man. Go you now with your brother, until he make an end of his supper; then return here in time to make up accounts and close. If this gentleman be the steady and sober man that his looks and your words promise, you can bring him hither to your chamber for the night."

"I thank you right heartily, Master.   He is sober as Mr. Vice-Chancellor, and good as an angel," said Aubrey.

Hans followed him, with an amused look, to the Golden Lion, where they supped on chicken and Banbury cakes, and Aubrey heard all the news—the one item excepted which Hans had come especially to tell.   The tongues went fast, but no sooner had the hour rung out from the clock of St. Ebbe's than Aubrey sprang up and said he must return.

"Thou canst wander forth for an hour, only lose not thyself," he said to Hans, "and when my work is done, I will join thee beneath the arch of West Gate."

Hans obeyed with amused pleasure.   This was an altered Aubrey.   When had he cared to keep promises and be in time for work?   They met presently under West Gate, and Aubrey played cicerone until dusk set in, when he took Hans to his own quiet little chamber at the book-seller's shop.   It was very plainly furnished, and Hans quickly saw that on the drawers lay a Bible which bore evidence of being used.

"Thou little wist," said Hans affectionately, when they were thus alone, "how glad I am to see thee, Aubrey, and to perceive thy good welfare in this place."

He did not add "good conduct," but he meant it.

"How much richer shouldst thou have been, Hans, if thou hadst never beheld me?" was the answer.

"I should have been poorer, by the loss of the only brother I ever had."

There was more feeling in Aubrey's look than Hans was wont to see, and an amount of tenderness in his tone which he had no idea how it astonished Hans to hear.

"My brother," he said, "you have had your revenge, and it is terrible."

Hans looked, as he felt, honestly surprised.   It was his nature to remember vividly benefits received, but to forget those which he conferred.

"Dost thou not know?" said Aubrey, reading the look. "After my unworthy conduct toward thee, that thou shouldst take my debts upon thine own——"

"Prithee, shut thy mouth," answered Hans with a laugh, "and make me not to blush by blowing the trumpet over that which but gave me a pleasure. I ensure thee, my brother," he added more gravely, "that I had a sufficiency to cover all was a true contentment unto me. As to revenge, no such thought ever crossed my mind for a moment."

"The revenge had been lesser if it were designed," was the reply.

"And how goeth it with thee here?" asked Hans, not sorry to change the subject. "Art thou content with thy work?—and doth Mr. Whitstable entreat thee well?"

"Mr. Whitstable is the manner of master good for me," responded Aubrey with a smile: "namely, not unkindly, but inflexibly firm and just. I know that from him, if I deserve commendation, I shall have it; and if I demerit blame, I am evenly sure thereof: which is good for me. As to content—ay, I am content; but I can scarce go further, and say I find a pleasure in my work. That were more like thee than me."

"And if it so were, Aubrey, that the Lord spake unto thee and me, saying, 'Work thus no more, but return unto the old life as it was ere ye came to London town' —how shouldst thou regard that?"

The momentary light of imagination which sprang to Aubrey's eyes was succeeded and quenched by one of wistful uncertainty.

"I cannot tell, Hans," said he. "That I were glad is of course: that I were wise to be glad is somewhat more doubtful. I am afeared I might but slip back into the old rut, and fall to pleasing of myself. Riches and liberty seem scarce to be good things for me; and I have of late—" a little hesitation accompanied this part of the sentence—" I have thought it best to pray God to send me that which He seeth good, and not to grant my foolish desires. Truly, I seem to know better, well-nigh every day, how foolish I have been, and how weak I yet am."

There was a second of silence before Hans said,—

"Aubrey, what God sees good for thee, now, is the old home at Selwick Hall. May He bless it to thee, and fit thee for it!"

"What mean you?" asked the bewildered Aubrey.

A few minutes put him in possession of the facts. Nothing which had passed convinced Hans of a radical change in Aubrey's heart, so completely as the first sentence with which he greeted the news of his altered fortune.

"Then my dear old grandmother can go home!"

"Thou wilt be glad to hear," added Hans, quietly, "that Mrs. Joyce Morrell hath sent her a caroche and horses wherein to journey at her ease. Mrs. Temperance and Lettice go back to Keswick."

"Not if I know it!" was the hearty response. "I lack Aunt Temperance to keep me straight. Otherwise I should have nought save soft south-west airs playing around me, and she is a cool north breeze that shall brace me to my duty. But how quick, Hans, canst thou get free of Mr. Leigh? for we must not tarry Grandmother at her years, and in this summer weather when journeying were least weariful."

"Wilt thou have me, then, Aubrey?"

"Hans, that is the worst cut thou hast ever given me. I have a mind to say I will not turn back without thee."

Hans smiled. "I thank thee, my dear brother. I dare

say that I can be quit with Mr. Leigh as soon as thou canst shake thee free of Mr. Whitstable."

Mr. Whitstable smiled rather cynically when the matter was laid before him.

"Well, young gentleman!" said he to Aubrey. "Methinks you shall make a better country squire than you should have done three months gone, and maybe none the worse for your tarrying with the old bookseller."

"Mr. Whitstable, I con you hearty thanks for your good and just entreatment of me," said Aubrey, "and if ever your occasions call you into Cumberland, I promise you a true welcome at Selwick Hall."

That night, Aubrey seemed to be in a brown study, and the sagacious Hans let him alone till his thoughts should blossom forth into words of themselves. They came at last.

"Hans, thou wist it is customary for chaplains to be entertained in great houses?"

"Ay," said Hans, smiling to himself.

"I desire not to ape the great: but—thinkest thou we might not have a prophet's chamber in some corner at Selwick—the chamber over the east porch, belike?"

"Truly, if the prophet were to hand," said Hans, looking as grave as if he were not secretly amused.

"The prophet is to hand rather than the chamber," was the answer. "Couldst thou not guess I meant Mr. Marshall?"

Hans had guessed it some seconds back.

"A good thought, truly," he replied.

"That will I ask my grandmother," said Aubrey.

It was the evening after Aubrey's return to the White Bear when that proposal was suggested to Lady Louvaine. A light of gladness came to the dim blue eyes.

"My dear lad, how blessed a thought!" said she.

"But what should come of Mrs. Agnes, then?" suggested Temperance.

"Oh, she could easily be fitted with some service," answered Mrs. Louvaine, who for once was not in a complaining mood. "Hans, you might ask of Mr. Leigh if he know of any such, or maybe of some apprenticeship that should serve her. She can well work with the needle, and is a decent maid, that should not shame her mistress, were she not over high in the world."

"Mother!"

The indignant tone of that one word brought the handkerchief instantly out of Mrs. Louvaine's pocket.

"Well, really, Aubrey, I do think it most unreasonable! Such a way to speak to your poor mother, and she a widow! When I have but one child, and he——"

"He is sorry, Mother, if he spake to you with disrespect," said Aubrey in a different tone. "But suffer me to say that if Mr. Marshall come with us, so must Mrs. Agnes."

"Now, Faith, do be quiet! I've been counting on Mrs. Agnes to see to things a bit, and save Edith,—run about for my Lady Lettice, see you, and get our Lettice into her good ways."

"You don't say, to spare *me*," wailed Mrs. Louvaine.

"No, my dear, I don't," replied Temperance, significantly. "I'll spare you when you need sparing; don't you fear."

Mr. Marshall and Agnes were as glad as they were astonished—and that was no little—to hear of the provision in store for them. To pass from those three rooms in Shoe Lane to the breezy hills and wide chambers of Selwick Hall—to live no more from hand to mouth, with little in either, but to be assured, as far as they could be so, among the changes and chances of this mortal life,

of bread to eat and raiment to put on—to be treated
as beloved and honoured friends instead of meeting with
scornful words and averted looks—this was glad news indeed.   Mr. Marshall rejoiced for his daughter, and Agnes
for her father.   Hers was a nature which could attain its
full happiness only in serving God and man.   To have
shut herself up and occupied herself with her own amusement would have been misery, not pleasure.   The idea
of saving trouble to Lady Louvaine and Edith, of filling
in some slight degree the empty place of that beloved
friend whom Selwick Hall called "Cousin Bess" and Agnes
"Aunt Elizabeth"—this opened out to Agnes Marshall
a prospect of unadulterated enjoyment.   To her father,
whose active days were nearly over, and who was old
rather with work, hardship, and sorrow, than by the mere
passage of time, the lot offered him seemed equally happy.
The quiet rest, the absence of care, the plenitude of books,
the society of chosen friends who were his fellow-pilgrims,
Zionward,—to contemplate such things was almost happiness enough in itself.   And if he smothered a sigh in
remembering that his Eleanor slept in that quiet churchyard whence she could never more be summoned to rejoice
with him, it was followed at once by the happier recollec-
tion that she had seen a gladder sight than this, and that
she was satisfied with it.

It was but natural that the journey home should be of
the most enjoyable character.   The very season of the
year added to its zest.   The five ladies and two girls
travelled in the coach—private carriages were much more
roomy then than now, and held eight if not ten persons
with comfort—Mr. Lewthwaite, Aubrey, Hans, and the two
maids, were on horseback.   So they set forth from the
White Bear.

"Farewell to thee!" said Charity to that stolid-looking
animal, as she rode under it for the last time.   "Rachel,

what dost thou mean, lass?—art thou crying to leave yon beast or Mistress Abbott?"

"Nay, nother on 'em, for sure!" said Rachel, wiping her eyes; "I've nobut gotten a fly into my eye."

Mrs. Abbott, however, was not behindhand. She came out to her gate to see the cavalcade depart, followed by a train of youthful Abbotts, two or three talking at once, as well as herself. What reached the ears of the ladies in the coach, therefore, was rather a mixture.

"Fare you well, Lady Louvaine, and all you young gentlewomen!—and I hope you'll have a safe journey, and a pleasant; I'm sure——"

"I'll write and tell you the new modes, Mrs. Lettice," said Prissy; "you'll have ne'er a chance to——"

"Be stuck in the mud ere you've gone a mile," came in Seth's voice.

"And where tarry you to-night, trow?" demanded Mrs. Abbott. "Is it to be at St. Albans or——"

"Up a-top of yon tree," screamed Hester; "there she was with a kitten in her mouth, and——"

"All the jewels you could think of," Dorcas was heard to utter.

The words on either side were lost, but nobody—except, perhaps, the speakers—thought the loss a serious one.

Under way at last, the coach rumbled with dignity up King Street, through the Court gates, past Charing Cross and along the Strand—a place fraught with painful memories to one at least of the party—past the Strand Cross, through Temple Bar, up Fetter Lane, over Holborn Bridge and Snow Hill, up Aldersgate Street, along the Barbican, and by the fields to Shoreditch, into the St. Albans Road. As they came out into the Shoreditch Road, a little above Bishopsgate, they were equally surprised and gratified to find Lady Oxford's groom of the chambers standing and waiting for their approach. As he recognised the faces, he stepped forward. In his hand was a very handsome cloak of fine cloth, of the shade of brown then called meal-colour, lined with crimson plush, and trimmed with beaver fur.

"Madam, my Lady bids you right heartily farewell, and prays you accept this cloak to lap you at night in your journey, with her loving commendations: 'tis of her Ladyship's own wearing."

It was considered at that time to add zest to a gift, if it had been used by the giver.

Lady Louvaine returned a message suited to the gratitude and pleasure which she felt at this timely remembrance, and the coach rolled away, leaving London behind.

"Weel, God be wi' thee and all thine!" said Charity, looking back at the great metropolis: "and if I ne'er see thee again, it'll none break my heart."

"Nay, nor mine nother!" added Rachel. "I can tell thee, lass, I'm fair fain to get out o' th' smoke and mire. Th' devil mun dwell i' London, I do think."

"I doubt it not," said Hans, who heard the remark, "but he has country houses, Rachel."

"Well!" said that damsel, in a satisfied tone: "at any rate, we shalln't find him at Selwick!"

"Maybe not, if the house be empty," was Hans's reply: "but he will come in when we do, take my word for it."

"Yo're reet, Mestur 'Ans," said Charity, gravely.

Four days' travelling brought them to the door of the Hill House at Minster Lovel. They had had no opportunity of sending word of their coming.

"How amazed Aunt Joyce will be, and Rebecca!" said Edith, with a happy laugh.

"I reckon they'll have some work to pack us all in," answered Temperance.

"Let be, children," was the response of Lady Louvaine. "The Hill House is great enough to hold every one of us, and Aunt Joyce's heart is yet bigger."

For a coach and six to draw up before the door of a country house was then an event which scarcely occurred so often as once a year. It was no great wonder, therefore, if old Rebecca looked almost dazed as she opened the door to so large a party.

"We are going home, Rebecca!" cried Edith's bright, familiar voice. "How fares my Aunt?"

"Eh, you don't mean it's you, mine own dear child?" cried the old servant lovingly. "And your Ladyship be-like! Well, here is a blessed even! It'll do the mistress all the good in the world. Well, she's very middling, my dear—very middling indeed: but I think 'tis rather weariness than any true malady, and that'll flee afore the sight of you like snow afore the warm sun. Well, there's a smart few of you!—all the better, my dear, all the better!"

"You can hang one or two of us up in a tree, if you can't find us room," said Aubrey as he sprang from his saddle.

"There's room enough for such good stuff, and plenty to spare," answered old Rebecca. "If you was some folks, now, I might be glad to have the spare chambers full of somewhat else—I might! Come in, every one of you!"

"We'll help you to make ready, all we can," said Rachel, as she trudged after Rebecca to the kitchen.

"Ay, we will," echoed Charity.

Warmer and tenderer yet was the welcome in the Credence Chamber, where Aunt Joyce lay on her couch, looking as though not a day had passed since she bade them farewell. She greeted each of them lovingly until Aubrey came to her. Then she said, playfully yet meaningly,—"Who is this?"

"Aunt Joyce," replied Aubrey, as he bent down to kiss her, "shall I say, 'A penitent fool?'"

"Nay, my lad," was the firm answer. "A fool is never a penitent, nor a penitent a fool. The fool hath been: let the penitent abide."

"This is our dear, kind friend, Mr. Marshall, Joyce," said Lady Louvaine. "He is so good as to come with us, and be our chaplain at Selwick: and here is his daughter."

"I think Mrs. Joyce can guess," said the clergyman, "that the true meaning of those words is that her Lady ship hath been so good as to allow of the same, to our much comfort."

"Very like you are neither of you over bad," said Aunt Joyce with her kindly yet rather sarcastic smile. "I am glad to see you, Mr. Marshall; hitherto we have known each other but on paper. Is this your daughter? Why, my maid, you have a look of the dearest and blessedest woman of all your kin—dear old Cousin Bess, that we so loved. May God make you like her in the heart, no less than the face!"

"Indeed, Mistress, I would say Amen, with all mine heart," answered Agnes, with a flush of pleasure.

There was a long discussion the next day upon ways and means, which ended in the decision that Aubrey and Hans, Faith and Temperance, with the two maids, should go forward to Selwick after a few days' rest, to get things in order; Lady Louvaine, Edith, Lettice, Agnes, and Mr. Marshall, remaining at Minster Lovel for some weeks.

"And I'm as fain as I'd be of forty shillings," said old Rebecca to Edith. "Eh, but the mistress just opens out when you're here like a flower in the sunlight!"

"Now, don't you go to want Faith to tarry behind," observed Temperance, addressing the same person: "the dear old gentlewomen shall be a deal happier without her and her handkerchief. It shall do her good to bustle about at Selwick, as she will if she's mistress for a bit,

and I'll try and see that she does no mischief, so far as
I can."

Aunt Joyce, who was the only third person present, gave
an amused little laugh.

"How long shall she be mistress, Temperance?"

"Why, till my Lady Lettice comes," said Temperance,
with a rather perplexed look.

"For 'Lady Lettice,' read 'Mrs. Agnes Marshall,'" was
the answer of Aunt Joyce.

"Aunt Joyce!" cried Edith. "You never mean——"

"Don't I? But I do, Mistress Bat's-Eyes."

"Well, I never so much as——"

"Never so much as saw a black cow a yard off, didst
thou? See if it come not true. Now, my maids, go not
and meddle your fingers in the pie, without you wish it
not to come true. Methinks Aubrey hath scarce yet read
his own heart, and Agnes is innocent as driven snow of
all imagination thereof: nevertheless, mark my words, that
Agnes Marshall shall be the next lady of Selwick Hall.
And I wouldn't spoil the pie, were I you; it shall eat
tasty enough if you'll but leave it to bake in the oven.
It were a deal better so than for the lad to fetch home
some fine town madam that should trouble herself with
his mother and grandmother but as the cuckoo with the
young hedge-sparrows in his foster-mother's nest. She's
a downright good maid, Agnes, and she is bounden to
your mother and you, and so is her father: and though,
if Selwick were to turn you forth, your home is at Minster
Lovel, as my child here knows"—and Aunt Joyce laid her
hand lovingly on that of Edith—"yet while we be here in
this short wilderness journey, 'tis best not to fall out by the
way. Let things be, children: God can take better care of
His world and His Church than you or I can do it."

"Eh, I'll meddle with nought so good," responded Temperance, heartily. "If the lad come to no worse than

that, he shall fare uncommon well, and better than he de-serveth. As for the maid, I'm not quite so sure : but I'll hope for the best."

"The best thing you can do, my dear. 'We are saved by hope'—not as a man is saved by the rope that pulleth him forth of the sea, but rather as he is saved by the light that enableth him to see and grasp it. He may find the rope in the dark ; yet shall he do it more quicklier and with much better comfort in the light. 'Hope thou in God,' 'Have faith in God,' 'Fear not'—all those precepts be brethren ; and one or other of them cometh very oft in Scripture. For a man cannot hope without some faith, and he shall find it hard to hope along with fear. Faith, hope, love—these do abide for ever."

The party for Selwick had set off, with some stir, in the early morning, and the quiet of evening found the friends left at the Hill House feeling as those left behind usually do,—enjoying the calm, yet with a sense of want.

Perhaps Mr. Marshall was the least conscious of loss of any of the party, for he was supremely happy in the library over the works of Bishop Jewell. In the gallery up-stairs, Lettice and Agnes sat in front of the two portraits which had so greatly interested the former on her previous visit, and talked about "Aunt Anstace" and "Cousin Bess," and the blessed sense of relief and thankfulness which pervaded Agnes's heart. And lastly, in the Credence Chamber, Aunt Joyce lay on her couch, and Lady Louvaine sat beside her in the great cushioned chair, while Edith, on a low stool at the foot of the couch, sat knitting peacefully, and glancing lovingly from time to time at those whom she called her two mothers.

"Joyce, dear," Lady Louvaine was saying, " 'tis just sixty years since I came over that sunshine afternoon from the Manor House, to make acquaintance with thee and Anstace. Sixty years ! why, 'tis the lifetime of an old man"

"And it looks but like sixty days, no doth it?" was the rejoinder. "Thou and I, Lettice, by reason of strength have come to fourscore years; yet is our life but a vapour that vanisheth away. I marvel, at times, how our Anstace hath passed her sixty years in Heaven. What do they there?"

"Dost thou mind, Joyce, Aubrey's once saying that we are told mainly what they do *not* there? Out of that, I take it, we may pick what they do. There shall be no night—then there must be eternal light; no curse—then must there be everlasting blessedness; no tears—then is there everlasting peace; no toil—then is there perpetual rest and comfort."

"Go on, Lettice—no sickness, therefore perfect health; no parting, therefore everlasting company and eternal love."

"Ay. What a blessed forecast! Who would not give all that he hath, but to be sure he should attain it? And yet men will fling all away, but to buy one poor hour's sinful pleasure, one pennyworth of foolish delight."

"And howsoe'er often they find the latter pall and cloy upon their tongues, yet shall they turn to it again with never-resting eagerness, as the sow to her wallowing in the mire. There is a gentleman dwells a matter of four miles hence, with whose wife and daughters I am acquaint, and once or twice hath he come with them to visit me. He hath got hold of a fancy—how, judge you—that man is not a fallen creature; indiscreet at times, maybe, and so forth, yet not wholly depraved. How man comes by this indiscretion, seeing God made him upright, he is discreet enough not to reveal. 'Dear heart!' said I, 'but how comes it, if so be, that man shall sell his eternal birthright for a mess of sorry pottage, as over and over again you and I have seen him do? Call you this but indiscretion? Methinks you should scarce name it thus if Mrs. Aletheia yonder were to cast away a rich clasp of emeralds for a piece of a broken bottle of green glass. If you whipped her not well for such indiscretion, I were something astonied.' Well, see you, he cannot perceive it."

"Man's perceptions be fallen, along with all else."

"Surely: and then shall this blind bat reckon, poor fool, that he could devise out of his disordered imagination a better God than the real. Wot you what this Mr. Watkinson said to me once when we fell to talking of the sacrifice of Isaac ? Oh, he could not allow that a loving and perfect God could demand so horrible a sacrifice ; and another time, through Christ had we won the right notion of God. 'Why,' said I, 'how know you that? Are you God, that you are able to judge what God should be? Through Christ, in very deed, have we won to know God; but that is by reason of the knowledge and authority of Him that revealed Him, not by the clear discernment and just judgment of us that received that revelation.' I do tell thee, Lettice—what with this man o' the one side with his philosophical follies, and Parson Turnham on the other, with his heathenish fooleries, I am at times wellnigh like old Elias, ready to say, 'Now then, O Lord, take me out of this wicked world, for I cannot stand it any longer.'"

"He will take thee, dear Joyce, so soon as thou shalt come to the further end of the last of those good works which He hath prepared for thee to walk in."

"Well!—then must Edith do my good works for me. When our Father calls this child in out of the sun and wind, and bids her lie down and fall asleep, must that child see to it that my garden-plots be kept trim, and no evil insects suffered to prey upon the leaves. Ay, my dear heart: thou wilt be the lady of the Hill House, when old Aunt Joyce is laid beneath the mould. May God bless thee in it, and it to thee! but whensoever the change come, I shall be the gainer by it, not thou."

"Not I, indeed!" said Edith in a husky voice.

"'As a watch in the night!'" said Joyce Morrell solemnly. "'As a vapour that vanisheth away!'" What time have we for idle fooleries? Only time to learn the letters that we shall spell hereafter—to form the strokes and loops wherewith we shall write by and bye. Here we know but the alphabet of either faith or love."

"And how often are we turned back in the very alphabet of patience!"

"Ay, we think much to tarry five minutes for God, though He may have waited fifty years for us. I reckon it takes God to bear with this poor thing, man, that even at his best times is ever starting aside like a broken bow, —going astray like a lost sheep. Thank God that He hath laid on the only Man that could bear them the iniquities of us all, and that He hath borne them into a land not inhabited, where the Lord Himself can find them no more."

"And let us thank God likewise," said Lady Lettice, "that our blessed duty is to abide in Him, and that when He shall appear, we may have confidence, and not be ashamed before Him at His coming."

HISTORICAL APPENDIX.

HISTORICAL APPENDIX.

ROBERT CATESBY.

HE was a descendant of another infamous Catesby, Sir John, the well-known Minister of Richard III., satirised in the distich—

> "The *Cat*, the Rat, and Lovel the Dog,
> Govern all England under the Hog."

This gentleman fought with his master at Bosworth, and was beheaded three days after the battle. His son George, who died in 1495–6, was father of Sir Richard, who died in 1552, and who was succeeded by his grandson Sir William, then aged six years, having been born at Barcheston in 1546. He was perverted by Campion in 1580, and developed into a famous recusant; was cited before the Star Chamber in 1581, chiefly on the confession of Campion, for being a harbourer of Jesuits and a hearer of mass; married at Ashby, 9th June 1566, Anne, daughter of Sir Robert Throckmorton of Coughton, Warwickshire; and died in 1598. The eldest of his children (four sons and two daughters) was Robert Catesby, the conspirator, born at Lapworth, Warwickshire, in 1573. At the age of thirteen—for boys went up to college then at a much earlier age than now—he matriculated, Oct. 27th, 1586, at Gloucester Hall (now Worcester College), Oxford, a house "much suspected," many of its undergraduates being privately Roman Catholics. It was probably during his residence in Oxford that he became a Protestant; and his change of religion being evidently of no moral value, he also led a dissipated and extravagant life. In 1592 he married a Protestant wife, Katherine, daughter of Sir Thomas Leigh of Stoneleigh Abbey, Warwickshire; she died before 1602. His talents were considerable, his will inflexible, and he possessed that singular power of attraction inherent in some persons. A portrait reputed to be his exists at Brockhall, near Ashby. "He was very wise," writes Gerard, "and of great judgment, though his utterance not so good. Besides, he was so liberal and apt to help all sorts, as it got him much love. He was of person above two yards high, and though slender, yet as well-proportioned to his height as any man one should see." Greenway adds that "his countenance was singularly noble and expressive, his power of influencing others very great."

In 1593, on the death of his grandmother, he came into possession of Chastleton, near Chipping Norton, co. Oxford, where he resided until 1602, when, in consequence of foolishly joining (like many other Romanists) the insurrection of Lord Essex, he sold Chastleton for £4000 to pay the fine of £3000 imposed on him for treason. He had in 1598 returned to his original faith, in defence of which he was thenceforward very zealous. Nine days before the death of Queen Elizabeth, Catesby, undeterred by his past experiences, and "hunger-starved for innovations," joined Sir Edward Baynham and the Wrights in a second plot, for which he suffered imprisonment. The Gunpowder Plot was his third treasonable venture; and to him principally is due the inception of this fearful project, though John Wright, and afterwards Thomas Winter, joined him at a very early stage. Until Easter, 1605, Catesby himself "bore all the charge" of the mine. During the summer, he was very busy gathering volunteers, arms, and ammunition, in the country, ostensibly for the service of the Archduke Albrecht in Flanders, but in reality for the purpose of creating a general commotion at the time of the intended explosion. About September, 1605, he met Percy at Bath, when they agreed to take into the plot two or three moneyed men, as their own means were fast failing. These were Digby and Tresham; Robert Winter, Rookwood, and Grant followed a little later. Catesby, however, never ceased to regret the admission of Tresham. (*See* Tresham.) In London he had three lodgings: a chamber in Percy's house in Holborn; apartments in the house of William Patrick, tailor, at the "Herishe Boy" in the Strand; and also "in the house of one Powell, at Puddle Wharf."

On the 26th of October, Catesby dined at the "Mighter" in Bread Street, with Lord Mordaunt, Sir Josceline Percy, and others; the last-named was a brother of Lord Northumberland, and a frequent visitor of Catesby. After this he met his servant William Pettye, "in a eeld called the common garden in London, by druerye lane." The story of the flight to Holbeach is given in the tale, and embraces many little details not before in print. Catesby was only thirty-three years of age at death. He left two sons, William and Robert, the latter of whom was with his father in London when the plot was discovered; they were subsequently sent in Mrs. Rookwood's coach, under charge of a lady not named, to their grandmother at Ashby. Robert alone lived to grow up, and married one of Percy's daughters; but he left no issue. "His posterity was cut off; and in the generation following, their name was blotted out."

SIR EVERARD DIGBY.

This weak and bigoted young man, who was only twenty-four at death, had really little part in the Gunpowder Plot. He was the son of Everard Digby, of Drystoke, co. Rutland, and Mary, daughter and coheir of Francis Nele, of Heythorpe, co. Leic. He was born in 1581, and lost his father, a Romanist, in 1592. His mother married again (to Sampson Erdeswick, of Landon, co. Staff., who was a Protestant), and young Digby was brought up in a Protestant atmosphere. Until his majority, he was much at Court, where he was noted for "graceful manners and rare parts," says Greenway; and

Gerard adds that "he was very little lower [in height] than Mr. Catesby, but of stronger making, . . . skilful in all things that belonged unto a gentleman, a good musician, and excelled in all gifts of mind." He is also described as "of goodly personage, and of a manly aspect." He was always strongly inclined to his father's religion, but did not openly profess it until he reached manhood. Sir Everard married, in 1596, Mary, daughter and heir of William Mulsho of Goathurst, co. Bucks, who survived him, and by whom he left a son, the famous Sir Kenelm Digby, who was little more than two years old at his father's death. If her piteous letter to Lord Salisbury may be believed, Lady Digby was treated with unnecessary harshness. She complains that the Sheriff has not left her "the worth of one peni belonging to the grounds, house, or within the walls; nor so much as great tables and standing chests that could not be removed without cutting and sawing apeses. He permitted the base people to ransack all, so much as my closet, and left me not any trifle in it. . . . He will not let me have so much as a suit of apparel for Mr. Digby [the little Kenelm], nor linens for my present wearing about my bodi." She implores to be allowed to retain Goathurst, her own inheritance, during the imprisonment of her husband, for whose life she would give hers or would beg during life. (*Burghley Papers*, Addit. MS. 6178, fol. 94.)

GUY FAWKES.

Guy Fawkes, whom his horrified contemporaries termed "the great devil of all" the conspirators, but who was simply a single-eyed fanatic, owes his reputation chiefly to the fact that he was the one selected to set fire to the powder. His responsibility was in reality less than that of Catesby, Percy, or Thomas Winter. His father, Edward Fawkes,—in all probability a younger son of the old Yorkshire family of Fawkes of Farnley,—was a notary at York, and Registrar of the Consistory Court of the Minster. He could not of course

have filled such an office, unless he had been a Protestant.
Edward Fawkes died in 1578, and was buried Jan. 17th
in the Church of St. Michael-le-Belfry, York. His widow,
whose maiden name was Edith Jackson, is said by some
to have subsequently married a zealous Roman Catholic, Mr.
Denis Bainbridge, of Scotton; but Sir W. Wade gives the
name of her second husband as "one Foster, within three
miles of York." She was living at the time of the plot. Guy,
who was baptized in St. Michael's Church, April 16th, 1570,
and educated at the Free School in the Horse Fair, did not
become a professed Papist until he was about sixteen years of
age. He had a step-brother of whom no more is known than
that he belonged to one of the Inns of Court in 1605. Guy
was not eight years old when he lost his father, who left him
no patrimony beyond a small farm worth about £30 per
annum; he soon ran through this, sold the estate, and at the
age of twenty-three went abroad, living in Flanders for eight
years, during which time he was present at the taking of
Calais by the Archduke Albrecht. In 1601 he returned to
England, with the reputation of one "ready for any enterprise
to further the faith." He now entered, along with the Winters
and the Wrights, into negotiations with Spain for a fresh inva-
sion of England, which was put a stop to by Elizabeth's death,
since the King of Spain declined to take up arms against
his old ally, King James. Fawkes's own statements in his
examinations have been proved to consist of such a mass of
falsehood, that it is scarcely possible to sift out the truth:
and all that can be done is to accept as fact such portions
of his narrative as are either confirmed by other witnesses,
or seem likely to be true from circumstantial evidence. His
contradictions of his own previous assertions were perpetual,
and where confirmation is accessible, it sometimes proves the
original statement, but sometimes, and more frequently, the
contradiction. This utter disregard for truth prepares us
to discount considerably the description given of Fawkes by
Greenway, as "a man of great piety, of exemplary temperance,

of mild and cheerful demeanour, an enemy of broils and disputes, a faithful friend, and remarkable for his punctual
attendance upon religious observances." So far as facts can
be sifted from fiction, they seem to be that Thomas Winter,
who had known Fawkes from childhood, came to him in
Flanders to acquaint him with the plot, and subsequently
introduced him to Catesby and Percy; that Fawkes was in
the service of Anthony Browne, Lord Montague, about 1604;
that in the summer of that year, when the mine was stopped
on account of the prorogation of Parliament, he went to
Flanders, returning about the 1st of September. During the
progress of the mine, he served as sentinel, passing by the
name of John Johnson, Mr. Percy's man; and he was the
only one of the conspirators allowed to be seen about the
house, his face being unknown in London. He said that he
"prayed every day that he might perform that which might
be for the advancement of the Catholic faith, and the saving
of his own soul." Fawkes provided the greater part of the
gunpowder, and stowed it in the cellar, as is described in the
story. His lodging when in London was at the house of
Mrs. Herbert, a widow, at the back of St. Clement's Inn.
Mrs. Herbert disliked Fawkes, suspecting him to be a priest.
On his return from Flanders, he took up his quarters in the
house at Westminster, where the mine had been, and brought
in the remainder of the gunpowder. At the end of October,
he went to White Webbs, whence he was sent to Town on
the 30th, to make sure of the safety of the cellar and its
dangerous contents. He returned at night to report all safe,
but came back to Town not later than the 3rd, when he was
present at the last meeting of the conspirators: but as to the
exact day he made three varying statements. The circumstances of his arrest are told in the story. It is difficult,
however, to reconcile some of the details. According to Greenway, Fawkes was taken as he opened the door of the vault;
according to the official report, he was "newly come out of the
vault;" while according to Fawkes himself, when he heard the

officers coming to apprehend him, he threw the match and touchwood "out of the window in his chamber, near the Parliament House, towards the water"—which can only refer to the room in Percy's house. The one certainty is that he was not apprehended inside the vault. He said himself that if this had been the case, he would at once have fired the match, "and have blown up all." The lantern (now in the Bodleian Library) was found lighted behind the door; the watch which Percy had sent by Keyes was upon the prisoner. Fawkes originally assumed an appearance of rustic stupidity; for Sir W. Wade writes to Lord Salisbury a little later that he "appeareth to be of better understanding and discourse than, before, either of us conceived him to be." (Addit. MS. 6178, fol. 56.) That Fawkes was tortured there can be no doubt, from the King's written command, and the tacit evidence of Fawkes's handwriting. Garnet says he was half-an-hour on the rack; Sir Edward Hoby, that he "was never on the rack, but only suspended by his arms upright." Nothing could induce him to betray his companions until he was satisfied that all was known: and with a base treachery and falsehood only too common in the statecraft of that day, he was deceived into believing them taken before they were discovered. Lying is wickedness in all circumstances; but the prisoner's falsehood was based on a worthier motive than the lies which were told to him. There was, indeed, in the fearless courage and unflinching fidelity of Guy Fawkes, the wreck of what might have been a noble man; and he certainly was far from being the vulgar ruffian whom he is commonly supposed to have been. In person he was tall and dark, with brown hair and auburn beard.

HENRY GARNET.

If Catesby be regarded as the most responsible of the Gunpowder conspirators, and Fawkes as the most courageous, Garnet may fairly be considered the most astute. Like the majority of his companions, he was a pervert. His father,

Brian Garnet, was a schoolmaster at Nottingham, and his mother's maiden name was Alice Jay. He was born in 1555, educated at Winchester College, in the Protestant faith, and was to have passed thence to New College, Oxford. This intention was never carried into effect: his Romish biographers say, because he had imbibed at Winchester a distaste to the Protestant religion; adding that "he obtained the rank of captain [of the school], and by his modesty and urbanity, his natural abilities and quickness in learning, so recommended himself to the superiors, that had he" entered at Oxford, "he might safely have calculated on attaining the highest academical honours. But he resolved, by the grace of God, upon embracing the Catholic faith, although his old Professors at Winchester, Stemp and Johnson, themselves Catholic in heart, together with another named Bilson, at first favourable, but afterwards hostile to Catholicity, made every exertion to persuade him to remain." Unhappily for this rosy narrative, the "other named Bilson," afterwards Bishop of Worcester and Winchester, has left on record his account of the matter: namely, that Garnet when at Winchester was a youth of such incorrigible wickedness, that the Warden dissuaded his going to the University, for the sake of the young men who might there be corrupted by his evil example. The reader can accept which version he may see good. On leaving school, Garnet proceeded to London, where for about two years he was employed as corrector of the press by the celebrated law-printer, Tottel. At the end of this time, he was received into the Church of Rome, and subsequently travelled abroad, first to Spain, and afterwards to Rome, where on 11th Sept., 1575, he entered the Society of Jesus. In the Jesuit College at Rome he studied diligently, under Bellarmine and others : and he was before long made Professor of Hebrew, and licensed to lecture on mathematics. In 1586, on the recommendation of Parsons, he was appointed to the Jesuit Mission to England, where he landed on July 7th. It is said that he was so remarkably amiable and gentle that Aquaviva, the General of the Jesuits, objected to his appointment on the ground that the post required a man of sterner and more unyielding character. Bellarmine records that his sanctity of life was incomparable; but Jesuits are apt to entertain peculiar notions of sanctity. As was then usual, Garnet on coming to his native country adopted a string of aliases—Walley, Darcy, Mease, Roberts, Farmer, and Phillips. Walley, however, was the name by which he was best known. Two years after he joined the Mission, he was promoted to be its Superior. For some years he lived in the neighbourhood of London, following various occupations to disguise his real calling, but chiefly that of a horse-dealer. That he was implicated in the intrigues with Spain before the death of Elizabeth, he never attempted to deny: but during the lull in the penal legislation which followed the accession of James, Garnet purchased a general pardon for all past political offences. He was frequently at Harrowden, the house of Lord Vaux, whose daughter Anne travelled everywhere with him, passing as his sister, Mrs. Perkins. About 1599, as "Mr. Mease, a Berkshire man," he took the house in Enfield Chase, named White Webbs, for the meetings of the Romanists, after which he was "seldom absent from it for a quarter of a year together." (Examination of James Johnson, servant in charge of White Webbs, *Gunpowder Plot Book*, art. 188.) This house was ostensibly taken for Anne Vaux, and was maintained at her expense; her sister Eleanor, with her husband Mr. Brooksby (whose alias was Jennings, and who is described as "of low stature, red beard, and bald head"), being often with her. Catesby was a frequent visitor. Anne Vaux had also a house at Wandsworth, where she and Garnet occasionally resided.

These details, gathered from the evidence of Anne Vaux herself, James Johnson, and others, do not, however, agree with some statements of Gerard. He asserts that Mrs. Brooksby was a widow, and was the real mistress of the house; and he compares the two to the sisters of Lazarus, "the two women who received our Lord"! It is impossible to avoid seeing the tacit further comparison as to Garnet. When a Queen's messenger arrived, Gerard writes, "rosaries, &c., all signs of piety [!] are thrown into a cavern; the mistress is hidden away: on these occasions the younger sister, the unmarried one, passed for the mistress of the house." (Gerard to Aquaviva, quoted by Foley, *Records of the English Province of the Society of Jesus*, vol. iv., p. 36.) All the evidence, apart from this, tends to show that Brooksby was alive, and that he and Eleanor were only visitors—though very constant ones—at White Webbs, where Anne was the real mistress. In 1603, Garnet was returned as living "with Mrs. Brooksby, of Leicestershire, at Arundell House. He hath lodgings of his own in London." (*Dom. State Papers*, Jac. I., vol. vii., art. 50.) These lodgings were in Thames Street. A large house at Erith was also a frequent meeting-place of the recusants.

That Garnet was acquainted with the Gunpowder Plot from its very beginning is a moral certainty, notwithstanding his earnest efforts to show the contrary. He not only made assertions which he afterwards allowed to be false; but he set up at different times two lines of defence which were inconsistent. He had been told nothing: yet, he had tried to dissuade Catesby and his colleagues from the execution of the plot. If the first allegation were true, the other must have been false. But Garnet's distinctly avowed opinions on the question of equivocation make it impossible to accept any denial from him. He believed that while "in the common intercourse of life, it is not lawful to use equivocation," yet "where it becomes necessary to an individual for his defence, or for avoiding any injustice or loss, or for obtaining any important advantage, without danger or mischief to any other person, there equivocation is lawful." He held, as some do at the present day, that "if the law be unjust, then is it, *ipso facto*, void and of no force:" so that "the laws against recusants . . . are to be esteemed as no laws by such as steadfastly believe these [Romish rites] to be necessary observances of the true religion. . . . That is no treason at all which is made treason by an unjust law." In other words, the subject is to be the judge of the justice of the law, and if in his eyes it be unjust, he is released from the necessity of obeying it ! This is simply to do away with all law at once; for probably no law was ever made which did not appear unjust to somebody : and it lays down the grand and ancient principle that every man shall do what is right in his own eyes. We have heard a good deal of this doctrine lately; it is of Jesuit origin, and a distinct contradiction of that Book which teaches that "the powers that be are ordained of God, and whosoever resisteth the power, resisteth the ordinance of God." Those who set up such claims, however they may disavow it, really hold that Christ's kingdom *is* of this world, since they place it in rivalry to the secular authority. "If thou judge the law, thou art not a doer of the law, but a judge." One great distinction of the Antichrist is that he is ὁ ἄνομος, the Lawless One. Even further than this, Garnet was prepared to go, and did go at his last examination. "In all cases," he said, "where simple equivocation is allowable, it is lawful if necessary to confirm it by an oath. This I acknowledge to be according to my opinion, and the opinion of the Schoolmen; and our reason is, for that in cases of lawful equivocation, the speech by equivocation being saved from a lie, the same speech may be without perjury confirmed by oath, or by any other usual way, though it were by receiving the Sacrament, if just necessity so require." (*Dom. State Papers*, James I., vol. xx., art. 218.) Garnet asserted that Catesby did him much wrong, by saying that in Queen Elizabeth's time he had consulted him as to the lawfulness of the "powder action," which was "most untrue;" but after the preceding extracts, who could believe their writer on his oath? Poor Anne Vaux, who undoubtedly meant to excuse and save him, urged that he used to say to the conspirators in her hearing, "Good gentlemen, be quiet; God will do all for the best :" and Garnet's own last confession

admitted that "partly upon hope of prevention, partly for
that I would not betray my friend, I did not reveal the
general knowledge of Mr. Catesby's intention which I had by
him." (*Dom. State Papers*, vol. xx., art. 12.) He allowed also
that about a year before the Queen's death, he had received
two briefs from Rome, bidding him not consent to the accession of any successor to her who would not submit to the
Pope : he had shown them to Catesby, and then burned
them. Catesby, said Garnet, considered himself authorised
to act as he did by these briefs ; but he had tried vainly to
dissuade him from so doing, since the Pope had forbidden
the action. (*Ibid.*, vol. xviii., art. 41, 42.) In September,
1605, Garnet led a pilgrimage of Roman Catholics to St.
Winifred's Well, in returning from which, he and Anne Vaux
visited Rushton, the seat of Francis Tresham. Sir Thomas,
his father, was then just dead, and the widowed Lady
Tresham "kept her chamber" accordingly. They stayed
but one night (Examination of Anne Vaux, *Gunpowder Plot
Book*, art. 212), and then returned to Goathurst, where they
remained for some weeks, until on the 29th of October they
removed, with the Digbys and Brooksbys, to Coughton, the
house of Mr. Thomas Throckmorton, which Sir Everard had
borrowed, on account of its convenient proximity to Dunchurch, the general rendezvous for the conspirators after the
execution of the plot. This journey to Coughton was considered strong evidence against Garnet ; and his meaning
has never been solved, in writing that "all Catholics know it
was necessary." (*Dom. State Papers*, vol. xix., art. 11.) At
Coughton was the Rev. Oswald Greenway, another Jesuit
priest, who has left a narrative of the whole account, wherein
he describes the conspirators and their doings with a pen
dipped in honey. In the night between November 5th and
6th, Bates arrived at Coughton with Digby's letter, which
afterwards told heavily against Garnet. Garnet remained
at Coughton until about the 16th of December, when at the
instigation of his friend Edward Hall (alias Oldcorne) he

removed to Hendlip Hall. Garnet and Hall made up between them an elaborate story describing their arrival at Hendlip, and immediate hiding, on Sunday night, Jan. 19th; but this was afterwards confessed both by Hall and Owen to be false, and Garnet was overheard to blame Hall for not having kept to the text of his lesson in one detail.

Nicholas Owen, Garnet's friend and servant, committed suicide in the Tower, on March 2nd, from fear of further torture. Mr. Abington, who had "voluntarily offered to die at his own gate, if any such were to be found in his house or in that sheire," was condemned to death, but afterwards pardoned on condition of never again quitting the county. Made wiser by adversity, he spent the rest of his life in innocent study of the history and antiquities of Worcestershire.

The remainder of Garnet's story is given in the tale, and is almost pure history as there detailed. In his conferences with Hall, he made no real profession of innocence, only perpetual assurances that he "trusted to wind himself out" of the charges brought against him; and when Lord Salisbury said—"Mr. Garnet, give me but one argument that you were not consenting to it [the plot], that can hold in any indifferent man's ear or sense, besides your bare negative"—Garnet made no answer. He persistently continued to deny any knowledge of White Webbs, until confronted with Johnson; and all acquaintance with the plot before his receipt of Digby's letter at Coughton, until shown the written confession of Hall, and the testimony of Forset and Locherson concerning his own whispered admissions. When at last he was driven to admit the facts previously denied with abundant oaths, he professed himself astonished that the Council were scandalised at his reckless falsehoods. "What should I have done?" he writes. "Why was I to be denied every lawful [!] means of escape?" That the Government did not deal fairly with Garnet—that, as is admitted by the impartial Dr. Jardine, "few men came to their trial under greater disadvantages," and that "he had been literally surrounded by snares"—may be allowed to the full; but when all is said for him that honesty can say, no doubt remains that he was early acquainted with and morally responsible for the Gunpowder Plot. The evidence may be found in Jardine's Narrative of the Plot; to produce it here would be to swell the volume far beyond its present dimensions. One point, however, must not be omitted. There have been two raids on the Public Record Office, two acts of abstraction and knavery with respect to these Gunpowder Plot papers; and it can be certainly stated, from the extracts made from them by Dr. Abbott and Archbishop Sancroft, that the stolen papers were precisely those which proved Garnet's guilt most conclusively. A MS. letter from Dr. Jardine to Mr. Robert Lemon, attached to the *Gunpowder Plot Book*, states that Mr. Lemon's father had " often observed to me that 'those fellows the Jesuits, in the time of the Powder Plot (not the *Gun*powder Plot) had stolen away some of the most damning proofs against Garnet.' That thievery of some kind abstracted such documents as the Treatise of Equivocation, with Garnet's handwriting on it—the most important of the interlocutions between Garnet and Hall in the Tower—and all the examinations of Garnet respecting the Pope's Breves, is quite clear. *The first thievery I have proved to have been made by Archbishop Laud*; the others probably occurred in the reigns of Charles II. and James II., when Jesuits and 'Jesuited persons' had free access to the State Paper Office." An old proverb deprecates "showing the cat the way to the cream;" but there is one folly still more reprehensible—placing the cat in charge of the dairy. Let us beware it is not done again.

JOHN GRANT.

Of this conspirator very little is known apart from the plot. His residence was at Norbrook, a few miles south of Warwick, —a walled and moated house, of which nothing remains save a few fragments of massive stone walls, and the line of the moat may be distinctly traced, while "an ancient hall, of large dimensions, is also apparent among the partitions of a modern farmer's kitchen." Before May, 1602, he married Dorothy Winter, the sister of two of the conspirators. He had been active in the Essex insurrection, for which he was fined; and with his brother-in-law, Robert Winter, he was sent for by Catesby, in January, 1605, for the purpose of being initiated into the conspiracy: but he was not sworn until March 31. Greenway describes him as "a man of accomplished manners, but of a melancholy and taciturn disposition;" Gerard tells us that "he was as fierce as a lion, of a very undaunted courage," which he was wont to exhibit "unto poursuivants and prowling companions" when they came to ransack the house—by which dubious expression is probably intended not burglars but officers of the law. "He paid them so well for their labour, not with crowns of gold, but with cracked crowns sometimes, and with dry blows instead of drink and good cheer, that they durst not visit him any more, unless they brought great store of help with them." Mr. Grant appears to have anticipated some tactics of modern times. All else that is known of him will be found in the tale. His wife Dorothy seems to have been a lady of a cheerful and loquacious character, to judge by the accounts of Sir R. Walsh and Sir R. Verney, who thought she had no knowledge of the conspiracy. (*Gunpowder Plot Book*, art. 75, 90.) It is, however, possible that Mrs. Dorothy was as clever as her brothers, and contrived to "wind herself out of" suspicion better than she deserved.

John Grant had at least two brothers, Walter and Francis, the latter of whom was apprenticed to a silkman; the relationship of Ludovic Grant is less certain. He had also two married sisters, Mrs. Bosse, and Anne, wife of his bailiff Robert Higgins. (*Gunpowder Plot Book*, art. 34, 44, 68, 90.) His mother, and (then unmarried) sister Mary were living in 1603.

Robert Keyes.

This man, who appears to have been one of the most desperate and unscrupulous of the conspirators, was the son of a Protestant clergyman in Derbyshire, who is supposed to have been the Rev. Edward Kay of Stavely, a younger son of John Kay of Woodsam, Yorkshire. His name is variously rendered as Keyes, Keis, and Kay; he himself signs Robert Key. His mother was a daughter of Sir Robert Tyrwhitt of Kettleby, a very opulent Roman Catholic gentleman of Lincolnshire, and through her he was cousin of Mrs. Rookwood. The opulence of the grandfather did not descend to his grandson, whose indigence was a great cause of his desperate character. He lived for a time at Glatton, in Huntingdonshire, but afterwards entered the service of Lord Mordaunt as keeper of his house at Turvey, his wife being the governess of his Lordship's children. He is described as "a young man with no hair on his face." (Addit. MS. 6178, fol. 808.) It was about June, 1605, when Keyes was taken into the plot, and his chief work thereafter was the charge of the house at Lambeth "sometimes called Catesby's, afterwards Mr. Terrett's, since Rookwood's" (*Ibid.*, fol. 62), where the powder was stored. His only other service was the bringing of the watch from Percy to Fawkes just before the discovery of the plot. Keyes left one son, Robert (Foley's *Records*, vol. i., p. 510), who was living about 1630, and was then a frequent visitor of his relatives the Rookwoods (*Dom. State Papers*, Chas. I., clxxviii. 43).

Humphrey and Stephen Littleton.

These cousins belonged to the family of the present Baron. Sir John Littleton of Hagley had with other issue two sons, of whom Gilbert, the eldest, was the father of Humphrey, while Sir George Littleton of Holbeach, the third son, was the father of Stephen. Humphrey was known as Red

Humphrey, to distinguish him from another of his name, and one of these two was a University man, of Broadgate Hall, Oxford, where he took his B.A. degree 29th Jan. 1580, and his M.A., 2nd July, 1582. His cousin Stephen was born in 1575. With the plot Humphrey at least was but partially acquainted, for Catesby "writ to Mr. Humphrey Littleton [from Huddington] to meet him at Dunchurch, but he, being then destitute of a horse, returned written answer that he could not then meet him, in regard of his unfurnishment before remembered: whereupon Mr. Robert Winter sent a good gelding to Mr. Humphrey Littleton, whereon he rode away to Dunchurch, and (saith himself) demanding of the matter in hand, and what it might be, Mr. Catesby told him that it was a matter of weight, but for the especial good of them all, which was all he would then disclose to him." (Harl. MS. 360.) The account given in the text, from this volume, of the escape and wanderings of Robert Winter and Stephen Littleton is somewhat varied by another narrative in the same MS., according to which Humphrey "bade the officers begone, or he would fetch that should send them packing." He affirmed in his confession, 26th Jan. 1606, that he "had intention to apprehend" the refugees, "in regard of the odiousness of their treasons and the horribleness of the offence, which this partie in his heart detested," and that he deferred doing so "out of love to his cousin and affection to their religion," until he should be able to obtain counsel of Hall. (*Ibid.*) Mrs. John Littleton, the lady of Hagley Park, was Muriel, daughter of Sir Thomas Bromley, and a Protestant; though renowned for her hospitality and benevolence, she contrived to pay off £9000 of debt left by her father-in-law and husband.

WILLIAM PARKER, LORD MONTEAGLE.

Lord Monteagle was of very distinguished and ancient race, being the eldest son of Edward third Baron Morley of his line (heir of a younger branch of the Lovels of Tichmersh) and Elizabeth, only daughter and heir of William Stanley, Lord Monteagle. Born in 1574, he succeeded his mother as Lord Monteagle, and his father in 1618 as Lord Morley. His wife was Elizabeth, daughter of Sir Thomas Tresham, and his sister Mary was the wife of Mr. Thomas Abington of Hendlip Hall.

The chief interest attaching to Lord Monteagle concerns the famous letter: and the two questions requiring answer are—Who wrote it? and, Was the recipient a party to the plot?

The second question, which may be first dealt with, must be answered almost certainly in the affirmative. Nay, more, Lord Monteagle was not only a party to the Gunpowder Plot, but there is strong reason to believe that in conjunction with Lord Salisbury and others, he got up a counter-plot for its discovery. The laying of the letter before Lord Salisbury on the night of Oct. 24th,[1] was probably not the first intimation which Salisbury had received, and assuredly not the first given to Lord Monteagle. The whole catena of circumstances, when carefully studied, shows that the episode of the letter was a cleverly-devised countermarch, designed at once to inform the public and at the same time to give a warning to the conspirators. The party got up at Hoxton, where Lord Monteagle was not living; the mysterious delivery of the letter; the placing of it in the hands of Thomas Ward, a known confidant of the conspirators: these and other circumstances all tend to one conclusion—that Monteagle was acting a part throughout, and that it was in reality he who gave warning to them, not they to him. If the conspirators had taken his warning, they might all have escaped with their lives; for the vessel designed to bear Fawkes abroad as soon as

---

[1] "Thursday, 24th Oct." (not 26th, as usually stated) is the endorsement on the letter itself (*Gunpowder Plot Book*, art. 2), and also the date given in the official account (*Ibid.*, art. 129).

he should have fired the mine was lying in the river, and there was abundant time for them all to have made good their escape, had they not foolishly tried to retrieve their loss at Dunchurch. This is made more certain by the fact that the Government were, as Garnet remarked, "determined to save Lord Monteagle," and that any reference in the confessions of the prisoners which tended to implicate him was diligently suppressed. In one examination, the original words ran, "Being demanded what other persons were privy [to the plot] beside *the Lord Mounteagle,* Catesby," &c. The three words in italics have been rendered illegible, by a slip of paper being pasted over them, and a memorandum in red ink made on the back. Time, however, has faded the red ink, and the words are again visible. (Criminal Trials, p. 67.) Garnet, too, confessed that "Catesby showed the [Pope's] breves to my Lo. Mountegle at the time when Mr. Tresham was with him at White Webbs." (Addit. M.S. 6178, fol. 161.) These facts raise a doubt whether the whole story of Tresham's anxiety to warn Lord Monteagle was not false, and a mere blind to cover something else, which perhaps is not now to be revealed. It remains to inquire, Who wrote the letter? It has been ascribed to three persons beside Tresham: Percy, Mrs. Abington, and Anne Vaux. If it really were a part of the Government counterplot, as is very probable, it was not likely to be any of them. If not so, Tresham seems the most likely, though it is customary to charge Mrs. Abington with it. Lord Monteagle would at once have recognised his sister's writing, and perhaps that of her intimate friend, his wife's cousin, Anne Vaux. Why Percy should be supposed to have written it is a mystery. The handwriting is undoubtedly very like that of Anne Vaux; indeed, for this reason I suspected her as the writer on the first investigation, and before I knew that she had ever been charged with it. Dr. Jardine votes decidedly in favour of Tresham. The real truth respecting this matter will in all probability never be known in this world.

Lord Monteagle was in the Essex rebellion, for which he was fined and imprisoned until the end of 1601; but he was in high favour with King James, probably owing to his strenuous efforts to secure his succession. He died in 1622, leaving three sons and three daughters.

A characteristic letter from this nobleman is yet extant, which shows his style and tone, and has not, I believe, been printed. It is that summoning Catesby to Bath, and if it were written in 1605, rather confirms the supposition that the writer was an accomplice. Dr. Jardine and others suppose it, I know not why, to belong rather to 1602. It runs as follows :—

"To my loving kinsman, Rob* Catesbye Esq., give these. Lipyeat. If all creatures born under the moons sphere cannot endure without the elements of aier and fire In what languishment have we led our life since we departed from the dear Robin whose conversation gave us such warmth as we needed no other heat to maintain our healths: since therefore it is proper to all to desire a remedy for their disease I do by these bind the by the laws of charity to make thy present aparance here at the bath and let no watery Nimpes divert you, who can better live with[out] the air and better forbear the fire of your spirit and Vigour then we who accumpts thy person the only sone that must ripen our harvest. And thus I rest. Even fast tied to your friendshipp, W*· MOUNTEAGLE." (Cott. MS. Titus, B. ii. fol. 294.)

THOMAS PERCY.

The exact place of this conspirator in the Northumberland pedigree has been the subject of much question. He is commonly said to have been a near relative of the Earl; but Gerard thinks that "he was not very near in blood, although they called him cousin." Among the various suggestions offered, that appears to be the best-founded which identifies him not with the Percys of Scotton, but as the son of

Edward Percy of Beverley, whose father, Joscelyn, was a younger son of the fourth Earl. The wife of Joscelyn was Margaret Frost; the wife of Edward, and mother of the conspirator, was Elizabeth, daughter of Sir Thomas Waterton of Walton, Yorkshire—of the family of the famous naturalist, Charles Waterton, of whom it was said that he felt tenderly towards every living thing but two—a poacher and a Protestant. The character of Percy, as sketched by one of the Jesuit narrators, is scarcely consistent with that given by the other. Greenway writes of him, "He was about forty-six years of age, though from the whiteness of his head, he appeared to be older; his figure was tall and handsome, his eyes large and lively, and the expression of his countenance pleasing, though grave; and notwithstanding the boldness of his mind, his manners were gentle and quiet." Gerard says, "He had been very wild in his youth, more than ordinary, and much given to fighting—so much so that it was noted in him and in Mr. John Wright . . . that if they heard of any man in the country more valiant than the others, one or other of them would pick a quarrel to make trial of his valour. . . He had a great wit, and a very good delivery of his mind, and so was able to speak as well as most in the things wherein he had experience. He was tall, and of a very comely face and fashion; of age near fifty, as I take it, for his head and beard was much changed white." The proclamation for his apprehension describes him as "a tall man, with a great broad beard, a good face, the colour of his beard and head mingled with white hairs, but his head more white than his beard. He stoupes somewhat in the shoulders, well coloured in face, longe foted, smale legged." Percy was steward and receiver of rents to his kinsman the Earl, whose rents he appropriated to the purposes of the plot—without the owner's knowledge, if his earnest denial may be trusted. Percy married Martha, sister of John and Christopher Wright, by whom he had three children: Elizabeth, who died young, and was buried at Alnwick, 2nd Feb. 1602; a daughter (name unknown), who married young Robert Catesby; and Robert Percy, of Taunton, who married Emma Meade at Wivelscomb, 22nd Oct. 1615, and was the founder of the line of Percy of Cambridge. Percy's widow lived privately in London after his execution.

AMBROSE ROOKWOOD.

Second son of Robert Rookwood of Stanningfield, by his second wife Dorothy, daughter of Sir William Drury of Hawkstead; he became eventually the heir of his father. Ambrose was born in 1578, and was educated in Flanders as a Roman Catholic. According to Greenway, he was "beloved by all who knew him;" Gerard describes him as "very devout, of great virtue and valour, and very secret; he was also of very good parts as for wit and learning." He was remarkable for his stud of fine horses. Coldham Hall, his family mansion, built by his father in 1574, is still standing, and is a picturesque house, about four miles from Bury St. Edmunds. Very reluctant at first to join the plot, (March 31st, 1605), when arrested he "denied all privity, on his soul and conscience, and as he was a Catholic." He was drawn into it by Catesby, with whom he had long been acquainted, and whom he said that he "loved and respected as his own life." Objecting that "it was a matter of conscience to take away so much blood," Catesby replied that he was "resolved that in conscience it might be done," whereon Rookwood, "being satisfied that in conscience he might do it, confessed it neither to any ghostly father nor to any other." (Exam. of Rookwood, *Gunpowder Plot Book*, art. 136.) Sir William Wade writes that "Rookwood can procure no succour from any of his friends in regard of the odiousness of his actions" (Addit. MS. 6178, fol. 34). He seems to have been fond of fine clothes, for he not only had a "fair scarf" embroidered with "ciphres," but "made a very fair Hungarian horseman's cote, lyned all with velvet, and other apparel exceeding costly, not fyt for his degree" (*Ibid.*, fol. 86). His wife, who was "very beautiful" and "a virtuous Catholic," was the daughter of Robert Tyrwhitt, Esq., of Kettleby, co. Linc. They had three children: Sir Robert Rookwood, who warmly espoused the cause of Charles I., and was buried 10th June, 1679; he married Mary, daughter of Sir Robert Townsend of Ludlow, and left issue: Henry: and Elizabeth, wife of William Calverley, Esq.

The Rookwoods of the Golden Fish, in the story, are all fictitious persons. The real brother of Ambrose was the Rev. Thomas Rookwood of Claxton, the correspondent of Garnet.

FRANCIS TRESHAM.

Sir Thomas Tresham, the father of Francis, had suffered much in the cause of Rome. Perverted by Campion in 1580, he was repeatedly imprisoned for recusancy and harbouring Jesuits, but remained the more resolutely devoted to the faith of which he speaks as "his beloved, beautiful, and graceful Rachel," for whom his "direst adversity" seemed "but a few days for the love he had to her." By his wife Muriel, daughter of Sir Robert Throckmorton, he had two sons, of whom Francis was the elder. He was educated at Gloucester Hall; and having been very actively participant in the rebellion of Essex, was on his trial extremely insolent to the Lord Chancellor. His life was saved only by the intercession of Lady Catherine Howard, whose services were purchased apparently for £1500. Catesby never ceased to regret the admission of Tresham to the conspiracy: but if, as is probable (see *ante*, Monteagle), Lord Monteagle were himself a party to the plot, the much-vaunted earnestness of Tresham to save him is in all probability a fiction, and a mere piece of the machinery. Gerard says that he was "of great estate, esteemed to be worth £3000 a year. He had been wild in his youth, and even till his end was not known to be of so good example as the rest." Jardine says, "He was known to be mean, treacherous, and unprincipled." He vehemently denied, however, the charge of having sent the warning letter to Lord Monteagle, of which he was always suspected by his brother conspirators. Catesby and Thomas Winter had determined to "poniard him on the spot" if he had shown any hesitation in this denial. He escaped the gallows by dying of illness in the Tower on the 23rd of November. Lord Salisbury has been accused of poisoning Tresham because he knew too many State secrets. But why then did he not poison Lord Monteagle for the same reason? The fact that Tresham's wife and servant were admitted into his prison, and allowed to nurse him till he died, is surely sufficient answer. By his wife, Anne, daughter of Sir John Tufton, Tresham left no issue. He "showed no remorse, but seemed to glory in it as a religious act, to the minister that laboured with him to set his conscience straight at his end: had his head chopped of and sent [to] be set up at Northampton, his body being tumbled into a hole without so much ceremony as the formalitye of a grave." (*Dom. State Papers,* xvii. 62.)

Robert, Thomas, and John Winter.

The Winters of Huddington are a family of old standing in Worcestershire; and Anne Winter, sister of the great grandfather of these brothers, was the mother of Edward Underhill, the "Hot Gospeller." His grandson, George Winter of Huddington and Droitwich, was a "recusant," yet was High Sheriff of his county in 1589. He married, first, Jane, daughter of Sir William Ingleby of Ripley, in Yorkshire, and secondly, Elizabeth, daughter of Sir John Bourne. By the first marriage he had issue two sons—Robert and Thomas; by the second, John, Dorothy, and Elizabeth.

Robert, the eldest son, was born in or soon after 1565. Gerard describes him as "a gentleman of good estate in Worcestershire, about a thousand marks a year (£666, 13s. 4d.), ... an earnest Catholic, though not as yet generally known to be so. He was a wise man, and of grave and sober carriage, and very stout (*i.e.*, courageous), as all of that name have been esteemed." He joined the conspirators, March 31st, 1605; but he, like others, objected at first to the "scandal to the Catholic cause," and was a half-hearted accomplice to the end. He is said to have been terrified by a horrible dream on the night of Nov. 4th, which made him more willing to desert the cause. He married Gertrude, daughter of Sir John Talbot (of the Shrewsbury line) and of Katherine Petre, by whom he had four children,—John, who died in 1622, leaving issue; Helen, of Cooksey, died 5th May 1670; Mary, a nun; and Catherine, died before 1670. All the daughters were unmarried.

Thomas Winter, one of the chief actors in the plot, was probably born about 1570, and seems to have died a bachelor. He may have been the "Thomas or William Wynter," apparently of Bradgate Hall, Oxford, who took his B.A. degree on 29th Jan. 1589. He had served in the Dutch army against Spain, and quitted it on account of religious scruples, but so long afterwards as 1605, he is spoken of as Captain Winter (Addit. M.S. 6178, fol. 62). After this he was secretary to Lord Monteagle. He was, says Green-way, "an accomplished and able man, familiarly conversant with several languages, the intimate friend and companion of Catesby, and of great account with the Catholic party generally, in consequence of his talents for intrigue, and his personal acquaintance with ministers of influence in foreign Courts." Gerard adds that his "elder brother, and another younger, were also brought into the action by his means. He was a reasonable good scholar, and able to talk in many matters of learning, but especially in philosophy or histories, very well and judicially. He could speak both Latin, Italian, Spanish, and French. He had been a soldier, both in Flanders, France, and I think against the Turk, and could discourse exceeding well of those matters; and was of such a wit, and so fine carriage, that he was of so pleasing conversation, desired much of the better sort, but an inseparable friend to Mr. Robert Catesby. He was of mean stature, but strong and comely, and very valiant, about thirty-three years or more. His means were not great, but he lived in good sort, and with the best. He was very devout and zealous in his faith, and careful to come often to the Sacraments, and of very grave and discreet carriage, offensive to no man, and fit for any employment." His "living was eight score pound by the year, by report of his man" (*Gunpowder Plot Book*, art. 41); namely, his annual income was about £160. Several letters of his are still extant; three have been published in Notes and Queries (3rd S., i. 341), and are all addressed to Grant. One written to Catesby has not seen the light hitherto, and as it is characteristic, I append it. (Cott. MS. Titus, B. ii., fol. 292.)

"To my loving friend, Mr. Ro. Catsby.

"Though all you malefactors flock to London, as birds in winter to a dunghill, yet do I, Honest man, freely possess the sweet country air: and to say truth, would fain be amongst you, but cannot as yet get money to come up. I was at Asbye to have met you, but you were newly gone; my business and your uncertain stay made me hunt no further. I pray you commend me to other friends. And when occasion shall require, send down to my brother's or Mr. Talbotts; within this month I will be with you at London. So God keep you this 12th of October. Your loving friend,   THO. WINTOUR."

John Winter, the youngest brother, seems to have had very little share in the plot, and most fervently denied any knowledge of it whatever. Gerard (see *ante*) asserts that he was engaged in it, and Gertrude Winter bore witness that he came to Huddington with the other conspirators on Nov. 7th. His own amusing narrative is to the effect that Grant asked him on the 4th of November, if he would go to a horse-race, and he answered that he would if he were well; that on the 5th, he went to "a little town called Rugby," where he and others supped and played cards; that a messenger came to them and said, "The gentlemen were at Dunchurch, and desired their company to be merry;" that at Holbeach he "demanded of Mr. Percy and the rest, being most of them asleep, what they meant to do," and they answered that they would go on now; and shortly afterwards he left them. (*Gunpowder Plot Book*, art. 110.) John Winter was imprisoned, but released. There is no evidence to show that he was married.

JOHN AND CHRISTOPHER WRIGHT.

Concerning the parentage of these brothers, I can find no more than that they were of the family of Wright of Plowland, in Holderness, Yorkshire. They were cousins of Robert Winter, perhaps through his mother; were both schoolfellows of Guy Fawkes, and "neighbours' children." John Wright originally lived at Twigmore, in Lincolnshire, and removed to Lapworth, in Warwickshire, when he became a party to the plot. He was the first layman whom Catesby took into his confidence, Thomas Winter being the second, and Fawkes the third. Like so many of the others, the brothers were involved in Essex's rebellion. They were perverts, and since their perversion John had been "harassed with persecutions and imprisonment." Greenway says he was one of the best swordsmen of his time. Gerard describes him as "a gentleman of Yorkshire, not born to any great fortune, but lived always in place and company of the better sort. In his youth, very wild and disposed to fighting. . . . He grew to be staid and of good, sober carriage after he was Catholic, and kept house in Lincolnshire, where he had priests come often, both for his spiritual comfort and their own in corporal helps. He was about forty years old, a strong and a stout man, and of a very good wit, though slow of speech: much loved by Mr. Catesby for his valour and secresy in carriage of any business."

Of Christopher he says that "though he were not like him [John] in face, as being fatter, and a lighter-coloured hair, and taller of person, yet was he very like to the other in conditions and qualities, and both esteemed and tried to be as stout a man as England had, and withal a zealous Catholic, and trusty and secret in any business as could be wished." But little is known of the relatives of these brothers. John Wright's wife was named Dorothy, and she was "sister-in-law of Marmaduke Ward of Newby, Yorkshire, gentleman;" they had a daughter who was eight or nine years old in 1605, and probably one or more sons, as descendants of John Wright are said still to exist. Christopher's wife was called Margaret, but nothing is known of his children. The brothers had two sisters,—Martha, the wife of their co-traitor, Percy; and another who was the mother of a certain William Ward, spoken of as Wright's nephew. (*Gunpowder Plot Book*, art. 44, 47, 52, 90.)

By Greenway, Gerard, or both, it is asserted of nearly every one of the conspirators that they were very wild in youth, and became persons of exemplary virtue after their perversion to Popery.

THE END.

Stories of English Life.

By EMILY S. HOLT.

Complete set 40 vols. £3 nett. Single vols. Half-a-Crown each.

For completion of List see other side.

Holt's Stories of English Life.

Complete set 40 vols. £3 nett cash.   Single vols.   Half-a-Crown each.

For completion of List see other side.

www.ingramcontent.com/pod-product-compliance
Lightning Source LLC
Chambersburg PA
CBHW030902270326
41929CB00008B/544